TINY TIM

Tiptoe Through a Lifetime

Lowell Tarling

Artwork by Martin Sharp

ETT IMPRINT
Exile Bay

ETT Imprint, PO Box R1906, Royal Exchange NSW 1225 Australia

ISBN: 978-1-922384-11-9 (eBook)
ISBN: 978-1-922384-10-2 (paper)
First published by Generation Books 2013

This edition published by ETT Imprint, Exile Bay 2020

Artwork © Martin Sharp
Cover Design © Joel Tarling
Cover photography: © Dave Newland 1982
Cover & interior formatting by Linda Ruth Brooks

Author Website: www.lowelltarling.com.au

For Tulip

Table of Contents

Table of Illustrations

Title Page: *Film Script* – painting: Martin Sharp

1. *Pop Art* – painting: Martin Sharp
2. *Beautiful Dreamer* – painting: Martin Sharp
3. *The Human Canary* – painting: Martin Sharp
4. *Hubert's Flea Circus in 1991* – photo: Lowell Tarling
5. *Steve Paul's Scene in 1991* – photo: Lowell Tarling
6. *Tiny Tim 1982* – photo: Dave Newland
7. *Tiny Tim - OZ magazine* – collage and drawings: Martin Sharp
8. *Tiny Tim & Miss Vicki - OZ magazine* – collage and drawings: Martin Sharp
9. *Tiny Tim - the Catalog* – collage and drawings: Martin Sharp
10. *Luna Park Non-Stop Singing Record* – poster/handbill: Martin Sharp
11. *Quadrant magazine cover* – painting: Martin Sharp
12. *Film Script* – painting: Martin Sharp
13. *Chameleon album cover* - design: Martin Sharp, photo: William Yang
14. *Martin, Lowell and the painting 'Film Script'* – photo: Peter Jensen
15. *Paddo – Masquerade Ball* – poster: Martin Sharp
16. *Tiny Tim, the Opera House Concert* – poster: Martin Sharp
17. *Late Show Kinselas* – poster Martin Sharp
18. *Tiny, press conference 1983* – Polaroid photo: Lowell Tarling
19. *Wonderful World of Romance* - album cover concept: Martin Sharp
20. *Brighton Festival Non-Stop Singing Record* – 3-cassette pack, Street of Dreams Productions
21. *Tiny outside the Olcott Hotel NY, 1991* – photo: Lowell Tarling
22. *Tiny in front of the Michael Bell poster 1992* – photo: Amber Tarling
23. *Rock album cover* – artwork: Martin Sharp
24. *Tiny Tim's Christmas Album* - album cover artwork: Martin Sharp
25. *The Southern Flyer cover* – photo: Dave Newland
26. *Lowell Tarling* – photo: Konrad Lenz
27. *Tiny Tim* – picture: Joel Tarling

Thanks

Artist, Martin Sharp made this book possible and I cannot thank him enough for his contribution. Since seeing Tiny Tim's Royal Albert Hall Concert in 1968, Martin has consistently encouraged friends to get behind Tiny with their creative energies. I was one of those.

To enable this, Martin provided the space, knowledge and opportunities to enable Tiny Tim film, music and writing projects. He literally turned his house into a Tiny Tim Resource Centre open to everyone who showed sincere interest. My tools of trade were the cassette recorder, electronic typewriter, and later – the laptop computer.

I would also like to thank publisher Michael Wilkinson who, for six months or so in 2002, tried to put together a Tiny Tim stage production, in the course of which he took me to America. Michael's involvement resulted in several key interviews, most notably more than two hours on tape in San Francisco with Tiny's third wife, Miss Sue.

Tiny's Cousin Hal Stein and his wife Sherry provided a genuine link with the family. Hal gave me a full and frank interview on tape. Later, he and Sherry visited Australia, visited Martin and saw the rooms, the posters and the memorabilia, that Martin had compiled into an archive museum. Hal also read through two of my drafts and made corrections. Sherry sent me some family DVDs – including Tiny's funeral service, and other material unavailable in Australia. Thanks Hal and Sherry.

My wife Robbie and children Amber, Joel and Zoë have all played a part in the creation of this book. Occasionally, they were even part of the story. As they didn't enjoy Tiny's music quite as much as I did, I thank them for many things, including their patience.

I also wish to thank the following people for agreeing to be interviewed. First - Tiny himself. Also Ernie Clark (manager of Tiny's official website), Chris Löfvén (musician), Sue Khaury (wife), Mark Mitchell (friend), Richard Perry (producer), Dave Rowe (Australian tour manager), Martin Sharp (artist), Bernie Stein (cousin), Tulip Stewart (daughter) and David Tibet (producer). Also, while watching Martin's *Street of Dreams* film, Eric Clapton explained to me how he was responsible for Martin's early interest in Tiny, but he didn't say it on tape.

Others who have helped in various ways include: Les Bean, Linda Brooks, Denny Burgess, Mic Conway, Phil Donnison, Pete Jensen, Al Jones, Marilyn Karet, Dave Newland, Mick Reid, Robbie Rollo, Peter Royles, Russell Sharp, Clayton Simms, Gordon Stinson, T-Bone, Carla Wilson, Ian 'Pee Wee' Wilson, Robert Wolfgramm, William Yang, Yensoon Tsai.

And Steve Elias, former editor of the *Southern Flyer,* who started me on this path, as you will read…

Foreword

A Word from Cousin Hal

Throughout his lifetime, Tiny Tim was a repository of recorded music stemming from the early days of vaudeville to the latest chart favorites.

But despite all these influences he remained a true original perfecting his performances as an outreach of his personality.

True, he had some strange traits, but they did not impede on his enthusiastic kindness to people he loved, to the musicians he accompanied, and to the many listeners he met. In the age of celebrity, he functioned as the complete entertainer.

Lowell Tarling has provided Tiny with a living biography and given us a definitive incentive to re-listen to his recording and re-visit his numerous You Tube postings,

You get the feeling that somewhere Tiny is standing on his tiptoes, strumming his ukulele, blowing kisses and saying, 'God bless you all'!

Hal Stein, April 2013

I always loved Pop music. We used to have Mum's old 78 player and her records and we used to play them a lot; maybe some Al Bowlly - but certainly Bing Crosby, Al Jolson and novelty songs. That's why I loved Tiny - he would always play our favourite songs!

Martin Sharp, 16 October 2003

Introduction

After I got to know him, Tiny always made me feel as if I was his biographer. I bet I'm not the only person who can say that. Many people have known Tiny better than me, people like Miss Vicki, Richard Perry, Mo Ostin, Jan Gianopoulos, Miss Jan, Mark Mitchell, Martin Sharp, Miss Sue, the Cappy Brothers, Mr Hollander, Nathan Waks, Dave Rowe, Gil Morris, Johnny Pineapple, Big Bucks Burnett, Howard Stern and more. But most of all, Cousin Hal. They grew up in the same apartment block in Washington Heights. Hal was present at the Wedding of the Century. Tiny sang at Hal's wedding to Sherry. And Hal delivered a well-appreciated speech at Tiny's funeral. Cousin Hal was always there. He should be writing this book, not me.

Another, with a bigger story than mine is Martin Sharp, without a doubt the No 1 documenter of Tiny's life. They enjoyed an extraordinary artistic relationship, which is why my story has a strong Australian slant. My best Tiny Tim moments were at Martin's house *Wirian,* where Tiny spent so much time when he was in the country. Martin enthused me, 'trained' me and opened lots of doors that would have been impossible for me otherwise. I watched Martin work. He taped all Tiny's phone calls, house concerts, studio-talk, gigs, sessions, etc. When Tiny was around, Martin taped everything. So I started taping everything too. He made approximately 1000 tapes of Tiny; I did a mere 78. However, Tiny would occasionally take me aside and talk on tape intimately, which is the core material for this book. He'd say, 'Is the recorder on?' and away he'd go. Tiny would start with whatever was on his mind right now, which was usually Miss Someone-or-Other - his current muse. Tiny would get this off his chest then switch to religion. Like so many artists, everything was sex and death.

I would always angle for something factual, like childhood, parents, cousins, comic books, movies, high school, first jobs, small-time gigs, getting a break or the pleasures of undiluted fame. Sometimes he'd respond to the question, other times he'd talk quite salaciously instead. One consistent theme was (*Oh Lord)* that he could 'make it twice!'

This book was initially supposed to be a 'biography' of Tiny. When my friend Robert Wolfgramm said Tiny deserved a biography 'like Barry Miles wrote for Allen Ginsberg', I realised I could never do that. I can't be objective about Tiny. Furthermore, I have an uneven flow of information. I was often on-the-spot when it happened in Australia but not so in America when something else happened.

Fortunately Justin Martell, a young writer and filmmaker from Connecticut picked up the torch. Justin has written a definitive Tiny Tim biography, saving me the embarrassment of writing what critics would have almost certainly damned as Tiny's 'hagiography'. In a way, Justin lifted my burden, leaving me free to now use my material as it naturally falls. When I miss a bit – and I miss lots – you've got Justin's less subjective and more comprehensive account to return to.

International readers may be surprised how central Martin Sharp is to my account. However, in Australia their names are often linked. When Tiny was in the country, a Tiny Tim event was also a Martin Sharp event. And a Martin Sharp event was a Tiny Tim event. I mean, concerts, tapes, media events, art openings, interviews and recordings. They even made a film.

As for me, I've been a fulltime writer since 1981. I've written books, written for magazines, edited magazines, written songs, plays for high school kids, occasional poems and all sorts of stuff. But unfortunately, I am probably best known as a ghostwriter. In fact, a few years ago – although I never said anything - I was hoping to ghost Cousin Hal's account on his cousin, Tiny.

As I write, new CDs keep slipping out and Youtube has lots of Tiny Tim clips…

For me, it started in 1968 when, staring into a record shop window, I spotted the *God Bless Tiny Tim* album cover and said to Clayton Simms, 'Check this one out!'

'That's Tiny Tim,' he replied. 'Bob Dylan's friend!'

Grandma was alive then. Although she didn't like my other Rock albums, she liked *God Bless Tiny Tim*. And then in the late-70s, when I was a schoolteacher, I heard that Tiny would be making a guest appearance at a shopping centre opening. I suggested to my wife Robbie that we should take the kids to see Tiny. However, what really affected the plot happened in August 1982. I interviewed Tiny for the *Southern Flyer* magazine, and photographer Dave Newland and I called on Martin to pick up a couple of posters. Martin gave us the *Chameleon* poster. We asked about the Sydney Opera House poster. He told us Tiny was holding a concert at the Sydney Opera House in a fortnight. Martin added he was making a film about Tiny.

'Anything else?'

'More recordings.'

And what recordings they were!

The sensational *Chameleon* LP!

I first heard it at Wirian - *Stayin' Alive, The Mickey Mouse Club March, Street of Dreams, The Great Pretender, My Way...!* After all these years, I still play it constantly. Another personal favourite is *Keeping My Troubles To Myself.* I tell ya, I was primed when Tiny came back to Australia 12 months later - August 1983.

A group of us formed a small welcoming party at the Sydney International Airport. Nine days later I interviewed Tiny for the second time. Now that we knew each other a bit, this was totally different. 'Is the recorder on?' Tiny asked, before showing me how to pray, followed by telling me – on tape – a few of his sexual fantasies. *Well, this is different!*

Rather than 'friend', I would describe myself as a hanger-on who Tiny was always pleased to see. I've been his chauffeur and his go-fer. I've gone to the TAB and placed his bets, I've been part of his retinue at an NRL football match at North Sydney Oval where he featured in the preliminaries. I've walked him through a public shopping mall. Everyone recognised him, spoke to him, photographed him and asked for the famous Tiny Tim left-handed autograph.

In New York, I hired a limousine and Tiny showed me his old neighbourhood. He pointed out the theatre where he first saw Sinatra, the cinema where he attended film matinees, his school, the location of *Hubert's Flea Circus* - where he played his first gig. And the rundown premises of what was *Steve Paul's Scene* in the 60s where Tiny was discovered.

In 2002, business friend Michael Wilkinson was in the process of buying a theatre in Melbourne and wanted me, and musician Mic Conway, to write a show about Tiny. We wrote preliminary drafts and Martin designed two sets. That's why Michael took me to America on the Tiny Tim trail. Consequently, I interviewed many of Tiny's closest associates, including his third wife Miss Sue and record producer Richard Perry.

Seeing the giant *Mamma Mia* billboards above us in New York, Michael fantasised about putting Tiny Tim on Broadway.

Fleetingly, it seemed possible.

Tiny Tim was everywhere - in my head, in Wirian, all the music that was played around Martin. After his death, I read in the newspaper that there was a sighting at the Byron Bay Festival. Tiny Tim was everywhere – there's no doubt about that. And almost no one else could see him.

This book is my account of what I taped and saw.

Lowell Tarling, 12 April 2013

1

'Maybe He's Musical?'

1932-1949

Harold (Hal) was the one who really knew him.
He was in constant contact with my brother.
My brother really knew him better than anybody else.
Cousin Bernie

Herbert Butros Khaury – aka Tiny Tim - was born 12 April 1932, at East Park Hospital Manhattan. He was born during the Depression, the year magnetic tape recording was being pioneered.

It was a difficult birth. 'I was a Caesarean. I came out of the stomach. I asked my mother "was I breast fed?" and the only answer she told me was "why would you want to know?"' (1)

What we do know is Tillie was in her forties when she gave birth. It was a difficult delivery. 'We only wanted one,' she says, 'one was enough'. (2)

On New Year's Day 1914 in her mid-late teens, Herbie's mother Tillie migrated from Brest-Livosk in Eastern Europe to join her mother, four sisters and one brother in America, Land of Opportunity. One sister remained in Poland.

Tillie was the daughter of a Jewish Rabbi. She must have been a bit of a rebel because her choice of husband was outrageous as far as her strictly Orthodox family was concerned. Butros Khaury was from Beirut Lebanon and his father was a Maronite Christian priest.

The relationship was thick with socio-religious tension from the start. It was a demanding marriage, based on deferred gratification, small pay and big arguments. Herbie's parents worked long hours in humble jobs.

In 1933 Adolf Hitler was elected Chancellor of Germany.

Beautiful Ohio

Herbie's first memory is not an event or a person, but a song. At the age of three he was enchanted by Henry Burr's 1919 hit *Beautiful Ohio*. He says, 'The first song I ever heard was when I was three years old. I wasn't five, I wasn't four, I was three and a half years old, *Beautiful Ohio*. I listened to it from a wind-up phonograph my father bought.' (3)

Henry Burr (1882-1941) was a Canadian tenor, the voice of the 1910s and 1920s. He made thousands of recordings and really caught little Herbie's ear. Around that time, Burr was on the comeback trail. Having lost his fortune in the 1929 Wall Street Crash, Burr returned to performing in 1935. Herbie heard him on a record bought by his father from a thift shop. 'I remember Henry Burr singing that song from a gramophone my father got me. I played it constantly, constantly, constantly,' he says. (4)

However, Tillie remembered a prior musical memory. 'When he was two years,' she recalled, 'I use to sing him Jewish songs. Right away he was singing after me, so I knew he has talent'. As a young girl in Poland, Tillie had often attended the opera and the ballet. (5)

Herbie got his first crush even before he attended school. She was a 21-year old Spanish girl who waved at him from the street on her way to work. 'I was four years old,' he said, 'Looking out of the tenement of my flat in New York City, I saw this girl going to work. She had long black hair. I waved to her from my window; she waved back. It seems I've always looked for that Fairy Princess,' Tiny sighed.

The first song I ever heard was when I was three years old. I wasn't five, I wasn't four, I was three and a half years old - Beautiful Ohio. I listened to it from a wind-up phonograph my father bought.

Tiny Tim, 4 April 1992

*

His second crush speedily followed - a fictitious radio character on the show *Let's Pretend.* Her name was White Cloud. She lived in the clouds as an innocent, pure and unattainable ideal, and as far as Tiny was concerned, she never really went away. (5)

Fire & Family Drama

Tillie was smarter than Butros with money, better at making it and better at stretching it. Butros was a practical man. He struggled to find work as a watch repairer, dye-maker and whatever he could get.

Tillie missed her eastern European family and Butros was constantly preoccupied with next week's rent. Such were the Great Depression years. Still, it was much better than the news coming from Germany.

In 1936 the Khaurys lived on the third floor of a six-floor tenement building on 81st Street. One day, with Tillie at work and Butros asleep, someone in the street lit a firecracker and threw it. The cracker sparked the clothes on their washing line, they caught alight and the fire spread towards the Khaury's window. Little Herbie screamed for help. Butros woke up and ran to the rescue but having no implements to extinguish the fire, he used his bare hands.

Herbie was upset to see his father in such pain. He said, 'On 4 July 1935 living on this third floor of a six floor tenement, when my Mother was away and my Father was sleeping - instead of sleeping, I thank Jesus Christ for having been awake so that I could see the fire. This happened near a window, a burning blaze. Someone lit a firecracker, clothes were hanging on the line above and it caught on fire and spread. When I woke him up my father went to the window and put it out with his hands before the firemen came. Burned both his hands.' (6)

Even more upsetting were the fights that Herbie remembered from age four. Tillie was a straight-talker with an irritating voice when riled. Butros was a patient man, who could only take so much. Plus, Tillie was Republican, Butros was Democrat. Rather than listen to all of this, Tiny retreated into his room, into the privacy of his dreams. One day Butros snapped, packed his bags, told Tillie the marriage was over and headed for the door. Herbie intervened, tearfully begging his father to stay. Butros couldn't go through with it. He put down his bags, hugged his little boy and promised that he would never leave.

Said Tiny, 'My parents were saints. I really mean it. My father worked hard, my mother worked harder. I can never do what they did with work. They were hard working people and because of the hardness they could never get along. It was screaming and fighting with each other from - I was aware from 1935 on.

'In fact, in that year -1936 - my father was ready to leave, and leave me with my mother because he couldn't take it no more. He was a quiet man, she was a hard working woman and when she talked she never stopped. And with the accent, it was very irritating. But she was working hard. I saw her cry and I said to my father, *Please don't leave.* He kept his promise of that day, he never left again. (7)

But the bickering never went away. Instead of noticing the unemployment queues and blaming the Great Depression, Tillie blamed their lack of prosperity on Butros' easy-going uncompetitive nature.

'It was just the hardness of their lives,' Herbie explains, describing them as 'great parents'. He found solace in popular culture, especially radio programs and Vicola records, which Butros sometimes brought home.

Washington Heights

After this, the Khaury family moved to 160th street near the East Rivers Polo Grounds (on the same block as George Washington's former residence). It didn't suit them, so the family did what they probably should have done in the first place - they moved into Charleston Court, 601 West 163rd Street, Washington Heights, where Tillie's sister and her family – the Steins - lived on the fifth floor.

With his complex ethnicity, up to now Herbie had been dissimilar to everyone around him. He was now no longer alone. Three generations of his family lived in the one apartment block. Herbie was in the same tenement as Cousin Harold (Hal). Herbie and Hal's grandmother lived with the Steins. Hal describes the place, 'I lived on the fifth floor, they lived on the ground floor. That apartment house had probably 15 apartments on each floor – that's 90 families.' (8)

Theirs was a close-knit extended family. Tillie had her mother and sister, Butros got to be king of kids and Herbie had a cousin to play with. They spoke Yiddish at family get-togethers. Tillie always felt more comfortable with Yiddish.

Herbie and Hal were mates. They discussed things no one else would understand. Growing up things, boy's stuff and also family things, like whatever happened to their grandfather who died back in the homeland? And whether their auntie who remained in Poland would be okay in the event of war? (9)

Describing the period, Hal said, 'The era between 1932 when Herbie was born, was tough times. It was the Depression era and the start of the World War. Our parents had to work hard, jobs were not plentiful. Uncle Butros went from job to job and it was tough.' (10)

Tillie's siblings were all more prosperous than the Khaurys. Her sister Mary (Herbie's godmother) owned a knitting mill on the Lower East Side. She offered Tillie a job as a machinist, which Tillie accepted and spent the rest of her working life. Butros was also offered a job at the garment factory, repairing machinery. (11)

Cousin Hal

In Charleston Court, Herbie developed a lifelong friendship with Hal, who is two months younger, born 9 June.

As boys living in the same tenement, Herbie shared all his fascinations with his cousin. They talked about baseball, Shirley Temple, religion, grandma, school, Captain America, *Let's Pretend*, Henry Burr, Mutt & Jeff, the Maple Leafs ice hockey team and did I mention the Dodgers? The baseball team that dominated Herbie's thoughts every weekend for the rest of his life? They also talked about the working life ahead of them both. Tiny had extremely soft hands. In discussing his parents, Herbie confessed to Hal, 'I could never work like that'.

Herbie saw himself as an uncoordinated misfit, who couldn't hit the baseball for nuts which explains why the neighbourhood kids left him out of the games. Hal doesn't remember it that way at all. He reckons Herbie was quite popular. (13)

Chicken Killers & Cheesemakers

Flash forward to 1992. Herbie – now Tiny Tim - has early childhood memories of New York evolving from poverty to prosperity. He recalls Jimmy Walker as the Mayor of New York. He rattles off the names of all nine daily newspapers - *The Daily News, The Daily Mirror, The New York Times, The Tribune, The Compass, The New York Post, The Journal American, The New York Sun* and *The Telegraph.*

Tiny recalls Shirley Temple as the biggest star in the country. Second to her (he says) was Bobby Breen who – in 1936 – was Eddie Cantor's 13-year old discovery. Tiny recalls the double-decker buses in the street, as well as the trolley cars, coming through Broadway all the way to 207th Street. He remembers all this, as well as the chicken killers out the back of shops and the cheese-makers out the front. (12)

Tiny has remarkable recall of the pop history of Washington Heights. It's George Gershwin's neighbourhood. Tango dancer George Raft, film actor James Cagney and bandleader Ted Lewis all came from here. It's the location of the Cotton Club.

Tiny's memories of being seven, eight and nine years old are also about newspaper comic characters, like *Mutt and Jeff* and *Nancy* in 1937. He reels off the names of *Marvel Comics, Prize Comics, Jumbo Jungle, Planet, Ranger, Captain Marvel, Whiz Comics, Captain Marvel Junior, Action Comics, Batman, Superman, Adventure Comics, All-American Comics, World's Finest Comics, Loony Tunes, True Comics, Blue Bolt, Dare Devil, Nickel Comics* all bought from Solomon's Candy Store.

But *Captain America* was the greatest of them all. There he is on the cover of the No 1 issue, with his chiselled jaw, dressed in skin-tight US flag-suit and punching out a bad guy with his red-gloved fist. The shield is what caught Herbie's interest. Describing the moment, Tiny said, 'like a woman, it attracted me right from the shop window'. He had to own this comic. He had to possess it and all subsequent issues, to store as a complete set in pristine condition.

However, like many parents of the time, Butros hated comics. 'Comics were an enmity to my father', said Tiny. 'In 1939-40, comic books were the rage of the age and my parents hated them. I tell ya, comic books were a trend - 64 pages for 10 cents'. (14)

With a headful of dreams, Herbie attended the local school and came home each day to play curb ball on the sidewalk and in the local park. He was a good-natured kid; he had no guile.

One day Tillie caught one of the local kids throwing dirt at Herbie. As she was about to rouse on him, Herbie stopped her. 'Don't worry', he said, 'it's all in fun'. Yes, Herbie was subjected to pranks and even some bullying, however the kids on his block – rough Irish types – were also his defenders and wouldn't allow anyone else to harm him. Ironically, he broke his nose playing baseball with his protectors. Curb ball with the kids on the block and going to movies was his social life.

On 7 December 1941 the two 9-year old cousins walked out of the Uptown Theatre on 170th Street Broadway having just seen *A Yank In The RAF*. A newsboy was spruiking 'Pearl Harbour had been attacked!'

Hal was transfixed, Herbie didn't say anything. They both stood on the street, perplexed. They knew this announcement would have enormous consequences on American lives. (15)

Violin? Piano?

While Hal started participating in athletic games and showing signs of being a smart kid in school, Herbie too was shaping up as a smart kid - for a time. 'Maybe he's musical?' thought Tillie, noticing the hours he spent listening to the gramophone player.

'I ask him, *whaddya wanna play*?' said Tillie, 'He says, *the violin*. So I send him to music class downtown wid his violin. Fifty dollars it costs me. He has a Russian teacher and, after a few lessons, he tells me, *You were right, he's very musically inclined. But he don't work, he don't want it*, so that was it wid the violin'. (16)

The violin was Herbie's first instrument. He took lessons at the Wurlitzer Music School and his teacher's name was Mickey Witek. Hal was in the audience at Herbie's stage debut at '169' (the local elementary school, so nicknamed because it is on 169th Street). Herbie popped out of a jack-in-the-box holding his fiddle and playing a little tune!

Cousin Hal said, 'He started violin lessons at the age of five or six and he was pretty good at it too. That naturally led to other string instruments'. Others also recall Herbie playing the violin 'very well'.

If he was so good, why did he quit? Says Hal, 'He quit because he didn't care for the classical tunes his mother expected him to play on the violin. He always went for the pop tunes'. Maybe he was more interested in singing? Hal recalls Herbie singing along with his records, songs like Russ Colombo's *Prisoner of Love*. (17)

Tiny dismisses the violin experience as insignificant, wishing he had learned piano or taken drawing lessons instead. He says, 'I can't draw. I wish I could draw. Do you know, if I could draw I'd want to sketch the faces of all these pretty women – that's the sort of thing I'd do: sketches.

'Another thing I miss is not playing piano. I wanted to be a pianist. If I had the time and the money to spend playing the piano I would learn that thing backwards so I could play in any key. The piano has many facets from Jazz to Classical, and of course Swing-time, Ragtime. To master every one of those facets takes a superb discipline to practice, practice, practice for maybe 10 years. And once you've mastered the labour pain, a great jazzman can play anything.'

Hal shrugs it off as unreality. He says, 'His parents weren't that well off that they could afford a piano.' (18)

During Herbie's childhood there was nothing but action around New York's underbelly. In his short stories, Damon Runyan gives insight into semi-fictitious characters like Milk Ear Willie, Harry the

Horse and Sky ('because no one can bet any higher') - types that were just 15 minutes away on the Subway from the Khaury's tenuous hold on their rented apartment. There were Puerto Ricans, comic sellers, horseplayers, hustlers, grifters, movie people, hot clubs and a new sound in music, a more intimate sound, thanks to the development of the microphone. All of this was in Herbie's ear.

On weekends, sometimes schooldays, Herbie caught the subway downtown and across Brooklyn Bridge to catch the Dodgers practice sessions and - when he could afford it - their games. These were his first forays away from the neighbourhood.

And then, to his shame, Herbie took to shoplifting. Tiny said, 'In 1940-41 these kids looked out in the stores. I walked in and they stole the comics. Sometimes I took one or two. I went into the same store again and the man there said, *You wanna steal another book?* That really got me, but that didn't stop me yet, it embarrassed me. I remember one time my Father caught me trying to steal one. He hit me right in public and I never stole again after that'. It took him years to shrug off the guilt. (19)

Jingle Jangle Jingle

With America now at war, 1942 was a difficult year for Herbie, as for everyone else. First, Herbie attended day camp, which he hated. Second, he gave up street-baseball because he reckoned he was hopeless. And third, he copped a bout of appendicitis that got him hospitalised.

Mount Sinai Hospital was a lonely place, somehow made worthwhile by a nurse – Miss Diana – a 'Florence Nightingale' with whom Herbie fell in love. Surprisingly, Herbie enjoyed his isolation.

Back home he closed himself away in his room and spent hours listening to records, organising his comic books and sometimes chatting to Hal. In 1942 Herbie's favourite hit was Kay Kyser's No 1 hit *Jingle Jangle Jingle.* It reminded him of Miss Audrey Dash with whom he fell in love (as well as her sister). She wore black shoulder-length hair and was 10 at the time, the same age as Herbie,. Her father was the superintendent of the school building. 'She was so beautiful,' moans Tiny.

In an effort to charm her in the playground, Herbie made a special concession and lent Miss Audrey No 8 of his complete 22-issue set of *Captain America* comics in mint condition. When she returned it, the comic was frayed. He asked why? To his horror, her father had beaten her with it. Herbie was appalled! He couldn't bear to own the thing so horribly defiled. Furthermore, the tattered No 8 broke up the perfect set, so he gave away his entire collection of Captain America comics. (20)

Christmas 1942, a woman in Herbie's tenement staggered from her room and accused him of stealing. He didn't know what she was on about, but the drunken crone insisted he was to blame. Always easily intimidated, she frightened Herbie into falsely blaming another boy. Billy Foody wore the blame and Herbie wore the guilt. He saw himself as nothing but a coward and for the first time in his life, Herbie prayed. 'There are better men than me...' he confessed.

'I was alone. I came back from a movie called *My Sister Eileen* with Rosaline Russell and Brian Aherne. It was 4.00 in the afternoon, 22nd December. My mother came home from work at 5.00 and a woman was drunk next door. She'd just moved in and she accused me of stealing, which I didn't. But she was living with a tough guy and I got scared. It was during the War of 42 and I never forgot that. Eventually she moved out, there was no problem, but I was a coward. I blamed this kid upstairs. His parents forgave me but he always felt uncomfortable near me. The Lord punished me with this trauma. I blame the punishment on the fact that I stole in the years before.' (21)

Here was something new – the Lord! Around this time Herbie occasionally attended synagogue, though not through any encouragement from Tillie. Herbie never had a Bah Mitzvah.

Flicking through the comics at Solomon's Candy Store Herbie picked one up called *Picture Stories From The Bible* 'featuring Jesus, Mary and Joseph' - New Testament Edition No 1, DC Comics, 40 pages. Herbie paid the 10 cents and took it home.

Sitting in his room alone, enjoying his wind-up gramophone records – Henry Burr, Rudy Vallee, Russ Colombo – Herbie read his comic and discovered that Jesus Christ is a type of superhero like Captain Marvel, 'but a real one!' he exclaimed. Tillie and Butros were seriously nonplussed. (22)

Sinatramania

Sinatramania began on the last day of December 1942 when Frank Sinatra opened at the Paramount Theatre. Everybody was suddenly talking about this singer who made women swoon. Swooning? That was new. They never swooned for Henry Burr, Irving Kaufman...

After the Paramount show the previous legend, Bing Crosby quipped, 'Frank's the kind of singer who comes around once in a lifetime, but why'd he have to come round in mine!'

Herbie caught the star at his peak. Tiny says, 'In 1943 I saw Frank Sinatra, he was getting out of a limousine, trying to get through the crowd and up to the concert hall and all the girls were screaming. The cop near me turned around and said, *What a sissy*. You can bet he owns all Sinatra's albums now!' (23)

The expression 'Swooner-Crooner' entered the national vocabulary, especially Herbie's. A Swooner-Crooner is what he told Tillie he was going to be when she hassled him about his career. 'Look at cousin Hal!' she'd exclaim, 'He's doing well for himself!'

Hal qualified into the prestigious Styversant High School from which he would go to college, pick up a degree in broadcasting and pursue a career in radio advertising and promotion. Herbie, on the other hand, attended the less exalted George Washington High School in Upper Manhattan and had no prospects other than to become a famous singer, which not even he himself quite believed. (24)

Being Clean

Next, Herbie became fascinated by Agatha Christie's new book *Evil Under The Sun,* particularly her Hercule Poirot character who was perfectly self-contained no matter how at odds he was with his environment. Poirot was full of mannerisms - he had an effete walk, a crafted moustache and spoke English with a strong Belgian accent. Said Tiny, 'I tried to be Hercule Poirot. I would lie at home in bed and read the dialogue aloud when he spoke. I would put on a French accent'. Herbie was trying on 'routines'.

Tillie was not someone who kept her opinions to herself. After years of working in a sweatshop, doting on the boy and hoping for a son with a career in law or accountancy, is this what she gets! Captain America, Frank Sinatra, Comic Book Jesus, now Hercule Poirot! What kind of role models were these! Oh, another thing - everything now had to be *clean!*

'I'll tell you the turning point', says Tiny, 'This is a trauma with my mother yelling, and my parents yelling at each other constantly because of the strain of work and hardship. So, with all this taking place I certainly lived alone with myself.

'I never wanted my parents to sit down at the table when I was eating, unless they were eating. I never wanted my father to come over when I was eating, and I'm talking about 12-13 years old. I always asked my mother when she prepared a meal, *Did you wash your hands with soap first?* That would infuriate her, and I was scared to eat anything if she hadn't washed with soap on the hand. From my own parents I would have a straw and my own glass. From my own parents I didn't want them to sit by me when I was eating, unless they were eating.

'My father pressed it and I hated that. Really, I hated the fact he did that. My mother said, *Leave him alone, you know who he is already.* And I liked that because she didn't press herself. But he was a very gentle man, and he thought that he could get me out of it. It got worse.' (25)

Alone in his room, Herbie practiced being Poirot until he mastered it. Then he tried Rudolph Valentino's phrasing until he mastered that. Next he copied John Barrymore's melodramatic way of saying the phrase, *Darling, how depressed I am* until he got that right too. He played records on the wind-up phonogram, sang along, picking up the voiceprints of Irving Kaufman, Russ Colombo, Henry Burr, Rudy Vallee and Bing Crosby. He didn't know why he was doing it, that's just what Herbie did, and he was enjoying himself.

Trouble At School

Then came a new addition to the family. In his early teenage years Herbie gained another cousin and Hal got a brother – Bernie. Herbie enjoyed playing with his little cousin. That part of family life was a delight. However Herbie started getting into lots of trouble at school where he was inattentive, unmotivated and seemingly carefree. While Hal achieved excellence at school, Herbie had to repeat two years.

'Leave the boy alone', said Butros, 'he'll be fine'.

'Ahh,' said Tillie, 'My husband thought I was too strict, he didn't like the way I talked to the boy, the way I got angry. *You'll see,* said my husband, *when he'll be 13, 14 years old he'll be a genius!* He had a real belief in him. Maybe he saw something I didn't!' (26)

Being strongly left-handed Herbie was frustrated that his teacher insisted he write with his right. It seemed a small issue but Herbie was digging in, or as the teacher saw it – being defiant. And that wasn't the only problem. Herbie kept getting crushes. He wooed Miss Lila (Cordian) in 1944 and Miss Anne (Hesse) in 1945 and probably others, dreamily entertaining them in stairwells with the speaking voice of John Barrymore and the singing voice of Russ Colombo – *I'm just a prisoner of love.* This annoyed the teachers. Quite a lot, actually.

Back in the days when 'men were men', Herbie was more attracted to so-called *girl's* subjects like Typing than a *boy's* subject like Woodwork. He was the only male in Typing Class. One day the teacher asked Herbie to open a window and when he couldn't do it, she mocked him in front of the girls. He chipped her and was sent to the principal.

Herbie described the incident, 'One teacher embarrassed me and I answered her back. She said, *I'll send you to the Principal.* I said, *He's an old man anyway!* She sent me to him.

Next - the Principal's office, '*What are you here for?*

I said, *I called you an old man.*

He said, *I'm ringing your Mother!*' And Herbie was expelled.

Expulsion is a substantial punishment for charge of mild insolence. Was the principal gunning for him? Either way, he was out. Tillie was livid. 'My Mother came to the school', Tiny explained, 'and the principal let me in again. He forgave me. But then I got into trouble with the Physical Education teacher because I was listening to baseball games on the staircase with a portable radio. And then they caught me singing to the girls during lunch break in the stairs. So that was the end of that and they told me to leave'.

Herbie's second expulsion was for real. He left school after completing his sophomore year. 'What's it gonna be?' says Tillie, 'Get out and get yourself a job!' (27)

'It was not easy leaving because then my father said, *Look at your cousin. He's going to College. You haven't graduated high school. So we have to work for you!* My mother said, *What kind of a son is this? What kind of boy is this? It came from you* (meaning my father). *We never had such an odd family.* She called me "Dope" here and there. She didn't mean to, but that did get me. Sure it would hurt. But it would hurt seeing her working. She was a very beautiful woman when she was young. My mother was a very very beautiful sensual woman. I saw pictures of her and for her to work and have the hard life - it hardened her.'

At family gatherings Herbie now preferred the company of his kid cousin. Bernie recalls Herbie playing with him every Friday night. One of his toys was an electric football game.

Bernie also recalls the kerfuffle around Herbie's expulsion. He recalls Butros taking sides with Tillie and calling Herbie a 'prick' to which Herbie responded most politely, 'Oh, thank you'. But Bernie isn't convinced that Herbie was actually expelled. He says, 'I don't think he was expelled. He was reprimanded and probably banned for a couple of days or something like that. You never could believe some of the things that Herbie said. Some of it became folklore after awhile.' (28)

Darling, how depressed I am! With the world seemingly against him, Herbie retreated into his music – where Rudy Vallee, Irving Kaufman and Henry Burr lifted his spirits to the heavens. 'What are you going to do with your life?' nagged Tillie. Herbie responded that one day he'll be a star. (29)

None of this impressed his parents, who could not see how their boy might earn a living in post-War America. How depressed *everybody* was during that terrible World War II.

One sad day, Herbie and Hal were shocked to overhear their aunt had been murdered by the Nazis. She, who stayed in Poland in 1914 when the rest of her family migrated to America.

Pied Piper

As the War drew to its end, good times kicked in again. There are many happy family photographs and memories, especially when Hal and Bernie's parents bought a 'bungalow colony' in the Catskills. Hal remembers Uncle Butros as a 'neat guy', someone who would engage them in jokes, conversation and activities. He sounds like everybody's favourite uncle.

Hal and Bernie's family holiday pad in the Catskills is where Herbie gathered his first audience, singing songs like *Ghost Riders In the Sky* to little Bernie and friends. Herbie sang, told them stories and they loved him. Bernie recalls the younger kids following Herbie around 'like he was the Pied Piper'. (30)

By now, Herbie was fully obsessed with the Top 10 radio hits and his 78rpm record player. He also loved movies that he and Hal continued to attend. To him, the world of Rudolph Valentino, Bing Crosby, Shirley Temple, Rudy Vallee and Miss Elizabeth Taylor was a perfect dream.

Miss Elizabeth Taylor

Then Herbie started writing his own songs and poems. He started at 14, with a song that he hoped the Dodgers might take up as their theme song. Their manager responded curtly, 'I'm sorry, the Dodgers only make music with bat and ball'.

At 15 (1947) Miss Elizabeth Taylor was Herbie's muse. At Hal's insistence, Herbie saw her new film *Cynthia,* after which he went back five times. 'And from that time on,' he says, 'she was so beautiful I had to meet her'. Those eyes. (31)

At the tender age of 14 Elizabeth Taylor wrote *Nibbles And Me,* a book about her pet squirrel. Herbie read and re-read that book, well aware that they were about the same age and she was a published author. If she could write at 14, maybe he could write too?

So he wrote a poem – his first – to Miss Elizabeth Taylor. The poem bursts with three four-line stanzas of flattery advising her to be 'good' and 'kind' before closing with the lines:

> *And sometimes when your thoughts are free*
> *Won't you kindly think of me.*

Fifteen-year old Herbie followed this by composing a song for her, possibly his second composition (after the Dodger's song). It was titled, You're the Only One. (32) Three months later, through a friend whose father worked at NBC Radio, Herbie was given a ticket to a radio program that featured Miss Taylor in person.

Four days later, a Wednesday afternoon, Herbie waited two hours at the St Regis Hotel until, at 3.00 in the afternoon, he was chosen from the crowd of fans and ushered upstairs into her presence. She signed Herbie's scrapbook and blew him a kiss. He found the gesture captivating and he started blowing kisses too. (33)

'She had the most beautiful violet eyes I'd ever seen. That day I said to myself, *I have to make it on her level. I want to meet Elizabeth Taylor at her level* – if ever there was a turning point in wanting to be a star, this was it.' Hal concurs, 'He had one ambition and that ambition was to be a star. He set a goal and aimed for that goal and never turned aside from that goal even though there were lots of years of hardship – but he made it.' (34)

'Ahh!' said Tillie, commenting on Herbie's employment prospects after dropping out of school, 'He'll promise and promise, then does what he wants. What can you do?' (35)

There were indeed lots of years of hardship. His next 12 years – from 1950 to 1962 – were absolutely fruitless. It is amazing that he persisted. (36)

Footnotes

1) Caroline Jones interview, 30 August 1983. Although Tiny frequently tells reporters his name is Herbert Buckingham Khaury, it is in fact Herbert Butros Khaury. Tiny's birth certificate and passport can be viewed on the Internet on the official Tiny Tim website, www.tinytim.org

2) Caroline Jones interview, 30 August 1983.

3) Martin Sharp tape 19 November 1978. Also Tiny Tim, interview with Lowell Tarling, 4 April 1992.

4) Tiny Tim, interview with Lowell Tarling, 4 April 1992.

5) Tiny Tim, interview with Lowell Tarling, 4 April 1992.

6) Tiny Tim, interview with Lowell Tarling, 4 April 1992.

7) Tiny Tim, interview with Lowell Tarling, 4 April 1992.

8) Tiny Tim, interview with Lowell Tarling, 4 October 1991. Footage can be seen of Charleston Court in the Martin Sharp film, *Street of Dreams.* Also, Harold Stein, interview with Lowell Tarling, 1 April 2002.

9) Harold Stein, interview with Lowell Tarling, 1 April 2002.

10) Harold Stein, interview with Lowell Tarling, 1 April 2002.

11) Sue Khaury, *Memories of My Husband Tiny Tim,* 1998 unpublished.

12) Tiny Tim, interview with Lowell Tarling, 4 April 1992.

13) Bernie Stein, interview with Lowell Tarling, 29 March 2002.

14) Tiny Tim, interview with Lowell Tarling, 4 October 1991. For more references to comic books, also Tiny Tim, interview with Lowell Tarling, 4 April 1992.

15) Harold Stein, interview with Lowell Tarling, 1 April 2002.

16) Harry Stein, *Tiny Tim*, p.16, Playboy Press, 1976.

17) Harold Stein, interview with Lowell Tarling, 1 April 2002. Also Bernie Stein, interview with Lowell Tarling, 29 March 2002.

18) Tiny Tim, interview with Lowell Tarling, 4 April 1992. And Harold Stein, interview with Lowell Tarling, 1 April 2002.

19) Tiny Tim, interview with Lowell Tarling, 4 April 1992.

20) Tiny Tim, interview with Lowell Tarling, 4 April 1992.

21) Tiny Tim, interview with Lowell Tarling, 4 April 1992.

22) Tiny Tim, interview with Lowell Tarling, 4 April 1992.

23) Tiny Tim, interview with *Ram* magazine, 14 June 1989.

24) Harold Stein, interview with Lowell Tarling, 1 April 2002.

25) Tiny Tim, interview with Lowell Tarling, 4 April 1992.

26) Harry Stein, *Tiny Tim*, p.17, Playboy Press, 1976.

27) Harry Stein, *Tiny Tim*, p.18, Playboy Press, 1976.

28) Tiny Tim, interview with Lowell Tarling, 4 April 1992. Also, Sue Khaury, *Memories of My Husband Tiny Tim,* 1998 unpublished. Bernie Stein, interview with Lowell Tarling, 29 March 2002. Harold Stein, interview with Lowell Tarling, 1 April 2002.

29) Harry Stein, *Tiny Tim*, p.18, Playboy Press, 1976.

30) Bernie Stein, interview with Lowell Tarling, 29 March 2002.

31) Tiny Tim interview with Lowell Tarling, 3 October 1991. Also, Elizabeth Taylor, *Nibbles & Me*, Duell, Sloan & Pearce, NY, 1946. Tiny Tim, *Beautiful Thoughts,* Doubleday & Company, Garden City New York, 1969. Also, Sue Khaury, *Memories of My Husband Tiny Tim,* 1998 unpublished.

32) In 1995 Tiny recorded *You're The Only One* on *Songs of an Impotent Troubadour.*

33) Tiny Tim, interview with Lowell Tarling, 4 April 1992. Also Mark Mitchell, interview with Lowell Tarling, 30 March 2002,

34) Harold Stein, interview with Lowell Tarling, 1 April 2002.

35) Harry Stein, *Tiny Tim*, p.17, Playboy Press, 1976.

36) For the earliest photos of Tiny, see photographs courtesy of Bernie and Hal Stein, on the Tiny Tim Memorial Site www.tinytim.org

2

Larry Love

Definitely the name I wanted was Larry Love
Tiny Tim

In January 1949 ukulele legend Arthur Godfrey was the first performer in television history to have two top-rated TV shows running simultaneously – *Arthur Godfrey's Talent Scouts* and *Arthur Godfrey and His Friends*. His show ran until June 1957. At the peak of his popularity in the early 1950s, Godfrey commanded a radio and television audience of 40 million per week. He was the most valuable single property in CBS. Advertising dollars from his shows comprised about 12% of the Columbia Broadcasting System (CBS) total annual revenue.

Before this, the ukulele had certainly had its moments, notably in Bing Crosby's 1939 film *Waikiki Wedding* in which Bing held a one but didn't play it. Bob Hope strummed a uke in his 1940 film *Road to Singapore*. And so-called 'uke player' George Formby didn't play one at all, it was actually a banjulele. But Godfrey was legit. He played it, gave lessons on TV and even proposed the instrument as an antidote to the rise of Post-War teenage delinquency. Godfrey said, 'A kid carrying a ukulele isn't going to get into much trouble' – which wasn't quite true of Herbie.

In addition to the broadcasts, there were many spin-offs, including 'How To Play Uke' books and, most significantly, Godfrey endorsed the famous plastic Maccaferri *Islander* ukulele. Herbie was one of nine million buyers who paid the $5.95.

It wasn't his first uke - that was a *Diamond Head*. The Maccaferri was his second one – the 'fashionable' one - and it played remarkably easily alongside Arthur Godfrey's *You Can Learn To Play The Ukulele* book. Tiny dismissed any suggestion that there was anything original about his main choice of instrument. He bought it because it was portable and because 'everyone was playing them then'. (1)

Herbie had a facility for learning stringed instruments - ukulele, 6-string guitar, later the banjo-mandolin and tenor guitar. The portability of the smaller instruments eased the inconvenience of public transport when he performed up to three times a week at parties and amateur nights under a range of stage names. One thing is for sure, he wasn't happy with his persona as Herbie Khaury and the outset of the decade saw him struggling to find an identity. 'I had to make it with this thing,' he said, tapping his hawk-nose. (2)

His school failures behind him, Herbie's real study was all ahead, and with his 78 records and gramophone player he was a diligent student, practicing the subtle difference between – say – early-Crosby and late-Crosby, as well as a range of songs from the past, especially love songs. Although many family members would have preferred him to have stuck with the violin, at this stage they were mostly supportive of Herbie's budding musical career. He was not the first in the family to follow this path, Auntie Leah's sons played in a wedding band and they were doing okay.

And so, Herbie was often asked to sing at family gatherings and parties. He would entertain Bernie and his friends with renditions of *Ten Little Indian Boys, Old King Cole* and *Playmates Come Out And Play With Me*. His parents encouraged the performances. (3)

Regular Employment

In 1950 Herbie registered with the Lawrence Employment Agency on 42nd Street. He got his first job working for the US Bead Company. It lasted just one day. 'I had to carry big boxes of beads with one of those truck wheelers,' said Tiny. 'I checked in at 9.00 and checked out at 5.00 forever. I tell ya, I couldn't lift my wife let alone a box of beads! I had to carry it all through that district down in 37th Street. The whole box fell and I quit my job right there and then'. (4)

He would continue in-and-out of bit-work for the following year. Jobs included delivering art supplies for Grand Central Art, delivering false teeth for Vogel & Parness, delivering phone books and a stint with the post office. Three weeks was the longest time he held a job. The three-week record was with Cam Photostats.

Around this time Herbie applied to join the Air Force to become part of the space program. He also tried the Army, the Coast Guard and the Marines. What was he thinking?

Amateur Shows

After work, Herbie would retreat to his room and absorb new songs. No more Al Bowlly, Al Jolson, Rudy Vallee. It was the 50s now and the hits were sung by Nat King Cole, Johnny Ray, Rosemary Clooney, Perry Como, Louis Armstrong, Frankie Laine, Kay Starr and Guy Mitchell. He always sang along, copying their phrasing and inflections.

Herbie's first time behind a microphone was in 1951 where – responding to an advertisement in the *Show Business* magazine - he performed on an amateur show called *Mom Grant's Riviera.*

While not the success for which he had hoped, from this he learned of other amateur shows where he also sang – like, the *Blue Haven* in Jackson Heights, *The Nut House* in Flushing, and if he couldn't find a booking he'd perform on the streets, in bars, at parties and simply anywhere. The 1929 Nick Lucas hit, *Tiptoe Through The Tulips* was already a part of Herbie's repertoire. He composed his own songs too, like *Who Stole Baby's Bottle From The Drawer?*

Metro-Goldwyn-Meyer (MGM)

In March 1951 Herbie got a $40-per-week job as a messenger boy for Metro-Goldwyn-Meyer (MGM), whose head office was in the Leows Building in Times Square.

It was as close to show business as Herbie had ever been and he tried to stick it out. He lasted almost a year and even got the attention of one of the honchos, not for his singing but his nudie pictures. Mr Emerling was the head of Leows Theatres, Tiny describes him as, 'So conservative, so private, no one spoke to him or saw him'. Emerling learned from his secretary that Herbie had a copy of the nude Marilyn Monroe calendar, 'He called me into his office to show him,' said Tiny. From there, it was a matter of getting the attention of the even bigger bosses, those who might influence his career. (5)

Every Christmas the 'big shots' would throw a party and invite their junior staff - messenger boys, lift operators, etc - to entertain them. It was an audition by default, a big deal for the little people to strut their stuff before a roomful of hitmakers. Herbie saw it as an opportunity to be discovered. He performed in front of the big shots and talent scouts but they passed him up. 'I bombed in the straight voice', Tiny said, to his great annoyance. (6)

Had this fairytale discovery happened, there might have been no falsetto because there would have been no pressure for Herbie to explore his extraordinary range. But that's not what happened. Instead, the MGM executives barely clapped.

After this, the MGM job became an effort. They sacked Herbie in August 1952 for turning up late because he'd slept overnight at Ebbet's Field baseball park, waiting to buy a ticket to the seventh game of the World Series Baseball. After this he was never again conventionally employed. The sacking gave him time to stay home and hone his act for the amateur nights.

It was on such an amateur night that he met Buddy Friar in 1952. Buddy was Herbie's first manager. He took Herbie around the clubs, the *Blue Room* in Elizabeth New Jersey, *The Park Terrace* in Brooklyn and the *Lighthouse Café,* Manhattan. Herbie didn't win anything and he did it all again next time.

Positive Thinking

His conventional working life behind him, Herbie decided to do a lot more work on himself. He scoured libraries reading about the history of popular song. He also read self-help books, especially *The Power of Positive Thinking* by Norman Vincent Peale, a philosophy that never left Herbie and is the corner-stay of his 1969 book *Beautiful Thoughts*.

Around this time, Herbie was also impressed with another book, *Life Is For Living* by Bishop Fulton Sheen. It brought Jesus-of-the-comics back into Herbie's life and he developed a crush on the Virgin Mary. (7)

Herbie's burst of religious enthusiasm coincided with a revival meeting held by Rev Jack Werston in a church on 8th Avenue and 44th Street. This is where Herbie formally accepted Jesus Christ as his Lord and was baptised into the Catholic faith. From then on Herbie peppered his speech with religious phrases like, 'thank God through Christ', 'Thank Jesus Christ for his blessings' and 'may s/he rest in peace' (when he spoke of the dead).

Prior to this, Herbie cursed and swore like a regular New Yorker. Now, he eliminated not only swear words, but rather than say words like 'sex', 'breasts' and even 'seed', he spelled them out.

Herbie also took to calling people 'Mr, Mrs and Miss'.

And then came the high voice.

Shattering Results

Why shouldn't Herbie have a stage-name? He probably knew that Bing was really Harry Crosby, Rudy was really Hubert Vallee, Tony Bennett was really Anthony Bendetto, Guy Mitchell was really Al Cernik, and Dorothy Lamour was really Mary Leta Dorothy Kaumeyer. Everybody had a stage-name. The fans knew that. Herbie began developing his inner-cowboy, Texarkana Tex.

One day - probably one night - while alone with his records in his room, Herbie prayed to the Lord for guidance. When Herbie arose from his knees he felt an urge to sing like a bird. He exploded into a piercing falsetto, with shattering results. Tiny described the moment, 'Suddenly I felt original. I didn't sound like Crosby or Guy Mitchell or Perry Como or Frank Sinatra, and I knew I had found a different way to interpret the same popular songs'.

The jigsaw pieces were really coming together for him now. He tried the piercing high voice for the first time at the Old Alliance Club in St Mark's Place. The audience was stunned. He was supposed to be singing a Texarkana Tex rendition of *High Noon,* but he sang it in his *Tiptoe-Through-The-Tulips* falsetto instead.

Tiny recalls a couple in the audience. The male was nonplussed, but his girlfriend was amazed. Tiny describes the incident, 'I sang it like that in front of this fellow and his girlfriend. The girl was looking at me and starting to swoon. The fellow said, Look at her, she actually liked that sound! And that's when I knew I had something different!' (8)

Opposite To Valentino

When Rudy Vallee said 'if you can get people in a bar to stop and look - then you've got something', he can't have imagined how this totally inspired Texarkana Tex.

In 1953 - after studying a photograph of heartthrob, Rudolph Valentino - as a way of being 'different', Herbie decided to part his hair the opposite way to Valentino. Once he started on the hair there was no stopping him. After a time, he even stopped cutting it.

Dropping Texarkana Tex, Herbie began to further experiment with his personae. After standing in front of the mirror for a long time with a brush, he gradually evolved into Larry Love. He really wanted to be Larry Love, the heavy-duty romantic crooner as portrayed on the back over of *Tiny Tim's Second Album*.

From the world of glamour, Herbie got the idea to wear white foundation face paint (white 'for purity') then clown-like splotches of rouge (soon abandoned). The perfumes swiftly followed. (9)

His father said, 'Now he *is* a sissy!' (10)

'There's only one reason I did it,' said Tiny. 'When I started doing this I started getting attention from women which I wanted in a silly way – *Who is that creep?* – whatever – but at least they were looking, which was very important because it kept me writing songs, poetry, to certain girls I liked.

'That wasn't all – I'm talking 1953-54 now – I had white make-up on, as white as a sheet. I'm not talking about at night when I went to amateur shows, I'm talking about in the day time. I went in the subways and actually looked for work. Now the make-up was as white as talcum powder, like you'd see Kiss on stage today, except I didn't have the eyebrows or anything on the lips. But the make-up was heavy. Not only that but I was starting to buy cosmetics to cleanse the skin, which I do eight times a day, and not only that but I would use night creams before I'd retire'. (11)

According to his relatives, 'the whole product was there in 1955' – the only missing element was the name. It was still Herbie off-stage and Larry on-stage.

Shortly afterwards, Larry Love won an amateur night contest! He had never won anything before. Greenwich Village was fast becoming his regular haunt, only 20 minutes away from Washington Heights by subway – eight miles or 160 blocks away - and the fare was only a dime. (12)

In mid-1954 Larry Love failed an audition at the Palace Theatre Broadway. He blew it in the straight voice and was most annoyed with himself. On his return to Washington Heights he was taunted by commuters, travelling (as he did out of necessity) in full make-up and stage clothes.

He had to cope with professional failure, plus the mockery of passing strangers, before returning home to disparaging parents who figured that without them Herbie would be homeless, because he couldn't hold down a straight job.

And as for his silly new look?

Rock N Roll!

The development of the Fender electric guitar in the early-50s made Rock and Roll music possible. Herbie heard this electric guitar-driven style of music for the first time in the mid-50s, while driving to a party with friends. He asked the driver to stop the car because he couldn't believe his ears!

Overnight, the music producers lost interest in acts like Larry Love, suggestive of the previous decade's Swooner Crooners. They didn't even want Sinatra. High voices, forget it. Harmony singers, buried as the fourth part of the doo-wop bands, were the only high voices of interest. Promoters were looking to project male teenage virility. Bill Hayley-style jive was the sound (as distinct from Benny Goodman jive). But the slightly flabby Bill Hayley was not the image they sought. It was to be Elvis.

Despite the press depictions of Rock and Roll as 'wild' music, it is an extremely conservative format. Each song usually comprises three chords wrapped around a fairly predictable blues-based progression. Most song constructions were cribbed from well defined Country, Blues and Gospel musical stereotypes. This was all part of Rock music's instant appeal to the senses.

Herbie's backdated song catalog and enormous vocal range now counted against him. The newer singers were only required to sing inside little more than one octave, with back-up vocalists handling the rest. The singers from which Larry Love derived were once the pillars of popular western music. Henry Burr was the biggest selling star of the pre-1920s. Billy Murray, Al Jolson, Irving Kaufman, Rudy Vallee, Gene Austin were all mainstream artists, as were – of course – Bing Crosby, Russ Colombo and Frank Sinatra. But in 1959 such songs were out of period, and thought (I suppose?) 'freakish' - where Gene Vincent, Little Richard and Jerry Lee Lewis were hep cats.

Furthermore the new music was powered by electric guitars which had grunt, an element not possible with plastic Maccaferri Islander ukes. It was as if Herbie, Texarkana Tex and Larry Love all had to go back to square one.

Are You A Fairy?

Herbie's relationship with his parents was going downhill. They couldn't understand why a man would wear make-up? Where once they applauded him at family parties, they now mocked him, except for Aunt Leah who said that he would 'make it' someday. Hal explained a reason for her belief in Herbie, 'Aunt Leah's sons were musicians. They played in local bands. That's why she knew what music meant and how to work into the system and how to encourage somebody to become a musician'. (13)

Sometimes Butros took Herbie's side. Cousin Bernie recalls, 'His father understood Tiny and it's funny that his mother didn't. His father used to come to bat for Tiny a lot with his mother saying *Leave him alone*. His father was a different kind of personality of course to his mother, but it was his father who also would go into New York City and pick up a lot of 78 records for Tiny.' (14)

One of the low points in his family life was when Herbie's godmother Mary called him a fairy. Tiny said, 'My godmother came in – she was the one my mother worked for - for years – and she said, *What are you, a fairy?* Just like that. I didn't like what she said. I wasn't warm with her for a long time. I knew what she was trying to do but I didn't like it.'

The accusation bit deep possibly because it wasn't entirely unfounded. In February 1956 Herbie had a relationship with a male friend. He probably wondered what it meant? The relationship had sexual overtones, yet it comprised only 'massages'. Years later Tiny thanked God-through-Christ for all the things they *didn't* do. This friend got married in 1961.) (15)

When I asked whether Tiny'd had a sexual relationship with a man, his third wife Miss Sue responded dismissively, 'Not much of one. He never did anything that could be called sex by anyone's definition'. (16)

Meanwhile, Herbie was upsetting people with his appearance and growing crop of mannerisms, which seemed without justification, as he was unable to convince anybody in the music industry to even give him an audition. Unfazed, Herbie continued performing throughout 1957-58 wherever there was a small audience. We're now talking no dollars and true grit.

May 1958 was hard. Herbie came home from a party at 6.00am and his father smashed his guitar (probably his tenor guitar). Later in the year Herbie had further physical conflict with his parents causing the Police to come to the house twice. (17)

Cousin Bernie explained, 'His father thought he was crazy. None of the older people encouraged him at all. They tried to discourage him. And yet he persisted. Later on they were all proud of what he accomplished, but he had no support. He was very courageous'. (18)

At first glance, 1958 is another in a string of bad years for Herbie's career. But it wasn't. It was a good year for song writing, a talent for which his later Tiny Tim incarnation is not known. His best, in his own estimation, is a song called *Stephanie* written for Stephanie Morgan, '…a gidget-type girl. She never fitted into my dream but you never known how songs come. This is the best one I thought I wrote at that time'. It is no 3-chord ditty, but a fully conceptualised pop arrangement with verse, middle eight, slick chords, gag words and a closing arrangement at the end.

Other songs written in this period are *Our Little Secret, Pretty Baby, Don't Call Me Anymore, Whispering Voices* and *Heaven Only Knows*. He continued writing songs, all his life, but 1958 may have been his most productive song-writing year. (19)

Even so, with his song-writing talent unrecognised (not even now), Herbie struggled on with no encouragement. Throughout most of the 50s, while his mother and father were working their difficult jobs, Herbie stayed home by day learning/writing new songs, and looking for gigs by night.

Hubert's Flea Circus

Times couldn't have been more difficult time for Herbie - in conflict with his parents, teased on public transport yet sticking to his guns.

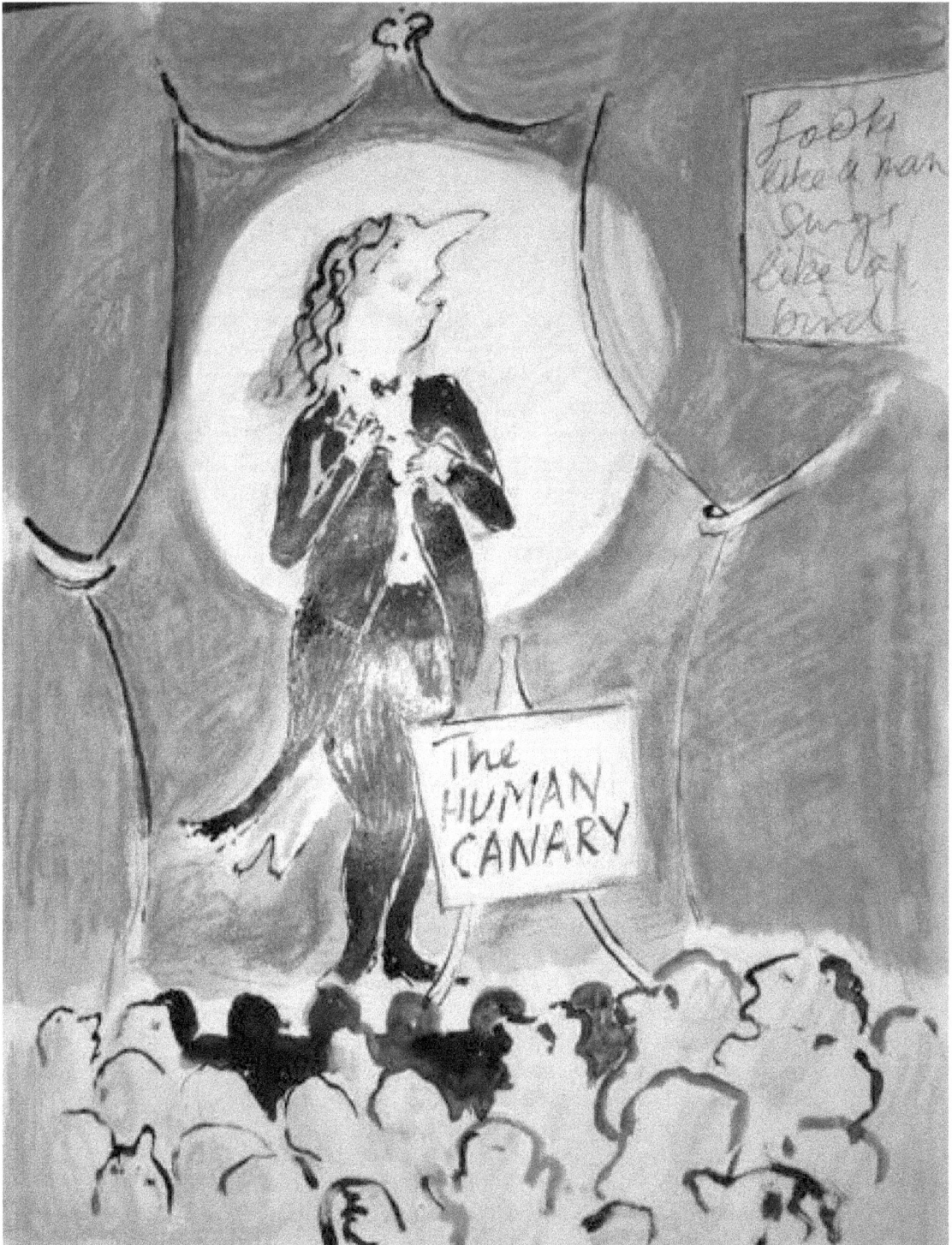

Tiny really sprang from the carnival. His first job was as the Human Canary in Hubert's Flea Circus on Times Square. Destin the Magician got him the job.

Martin Sharp, 13 April 1983

Then Herbie got another great idea. He grew his hair long when crewcuts were in vogue!

'Don't ask me what it is, it's sick!' Tiny recalls people sneering as they walked past him on public transport. (20)

Although the word 'freak' never seemed to bother him, in Herbie's case there was one slight justification. His first paying gig was in 1959 at Hubert's Flea Circus (variously called Hubert's Museum) in 42nd Street where he appeared as Larry Love 'The Human Canary'. He was on the same bill as Estelline Pike the Sword Swallower, Lydia the Contortionist, Sailor White the Strong Man, Congo the Jungle Witch Doctor, the Elephant Lady (with elephant feet) and a man who played *Anchors Away* on 10 glasses. 'They were freaks of nature,' recalled Tiny. (21)

Tiny would stand behind the curtain, waiting for the barker to announce, 'And now ladies and gentlemen, I want to introduce this man here. He looks like a man but he sings like a canary! The voice of a bird!' And Tiny would chirp his way through one song. There was nothing particularly freakish about the Human Canary act. Just a little makeup and a falsetto voice, that was about all. (22)

Through he trudged from one record company to another, and from gig to gig – sometimes walking miles after hours if he didn't have the subway fare – Hubert's Flea Circus was to be Larry Love's only professional job to date. Tillie would yell at him, 'Sleeping all day, coming home at five in the morning, is this how a nice boy acts?' (23)

Although he didn't know Tiny yet, comedian and raconteur Lenny Bruce was fascinated by Hubert's Museum – a place he would often cite in his outrageous stand-up monologues - having been taken there at a young age by his mother.

And so Herbie/Larry took his first step on the show business ladder by performing at a Freak Show. 'It was only a week, my friend…', he told me dismissively, '…only a week'. (24)

Perhaps so, but a week in which he met Destin the Magician, who introduced him to his second manager – maybe his first 'proper' manager, George King.

1960

For as long as anyone can remember, Herbie assiduously studied popular song and visited music stores from Broadway to Greenwich Village. When interviewed, Mr Meltzer at the Merit Music Shop recalled Herbie buying difficult-to-obtain 78 records from his store in the early 1960s.

Six years after Tiny's death – in 2002 – I visited a sheet music store in New York who also claimed Tiny Tim as a regular customer for decades. No wonder he was reputed as knowing around 10,000 songs!

1960 was also the year when Herbie, now 27, first contemplated marriage. He described the object of his affection, Miss Nancy Prince, as 'strong'. She was probably a lesbian, attracted to Herbie because 'she knew I wouldn't touch her' said Tiny, 'I'd have loved to have married her'. But no marriage ensued, because she never asked him.

Having experienced much public derision, Herbie was toughening up. This time around the wheel Herbie was no longer scared of being seen as 'weird', he seemed to welcome it ('at least they were noticing!'). He certainly enjoyed telling me about freaking out the subway commuters with his long hair and white face. He probably looked like the Charles Dickens character, Fagin!

It's a wonder he wasn't beaten up, but somehow he seemed to talk his way out of it when trouble came his way. He was held-up several times. On one occasion when he had no money, he offered his assailant the only thing in his pocket – breath freshener. 'This guy is *weird,* man', he reported to the gang. They fled.

Said Miss Sue, 'Tiny had a tremendous need for recognition and to be noticed. Tiny noticed the things that made people pay attention to him, which he did even more. Apparently one time his hair started to get long and people started to comment on it. He wanted the attention. Whether it was positive or negative, he wanted people to know he was there. He wanted to be somebody. Even if it was somebody notorious and absurd, he still wanted to be somebody that people would remember'. (25)

Also around this late-50s/early 60s period he teamed up with a 19-year old student, a girl 'who needed $35 to pay for her schooling'.

They performed together for a time, and Tiny recalls the audience throwing dollars when she sang while yelling at him, 'What are you there for?' The duo didn't last. Larry Love was nobody's backing band. He was his own act.

Darry Dover

Around 1960 Herbie dropped Larry Love for a worse idea - Darry Dover. It didn't work for him at all. 'I had shoes thrown at me,' Tiny told a *Newsweek* reporter in 1968. 'A hired man in black would set off a siren to stop me, but I always finished the song. I was booed for years. I went from dive to dive and bar to bar all over New York and New Jersey.' (26)

Although Tiny never described them as such, 1950-1962 must have been terrible. Twelve years is a long time without a real bite. Larry Love only had one nibble, a booking in a freak show. Then as Darry Dover, he lost ground.

Tiny said, 'I sounded like nobody else and I certainly wasn't good looking. I did not look like Rock Hudson. I've always wanted to appeal to women. I've always wanted women to notice me. But more than that, I couldn't live with myself the way I was, I didn't want to take this *nose* off because I wanted to take a challenge and make it with this thing. So I definitely needed something else to go with my looks. There's a reason for it. I did have an inferiority complex. I felt that something was not right.' (27)

Tiny reminds us that this was more than a decade before Alice Cooper wore make-up and years before the Beatles turned long hair into high fashion. In those times, Tiny looked like the cover of his 1982 album *Chameleon,* and he stayed in character off-stage as well as on.

Sir Timothy Thames

Twelve barren years, I can't leave this thought alone.

Surely, being a messenger boy or working in a factory would have been better than these nightly humiliations? But this is the period when Herbie did his 'PhD' in music, having the daytime to learn and the night time to struggle from amateur show to amateur show, for – not 'little' reward – I'm talking NO reward. There is nothing in these years to suggest that Herbie would become anything more than a guy with a genius for reproducing songs that nobody wanted to remember. By 1962 after earning virtually no income for more than a decade most people would have taken the hint and given up.

But Destin the Magician had introduced Herbie to George King a toupee-wearing man who carried a flask of whisky in his pocket and saw some potential in Tiny. (27) He told Herbie to forget Texarkana Tex, Larry Love, Darry Dover and other alter-egos I forgot to mention, like Judas K Foxglove, Vernon Castle and Emmett Swink.

In Mr King's great moment of genius, because Britpop was invading America – he christened Herbert Khaury…*Sir Timothy Thames*! But Herbie never mastered the British-accent, which left King struggling for a new idea.

'Okay,' he said. 'We're gonna call you Tiny Tim'.

A star was born.

But Herbie didn't want to be Tiny Tim. He explained, 'A man by the name of George King gave me that name back in 1961. I didn't like Tiny Tim because it was not original, but I had it when I started working Greenwich Village in New York and it caught on. And by the time I tried to change it I couldn't change it no more.

'Definitely the name I wanted was *Larry Love'*. (28)

Footnotes:

1. Tiny Tim, interview with Lowell Tarling, 4 April 1992.
2. Tiny Tim, interview with Lowell Tarling, 4 October 1991.
3. Tiny Tim interview with Lowell Tarling, 4 April 1992. 'Those were the songs I sang to people in the country when I went up to the Catskills for the summer for two months.' Harold Stein, interview with Lowell Tarling, 1 April 2002 recalls Aunt Leah's sons band and Tiny's early musical interests.
4. Tiny Tim, interview with Lowell Tarling, 4 October 1991.
5. Tiny Tim, interview with Kate Fitzpatrick, *Sydney Morning Herald*, 3 September 1983.
6. Tiny Tim, interview with Lowell Tarling, 24 August 1982.
7. Tiny Tim, 'The Perfect Mother', *Esquire*, December 1970, pp. 144-145. He writes, 'First of all, the greatest of all mothers was the mother of Christ, the Virgin Mary.'
8. Tiny Tim, interview with Lowell Tarling, 24 August 1982. For a different account, Sue Khaury, *Memories of My Husband Tiny Tim*, 1998 unpublished. She said the breakthrough song was *You Are My Sunshine*.
9. Tiny Tim, interview with Lowell Tarling, 24 August 1982.
10. Sue Khaury, *Memories of My Husband Tiny Tim*, 1998 unpublished.
11. Tiny Tim interview with Lowell Tarling, 4 April 1992.
12. Harold Stein, interview with Lowell Tarling, 1 April 2002.
13. Harold Stein, interview with Lowell Tarling, 1 April 2002.
14. Bernie Stein, interview with Lowell Tarling, 29 March 2002. Also Mark Mitchell, interviewed by Lowell Tarling, 30 March 2002 .
15. Stein, Harry, *Tiny Tim*, Playboy Press 1976. And, Sue Khaury, *Memories of My Husband Tiny Tim*, 1998 unpublished.
16. Sue Khaury, interview with Lowell Tarling and Michael Wilkinson, 30 March 2002.
17. Stein, Harry, *Tiny Tim*, Playboy Press 1976.
18. Bernie Stein, interview with Lowell Tarling, 29 March 2002.
19. Tiny Tim, Songs from an Impotent Troubadour, the core of this album is Tiny singing his own compositions. Tracks 3-23 (of this 35 track CD) cover compositions from 1947-1964.
20. Tiny Tim interview with Lowell Tarling, 4 April 1992.
21. Tiny Tim, interview with Lowell Tarling, 4 October 1991.
22. Tiny Tim, interviewed by Caroline Jones, *ABC Radio*, 25 October 1978.
23. Sue Khaury, *Memories of My Husband Tiny Tim*, 1998 unpublished.
24. Tiny Tim, interview with Lowell Tarling, 4 October 1991.
25. Sue Khaury, interview with Lowell Tarling and Michael Wilkinson, 30 March 2002.
26. Tiny Tim, *Newsweek*, 20 May 1968.
27. Tiny Tim, interview with Lowell Tarling, 4 October 1991.
28. Tiny Tim, interview with Lowell Tarling, 24 August 1982. Also, Sue Khaury, *Memories of My Husband Tiny Tim*, 1998 unpublished.

Taken in 1991, Tiny wasn't sure which of these was the actual site of Hubert's Flea Circus. Was it Roxy XXX Movies? Clothes Encounters? Photo ID Center? Peep Land? It was one of them, though Tiny couldn't pinpoint which one.

3

Answer To The Beatles

He was ahead of his time, the hair and the style of clothes. He had that a long time ago. That's why, when it came to the 70s and 80s, he fitted right in. He was a natural.
Cousin Hal

Tiny never made a big thing about his early connection with Bob Dylan. To hear Tiny tell it, you'd think their first encounter was in 1968 when Dylan invited him to jam on the Big Pink sessions, in Woodstock, upstate NY.

In fact, they knew each other six years before, which Dylan writes about in his *Chronicles.*

Bob Dylan

Dylan arrived in Greenwich Village in February 1961 and he didn't know anybody. He took to hanging out at *Café Wha?* where Tiny often tried to get a spot too. Both were desperate to get paying gigs, both were keen to learn a repertoire of songs that was nothing like the current Pop charts, and neither had any money.

Dylan describes the *Café Wha?* audience as, 'mostly college types, suburbanites, lunch-hour secretaries, sailors and tourists'. The daytime show featured 'anyone and anything – a comedian, a ventriloquist, a steel drum group, a poet, a female impersonator, a duo who sang Broadway stuff, a rabbit-in-the-hat magician, a guy wearing a turban who hypnotised people in the audience, someone whose entire act featured facial acrobatics – and just about anybody who wanted to break into show business… one of the guys who played in the afternoons was the falsetto-speaking Tiny Tim'.

These afternoon performers did it for little or no money. The night time show was the bigger draw, featuring comedians on their way up, like Richard Pryor, Woody Allen, Joan Rivers and Lenny Bruce - whom Tiny got to know.

Tiny and Dylan would occasionally hang out together in the Café Wha? kitchen, hoping for a feed. Norbert the Cook would take care of them, giving them all the French fries and hamburgers they could eat. One day, Dylan questioned Tiny about being the Human Canary at Hubert's Flea Circus. Who knows what was on Dylan's mind? (1)

In September 1962 Dylan performed Carnegie Hall. Two weeks later he topped the bill in a Town Hall concert with Ian and Sylvia, John Lee Hooker, Judy Collins, Lynn Gold and instrumentalist Sandy Bull. Allan Grossman became his manager and *whoosh*, Dylan was gone. No more scratching for meals with Tiny.

Beautiful Tuesday

Grossman was on a roll, with a stable of chart-toppers that included Peter, Paul and Mary and now - Dylan. As one of Grossman's scouts, Roy Silver ran into Tiny's performance at *The Bitter End* and kept an eye on him ever after, reporting all developments back to his boss. For the next five years, leading to hit records on Frank Sinatra's Reprise label – whether Tiny knew it or not – he was being watched by the music industry.

In 1961 Tiny recorded his first 45 rpm record, *Beautiful Tuesday* for Tuesday Weld, who had replaced Elizabeth Taylor as the star of his affections. Now he wanted to present it to her.

For 17 episodes (1959-1962) Miss Tuesday played a money-hungry character called Thalia Menninger in the Dobie Gillis TV program. At the close of 1961 she was visiting New York to promote the show. On New Year's Day 1962 Tiny arranged a meeting to present her with the record. Tiny arrived at the Algonquin Hotel on 59 West 44th Street as agreed but Miss Tuesday did not.

Someone said she had headed to Greenwich Village so Tiny chased after her. There he ran into Miss Cynthia, whom he knew. *Why the rush?* She asked. Tiny explained that he'd written a song for Miss Tuesday but then he'd lost her. Tiny was enchanted by Miss Cynthia's response, 'Why don't you write a song for me?' So that was Tiny's next song.

He also cut another record, *Be My Love,* which he describes as 'atrocious' (which it probably wasn't). He joked, 'The writer wanted to sue me for defamation of song'. Under various guises, Tiny made perhaps 30 independent recordings prior to *Tiptoe Through The Tulips.* They show both consistency and diversity. His five 1963 recordings were: *On The Old Front Porch, If I Had a Picture of You, This is the Missus, 10 Little Fingers 10 Little Toes* and *I'm A Nut.*

Having discovered the high voice, Tiny was certainly not going to drop that. However, Tiny sounds most comfortable when crooning. Elements of crooning appeared in all his songs, through all his life.

There is diversity too. He constantly tried new vocal tricks. He skatted remarkably well, he slid and skipped through various numbers. Unexpectedly his backing band sometimes moved towards elements of Britpop, which was beginning its invasion of the US charts. Was this Sir Timothy Thames?

Page Three

Things were now picking up. Tiny was being paid on a semi-regular basis, for example - two nights at $10 per night at *Café Bizarre* in the Village. It might seem like peanuts, but it was real money at last. Tiny also picked up six months work in another coffeehouse, where he earned $20 each weekend. Plus, talent shows, parties and other venues around Bleeker and MacDougal Streets. He roamed from gig to gig. And while most of the other performers were folkniks who lived in the Village, each night Tiny would catch the subway home to Washington Heights.

Herbie played wherever he could under his new name – Tiny Tim. George King insisted that he hold the Tiny Tim image because, where once there was no money coming in, there was now a trickle. Tiny had gradually reinvented himself. He was becoming known around the Village. Robert Zimmerman did the same thing when he became Bob Dylan.

Tiny's third wife, Miss Sue described Tiny's management of the time, 'Tiny was surrounded by two-bit hustlers and con men, each with a new scheme. The one who named him was George King. He always wore a toupee, "from Woolworths" as Tiny described it, and carried a bottle of whisky in his back pocket. He cheated young acting students by posing as a director. They paid to be in a "movie" which consisted of nothing more than a disconnected series of screen tests.

'King taught Tiny how to hustle for cash by reading the palms of pretty girls in the Village. Tiny used these opportunities for endless flirtations, though he seldom dated. He sometimes took his guitar, explaining that it was cracked because his father smashed it against his backside. Nevertheless he said it was "still a great instrument" and proceeded to serenade them. He started presenting a trophy to the prettiest girl he met every year.

'George King might have been in show business for a dollar, but for Tiny show business was about meeting girls. That was fine with guys like King who got Tiny jobs for ten bucks a night and took five in commission. One of Tiny's managers posed as a Catholic priest, hustling donations door-to-door. He went on to manage Procol Harem. Tiny signed multiple conflicting contracts with many of these men. Those contracts later cost Warner Brothers many lawsuits. Tiny seemed to feel that when these hustlers disappeared out of his life, their legal rights went with them'. Lyons tried to sign Tiny to Buddha Records but they turned him down. (2)

And then Tiny met a hydrocephalus man named Kiki Hall, whose boyfriend Ronnie Lyons knew Lenny Bruce. Hall worked as a part-time music hustler and part-time waiter at the *Page Three.* He introduced Tiny around. This gig became the staple of Tiny's income for the next two and a half years, $40 per week for performing four songs 10.00pm-4.00am six days a week. Three were sung in the high voice, and the fourth was *Hey Paula,* a duet with himself. On his *Impotent Troubadour* CD, Tiny described the Page Three as 'the starving amateur artist's *Copacabana* of the Village'. Drop-in visitors included celebrities like Mitzi Gaynor and her husband, Mick Jagger, Sarah Vaughan, Shelley Winters and financier and banker, Pierpont Morgan.

The Page Three was a Lesbian club where Tiny became extremely popular, really honing his act and perfecting his stage persona with beguiling songs like *I Enjoy Being a Girl.* It was here that Tiny added to his persona even more campy mannerisms for which he became known. He was louche, coy and virginal. Being Tiny, he always had crushes on various girls who liked him very much in return and, as he didn't want to 'do anything', that was all fine.

Within two days at Page Three he developed a big crush on Miss Snooky. (This of course did not preclude him simultaneously having a crush on Miss Ronnie, a more muscular type.) For Miss Snooky, Tiny wrote *The Spaceship Song* (recorded as a single in 1971). At Sanders Recording Studio on West 48th Street he also recorded *You Are Heaven Here On Earth*, plus other songs.

He also awarded to Miss Snooky the first of what became known as Tiny Tim's 'trophies'. They were literal trophies, which Tiny awarded annually and presented at the end of December. They cost him $25 (more than half his week's wage) for an angelic statuette featuring a white tile on which words like '1963 Miss Snooky – Girl of the Year' were inscribed.

To date, most of Tiny's crushes were unrealistic muses whom he could keep at bay so as not to conflict with his religious beliefs. Although Tiny played the part of the shocked innocent, in reality he saw it all at the Page Three, if not before. Within 12 months of being Tiny's 'Girl of the Year', Miss Snooky got into drugs and prostitution and probably died as an addict.

Gigs were now coming in. George King scored him a great spot at the *Ratfink Room,* which paid a decent fee for a change. But it clashed with a previous Page Three booking that Tiny refused to cancel out of loyalty. Tiny loved the Page Three, possibly because he had never found acceptance like this before – wearing make-up was okay, no one called him 'sissy' and he was free to project his feminine side to startling advantage.

In June, Tiny started picking up even more gigs - among them, the *Little Theatre.* But always he played the Page Three, which is where became friends with Lenny Bruce.

Mr Lenny Bruce

Ronnie Lyons was the link. Lyons was a small time promoter who started managing Tiny while acting as Bruce's go-fer. He taped Tiny's act for Bruce because, according to Lenny Bruce's biographer, Albert Goldman, '…always a sentimentalist about old things and camp things and things fragrant with the musty odours of nostalgia, Lenny's heart leaped up the first time he heard Tiny Tim sing'. Bruce was the biggest name to date to show interest in Tiny's act. And, the first to become openly fascinated.

A meeting between Tiny and Lenny was arranged at Lyon's place in Greenwich Village. The meeting was a great success. Said Tiny, 'I was waiting for Mr Bruce and he came out of the bathroom. He had a favourite song of mine, *When Will The Sun Shine For Me?* It was done by Irving Kaufman in 1924 - the Bing Crosby of his day. I left feeling bad after realising that I had auditioned for somebody who it would seem like I wanted something from.' Tiny kinda regrets performing for Lenny, he later added, 'I never like to use any star for success'.

Tiny continued the story, 'Mr Lyons came to the Page Three a day later and said, "Mr Bruce *loved* you! He wants you to sing on the bill with him". The night we opened I really tore the place down. I did *Tiptoe,* and several songs in my high voice and a duet with myself. After that I went into heavier ballads, which I never did except at parties. I sang one of Russ Colombo's songs, Jolson's *Avalon, Sonny Boy* and *Walk Like A Man* in a high voice. After that tragedy came.'

Bruce was the most controversial stand-up comedian around. He talked like this, '*Fuck* you – I never understood that insult, because fucking someone is actually really pleasant. If we're trying to be mean, we should say *unfuck*…'. He famously sprayed a room with a vocabulary of '*kikes, wops, guineas, spicks, micks, niggers…'* (and so on). Meanwhile, his innocent friend Tiny couldn't even say the word 'breast'. Tiny went to extremes to make prudishness fashionable, spelling out B-R-E-A-S-T rather than saying it.

The tragedy came in the form of a small dapper undercover detective in a dark suit who dropped into the Page Three and Café Au Go Go with a notepad in which he made notes throughout Bruce's performance. He paid particular attention to Bruce's vocabulary, as well as Bruce's 'blasphemy' of two of New York's leading priests and a description of Jackie Kennedy 'hauling ass'. After typing up these notes, he took the document to his boss, Frank Hogan, District Attorney, and so began the prosecution/persecution of Lenny Bruce. In April 1964, Bruce was arrested after leaving the stage at Café Au Go Go.

During the hearings Bruce was hospitalised and subjected to major surgery. Two days later, who should wander in to see him but Tiny, carrying a shopping bag from which he produced his ukulele. Tiny began singing his great syrupy version of *On The Good Ship Lollipop* followed by *Tiptoe Through The Tulips*. Bruce, who was remarkably alert considering his medical circumstances, taped him with his Uher hand held recorder. After this, he introduced Tiny to Kenny Hume, another guest in the room. 'Here's a producer from Hollywood,' said Bruce. At the time, Hume was working on a musical LP called *Little Bird*.

Tiny always confessed his sexual fantasies to friends - now Bruce was on the receiving end. They became more than just fantasies when Tiny developed a crush on Miss Betty Wallace. Tiny and Miss Betty were friends for about nine months, but 'the night after Page Three' one thing led to another and Tiny found his arms wrapped around Miss Betty and his lips on hers (his first kiss). 'I exploded within me, Mr Tarlin,' he told me, *'know what I mean?'* He had prematurely ejaculated and was devastated by the sin. Plus he now had to confess to Mr Lenny Bruce who probably couldn't care less.

In time, Tiny and Miss Betty formalised their relationship and 'went steady'. Soon after she said the hand creams had to go, she didn't want him wearing perfumes, she didn't want the make-up. Nag, nag, nag. The rules had all changed. Tiny couldn't understand why she talked like that - after all *before* going steady Miss Betty admired the softness of his hands.

Furthermore, Tiny felt Miss Betty presented a great temptation because she had such magnificent B-R-E-A-S-T-S. Either way, notwithstanding a tearful parting, he didn't want her any more. Tiny'd had enough of being nagged. (3)

Over the course of his life, lots of people made an effort to tape Tiny. First Lenny Bruce, seriously hospitalised, lying in bed and organising the Uher recorder, monitoring the ups and downs of Tiny's voice with his hand on the level control.

Then, as you will read, record producer Richard Perry 'lunged' for his tape recorder as soon as he heard Tiny sing. Bob Dylan ran tape on Tiny and filmed him for a film that was never released. George Harrison taped Tiny for the Beatles 1968 Christmas record. Artist, Martin Sharp is Tiny's most dedicated tape-person - he taped their first meeting in 1973 and continued to do so for the rest of Tiny's life. Miss Sue, Ernie Clark, David Tibet and I also taped Tiny, all on our *first* meeting. Martin sums it up well, 'It seemed like a totally natural thing'.

After his release from hospital and a period of convalescence, it was back to the courtroom for Lenny Bruce. Instead of backtracking, he challenged his accusers. Bruce began to organise a stint at The Village Theatre for three nights with Tiny on the same bill, after which he planned another series of concerts to be titled, *Lenny Bruce Speaks For Money, Tiny Tim Sings for Love.* (3)

Ronnie Dell

September 1964, Tiny rushed out of a Maple Leafs game to get to the Page Three on time. There he found out that Lenny Bruce had been re-arrested and the place closed down. There would be no Lenny

Bruce Speaks For Money, Tiny Tim Sings for Love. Tiny's regular Page Three gig venue was closed. And his friend was in jail.

Lenny Bruce and club owner Howard Solomon were both found guilty of obscenity on November 4, 1964. Bruce was sentenced to four months in a workhouse; he was set free on bail during the appeal process and died before it was decided. (Bruce was granted a posthumous pardon in 2003.)

Tiny was back to chasing gigs and for the next six months he had barely a nibble. He tried changing his name to Ronnie Dell, which didn't help.

It was probably in this guise that Mark Mitchell (a friend later in life) saw him when Mitchell visited New York and poked his head inside a club. Mitchell isn't quite sure whom he saw. He says it was not Texarkana Tex, Larry Love or Tiny Tim – probably Ronnie Dell. Mitchell said, 'I was in New York with my parents during the New York's World Fair, which was 1964. I didn't meet him. I poked my head into a nightclub and Tiny was there. I didn't think too much of it, I was only very small, and then of course in 1968 when he came out I knew right away when I saw him, that I had seen him somewhere before.' (5)

Around this time Ronnie Dell – perhaps Larry Love – or Darry Dover – sometimes Tiny Tim - recorded a dozen demos with George Goldner and producer Johnny Ponz. The tracks included poor recordings of two trademark songs, On The Good Ship Lollipop and Animal Crackers and another 10 songs. Never intended for commercial release, the thin ukulele backing and would totally clash with Tiny's later image as someone who sang with lush 30-piece orchestral backing.

When Tiny was famous, this collection would haunt him. It was released as a bootleg album under the title, Concert In Fairyland and it was such a poor quality recording that it wrought havoc with Tiny's reputation.

After his ill-fated spell as Ronnie Dell, Herbie was back to being Tiny Tim again. That always seemed to work.

The Fat Black Pussycat

Tiny was also a regular at *The Fat Black Pussy Cat*, the beatnik club on West 3rd Street where Bob Dylan wrote *Blowin' In The Wind* just 12 months earlier. Bill Cosby and Ritchie Havens performed there. Tiny was another regular. Someone taped his February 8-song 16-minute set (recently released as a CD - available: www.tinytim.org). As one of Tiny's earliest known recordings, it reveals a performance and selection of song consistent with Tiny's persona at the peak of his fame five years later. The compère introduces Tiny as 'a different kind of personality…very serious about his talents, about his music and his art and he's very quickly picking up a following – Mr Tiny Tim!' (applause).

Tiny hops up to the mike and introduces his first song as 'a very serious number…' immediately getting the laugh he expected. The song is *I Enjoy Being a Girl,* which gets a good response from an audience of maybe 40.

The second song is *Animal Crackers,* which later became something of a Tiny Tim standard. Ha ha, very good. But the third song is Al Jolson's *Swanee,* which Tiny sings authentically. This time, it's a different type of applause. The fifth song, *We Could Make Believe* is one of Tiny's duets with himself. It is meant to be his closing song, but he is returned for three encores – *Million Dollar Baby, Maine Stein Song, You Called it Madness.* Although variously intrigued and amused by Tiny's effeminate attention-getting routine, it is his authentic renditions of Bing Crosby, Rudy Vallee and Russ Colombo songs that makes this Fat Black Pussycat audience keep bringing him back.

And then eventually - at last - Tiny was properly introduced to Miss Tuesday Weld by Warren Beatty. Tiny presented her with the *Beautiful Tuesday* single. He shrugged, 'I don't know if she ever played it'.

They were to meet again, when Tiny was a bigger star than she was, but she never acknowledged the song. He referenced her again in 1989 on *Then I'll Be Satisfied With Life* (…if Tuesday Weld would only be my wife…'). And on his 1995 *Impotent Troubadour* album he re-recorded *Dear Tuesday.*

35

Rolling Stones

In the crucible of a folk revival, in and around Greenwich Village, Tiny brushed shoulders with Ramblin' Jack Elliott, Sonny Terry & Brownie McGee, Joan Baez, Karen Dalton, people who'd been on the road with Woody Guthrie, beatnik poets and artists. These people were the cornerstones of the coming folk revival, and Tiny Tim appeared to be the only person untouched by it. He derived from another era. The folkies nasalised their songs in 'of-the-people' voices, Tiny crooned and sang falsetto. They wore workshirts, he powdered his cheeks. They re-worked old slave and work songs, Tiny sang chart hits from as far back as the 1910s.

By November 1964 Tiny Tim was the talk of the underground. After seeing him at the Page Three, Mick Jagger invited Tiny to a party at musician Bob Crewe's place at the Dakota Hotel (where *Rosemary's Baby* was shot - as was John Lennon).

Tiny – who was used to playing parties - proceeded to entertain the Rolling Stones with high-pitch renditions of their own songs, most notably *Satisfaction* and *Time Is On My Side*. It was typical Tiny - showing them how Henry Burr, Rudy Vallee, Bing Crosby and Frank Sinatra would have rendered their songs and taking off their respective voices perfectly. Tiny particularly remembers Brian Jones being astonished.

'Mick Jagger came to see my show in 1964 at the *Page Three* - a place where the girls liked each other. He liked me and took me to a party in the November/December period, and to pay his respect after he saw me at the party, which was held in the Dakota, ironically where John Lennon was killed years later. I can honestly tell you, I was in the Dakota and it's a wild place. You can't get in there. It was preserved for over 100 years. I sang *Time Is On My Side* to Mick Jagger when I had the high voice. They came over to plug the song. And Brian Jones looked at me and couldn't believe what he saw! So I had a big following.' (6)

Steve Paul's Scene, MacDougal Street, New York - as pointed out to me by Tiny, 4 October 1991

Photo credit: Lowell Tarling and a disposable camera

Steve Paul's Scene

On 5 December 1965 Tiny won first prize at an amateur show in MacDougal Street - a bottle of champagne that he promptly gave away. In the excitement of the moment someone pulled Tiny aside and told him about *Steve Paul's Scene,* a breeding ground of new talent.

The club featured bands whose next stop was chart success. The Young Rascals was just one example. The Scene was one of Jimi Hendrix's favourite clubs for impromptu jam sessions. It was also known for featuring acts like The Velvet Underground, Pink Floyd, Jeff Beck, Traffic and Fleetwood Mac. The writers of the musical *Hair* – James Rado and Gerome Ragni - were among the regulars. The Scene was the kind of place where one might find Paul Newman chatting to Jim Morrison. It was the trendiest club in New York and when Tiny wandered in he created a great impression. (7)

Blues-Rock musician, Corky Siegel writes, 'Steve Paul's Scene in New York City was an outrageous nightclub. Our opening acts were a fire-eater and Tiny Tim. People would actually dance on the tables and Tiny Tim would make them laugh and cry. It was surreal to say the least. Actually in this place Rado and Ragni would have a somewhat chance of blending than most anywhere else. But this was just before young Americans began to grow their hair in the eastern seven eighths of our country. When Rado and Ragni popped into this place of places, their hair was matched only by Tiny Tim's waist long strands.' (8)

At the Scene, Tiny's reputation was massive. He was booked virtually every night. The marquee outside read *Tiny Tim: The Answer To The Beatles.* As a response to his billing he also sang some Beatles songs like *She Loves You* and *I Want To Hold Your Hand* in the high voice. Backed with nothing but his uke Tiny Tim brought down the house, night after night.

Like the Rolling Stones beforehand, a lot of important people were showing up and saying, 'You've gotta hear this guy!' The act was by now honed to perfection, the patter, the image and the songs. Summing up the Scene in her *Encyclopedia of Rock* Lilian Roxon wrote, 'The fee was modest, the exposure fantastic'. (9)

Another regular, Jim Morrison of the Doors, was drawing enormous crowds. Morrison liked Tiny and offered him the song, *People Are Strange* – however, before Tiny could record it, the Doors had soared to the top of the charts with their hit song *Light My Fire* and became out of reach overnight.

Tiny describes Jim Morrison as, 'One of the best-looking men I've ever seen. Unfortunately, he passed away too. The Lord giveth, the Lord taketh away. Praise be the name of the Lord. I tell ya, whatever the gift is – you only have it for a season.' (10)

Footnotes:

1) Bob Dylan, Chronicles Volume One, pages 11-15, Simon & Schuster, 2004.
2) Sue Khaury, *Memories Of My Husband Tiny Tim,* 1998, unpublished.
3) Tiny Tim, interview with Lowell Tarling, 4 April 1992.
4) Albert Goldman, *Ladies And Gentlemen – Lenny Bruce,* pp. 448-449
5) Mark Mitchell, interview with Lowell Tarling, 20 March 2002.
6) Tiny Tim, interview with Lowell Tarling, 6 September 1983.
7) A good summary of Steve Paul is on Ernie Clark's Tiny Tim Memorial Site, www.tinytim.org under the headline 'Steve Paul Dies at 71'. Also Greg Shaw, article 'The Scene', www.waiting-forthe-sun.net
8) Corky Siegel, 'Corky's Stories', *Before Hair With Rado and Ragni.* www.chamberblues.com/adventures/corkhair.html
9) Lilian Roxon, *Rock Encyclopedia* pp. 508-509.
10) Tiny Tim, interview with Lowell Tarling, 4 October 1991.

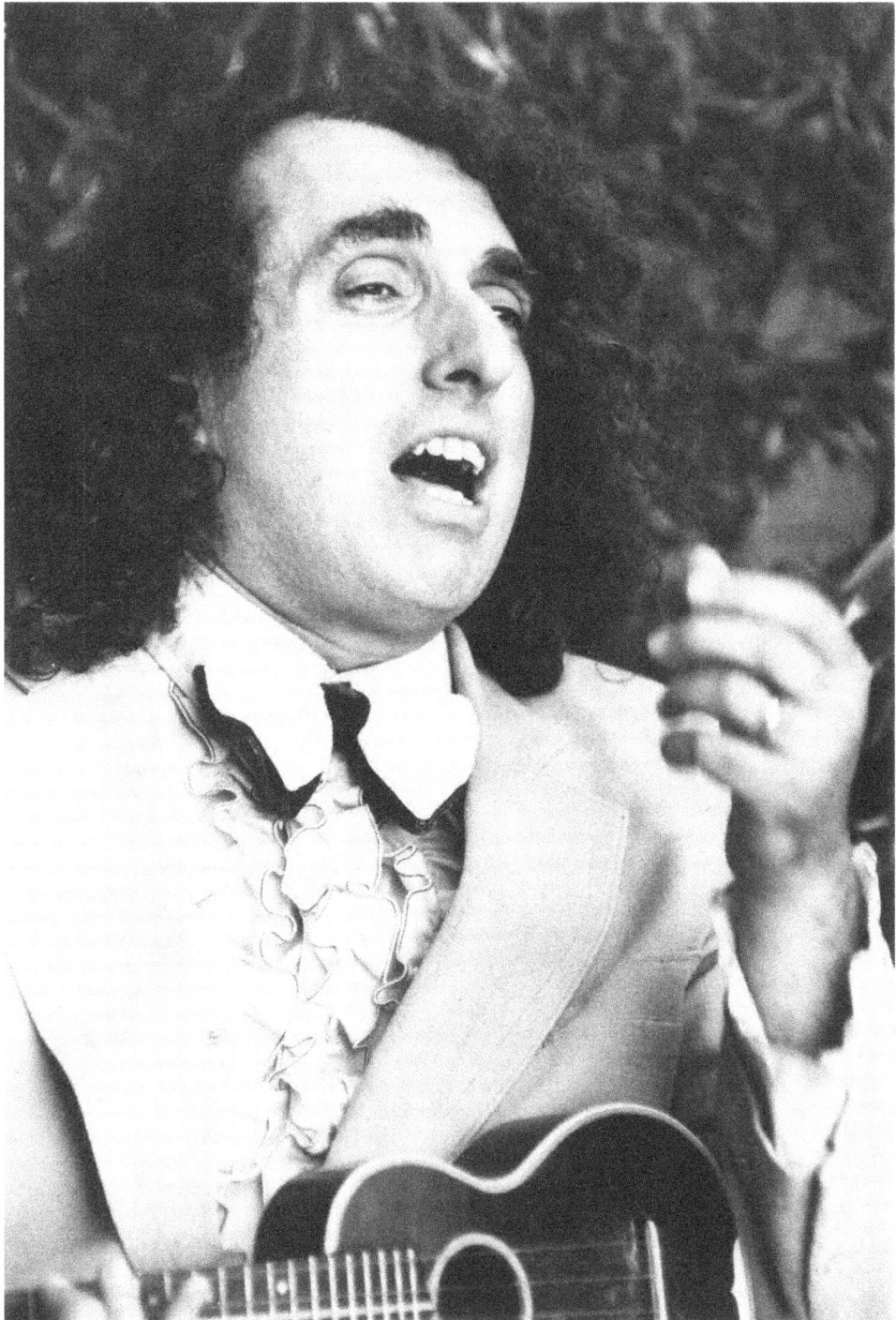

Photo Credit: Dave Newland

4

Richard Perry

I was deeply involved in Tiny's career. The years between 65-69 really is the heart and soul of the Tiny Tim story. By 1969 his career for the most part was over.
Richard Perry, producer

Born in Brooklyn 18 June 1942, Richard Perry shares a birthday with Paul McCartney. Perry's musical taste ran a lot wider than most of his peers. He did not lock into Rock. He was as eclectic as Tiny. He had an ear for jazz, orchestras, country and western, bobbysox, everything.

Perry went on to produce some of America's best known albums, including Rod Stewart's Great American Songbook series, which always seemed to me what he may have intended for Tiny. Perry is the only producer, apart from George Martin, to work with all four Beatles.

Perry has also produced Captain Beefheart, Ray Charles, Neil Diamond, Fats Domino, Ella Fitzgerald, Art Garfunkel, Julio Ingesias, Tom Jones, Patti LaBelle, Manhattan Transfer, Johnny Mathis, Harry Nilsson, the Pointer Sisters, Diana Ross, Leo Sayer, Carly Simon, Barbra Streisand, Donna Summer, the Temptations, Tina Turner, Andy Williams and many more. But it all started with Tiny. (1)

The Escorts

Perry's first band was a Bar Mitzvah group formed in a Brooklyn high school. First named *The Legends,* it soon became *The Escorts.* The other band members were Richard Berg and Richard Rosenberg. Yes, the three Richards. They all sang and played instruments. In 1961 they recorded for Corol Records with a fourth member Rodney Garrison, who worked in Perry's father's instrument business. Their first release was a fast version of *Gloria* with novelty value that won radio airplay, though not hit-making sales. The group's second record was *Gaudeamus,* an uptempo reworking of a traditional graduation processional.

Perry got them gigs around New York City. Good gigs, like the Peppermint Lounge and Coney Island. They peaked with a No 1 hit in Detroit (*Somewhere*), which led to an offer to appear on the Murray The K Easter Show. The band clumsily knocked back Murray the K, which lead to arguments among its members. After all, weren't they only doing it for pocket money, to ease their passage through college? The group disbanded after they each graduated in 1965. They all pursued different careers, with Perry starting in writing and production. He rented a small office at 1650 Broadway, trying to get a break and seeking opportunities where he could scratch them up.

Around this time, Perry met Tiny. He was introduced by Ken Vance, who had early-60s hits with the band *Jay & The Americans.* Tiny agreed to call on Perry while doing his round of music publishers, song pluggers and booking agents. He received a huge reception. From the moment Tiny started playing his uke, Perry recalled, 'I lunged for my tape recorder'.

Tiny Tim had found a musical collaborator, someone who knew what he was talking about, someone with a vision of what could happen, someone who loved Tiny's variety of song and vocal versatility. Although 10 years younger than himself, Perry understood Tiny's musical references. While Perry might have preferred – say - Russ Colombo to Rudy Vallee, he was a bright young person who actually knew the difference!

Perry was amazed at the breadth of Tiny's repertoire like, says Perry, 'his ability to sing country music. It always fascinated me how he came to know that music sitting in his apartment in New York'. Furthermore, in the back of his mind, Perry was intrigued by Tiny's theatrical potential? Says Perry,

'Even in those days he was a very bizarre looking person. He used to wear clown-white make-up and rouge, and he looked more bizarre than he did in later years'.

Perry and Tiny hung out together. They partied with record producer Phil Spector (now *there's a story!*) and enjoyed fun times. Tiny was such a phenomenon that being around him was exciting for Perry, watching his effect on audiences and the startled reaction from people on the street. Tiny understood his impact; he'd worked on it for years. One thing he could never conceal was that intelligent flash in his eyes that told you that he knew *exactly* what was going on. Perry claims, 'I know Tiny Tim like nobody in the world knew him'.

Six months after their meeting, Perry borrowed some money from his parents and took Tiny into a studio to record three tracks, *April Showers, Little Girl* and the Tom Paxton song, *I Can't Help But Wonder Where I'm Bound.* With shades of the Animals' *House of the Rising Sun,* Tiny's *Little Girl* is a particular favourite of mine, and worth chasing down on youtube even just for the end, with Tiny weeping and magnificently howling. It was released as the B-side of *April Showers* which former Escort, Richard Berg, recalls rehearsing with Tiny. (2)

Perry, who was looking for a job as a record producer, took these demos with him when he moved to Los Angeles soon afterwards, and used them to get work. (3) Back in New York, Tiny did what he always did - he prayed, read his Bible, listened to records and learned songs, thousands of them.

Better Parties, First Class Gigs

Things began to improve. Tiny started playing A-list parties. He sang for screen stars Ruth Ford and Zsa Zsa Gabor, and playwright Tennessee Williams (who tipped him $10). His first television appearance was *The Merv Griffin Show* on 7 March 1966, a booking organised by Wally Cedar, the publicity manager from The Scene. Tiny shared the spot with Douglas Fairbanks Jnr, after which bookings came in thick and fast.

A regular at the Scene, Peter Yarrow (of Peter, Paul and Mary) featured Tiny in his underground movie, *You Are What You Eat.* Tiny sang *Be My Baby,* now one of his standards. He also sang the high voice in *I've Got You Babe,* a duet shared with Eleanor Baruchian, member of the all-girl *a cappella* group The Cake. Yarrow cast them after seeing them perform together at The Scene. She sang the male voice.

Later in 1966 Tiny nervously took his first plane trip, a flight to California where he remained for one month for a series of bookings. It gave him the opportunity to renew two old acquaintances, first Lenny Bruce - at whose home he stayed for a couple of nights. And Bob Dylan - who attended Tiny's concert at *The Hollywood Ranch Market.* (Also in that audience were Donovan and Lenny Bruce's Mum.)

Before singing a Dylan song, Tiny acknowledged his presence with, 'Ladies and gentlemen, I have a great star in the audience. I'm sorry to embarrass him but it is the famous Bob Dylan. I want to thank Mr Dylan for coming down to see the show'. 'Then', recalls Tiny, 'I pulled out some sheet music from my pocket called *Positively Fourth Street* and I just did a snip but I added at the end, "It's not 10th Street, 9th Street, 8th Street, 7th Street, 6th Street, 5th Street…". Now that brought down the house. He came backstage and was so nice.' (4)

Tiny was on the same bill as entertainer-comedian-activist Wavy Gravy, managed by Bruce. Tiny's performance was stunning enough to win him a booking at Bill Graham's legendary Fillmore Stadium, which featured the newest bands like *The Grateful Dead, Moby Grape, Janis Joplin & Big Brother & the Holding Company, Jefferson Airplane* and the like. Tiny Tim was suddenly finding a niche with a Rock audience.

Around this time Tiny sat for a series of portrait shots for the celebrated photographer Diane Arbus, famous for eerie portraits of offbeat subjects.

You'll find 11 frames on www.michaelhoppengallery.com/artist captioned with Arbus saying, 'Freaks was a thing I photographed a lot. It was one of the first things I photographed and it had a terrific kind of excitement for me. There's a quality of legend about freaks. Like a person in a fairy tale who stops you and demands that you answer a riddle. Most people go through life dreading they'll have a traumatic experience. Freaks were born with their trauma. They've already passed their test in life. They're aristocrats'.

I'm not sure why Arbus said that. She makes Tiny look like a louche band member of a fashionable band, like the Kinks or the Sir Douglas Quintet. Diane Arbus said those words just a tad before the word 'freak' became a lazy, commonly-used adjective to describe Tiny.

The Basement Tapes

On 29 July 1966 Bob Dylan had a motorcycle accident and spent a week in hospital. After having been such a public figure for so long, Dylan now sought privacy. He, wife Sara and family, moved to Woodstock with his band – The Band – and recorded what came to be known as *The Basement Tapes* in a house famously dubbed The Big Pink. Dylan had all sorts of new ideas, among them he wanted to make a film.

In January 1967, fired up from seeing Tiny's performance in *You Are What You Eat,* the Band's guitarist Robbie Robertson told Dylan about Tiny Tim. Well, Dylan already knew all about Tiny but Robertson's enthusiasm gave Dylan the impetus to include him in his current work-in-progress-film called *Stage 67.*

Dylan brought Tiny to Woodstock. Dylan was there to welcome him and showed him to his room. They discussed the Toronto Maple Leafs ice hockey team and Dylan offered him a banana. Later, they jammed together. Tiny and the Band did some recordings, among them Chuck Berry's *Memphis Tennessee,* Al Jolson's *Sonny Boy* and Sonny & Cher's *I Got You Babe* – which, in the absence of Baruchian, had become Tiny's duet with himself.

Said Tiny, 'Bob Dylan invited me privately to Woodstock, his house, in the beginning of 1967 – February - where The Band was first forming with him. I came there at night. They took me in a limousine. I couldn't even see, I was just ushered in and I had my cosmetics. They led me up to a room for a night or so.

'He was making a movie called *Stage 67* and he wanted me in that movie. He paid me $22 a day. But he made this movie. It's footage that he did of me in Woodstock when it was still virgin territory, in the beginning of 1967. There was about two days of shooting. He called me Phillip Granger and the film never got off the ground. That footage is in his hands.' (5)

Over the years Dylan has participated in and produced a string of hit-and-miss films, including *Don't Look Back (1967), Eat the Document (1972), Renaldo And Clara (1978), Hearts of Fire (1987)* and *Masked And Dangerous (2003).*

Monterey Pop

Everywhere Tiny sang, the people loved him. They laughed with amazement and, most important of all, they applauded. However, Tiny miscued in public at least once. It was at a Dodgers rally against the Phillies, where Tiny got so excited that he leapt to his feet and burst into song, singing *Living In The Sunlight.* He was promptly ejected from the Connie Mack Stadium.

In June, Steve Paul could see that Tiny had enormous potential. There was literally nothing like him. Paul took him to the 1968 Monterey Pop Festival, the festival that telescoped the hippie cult of the West coast into a worldwide phenomenon. Paul *almost* got Tiny a spot onstage alongside the Who, Jimi Hendrix, Eric Burdon & the Animals, Booker T & The MGs, Simon & Garfunkel, Canned Heat, Big Brother & The Holding Company (with Janis Joplin), Country Joe & the Fish, Steve Miller,

Quicksilver Messenger Service, the Byrds, the Grateful Dead, the Mamas & the Papas and a stunning performance by Otis Redding.

It was a real long shot and almost unthinkable that an unknown like Tiny, without a hit record, could take his place alongside Jimi Hendrix burning his red Stratocaster guitar. It was a 'might-have-been moment' that never was. However, every one of the stars on the bill that night knew who Tiny Tim was, even though Tiny wasn't always sure who they were. For example in Vancouver 1968, when he introduced 'Country Joe Fish and his band' (ie. 'Country Joe and the Fish').

Never Let That Golden Break Go By

Five weeks later, the Scene fell on hard times. Lenny Bruce was dead. Paul was scratching to pay his acts. The big names had gone to bigger success. The Doors were top of the charts. The Scene looked like closing, and Tiny offered to bow out. However, Paul insisted Tiny stay because Yarrow had persuaded the Chairman of Warner Bros, Mo Ostin, to show up to see his extraordinary act. The night Yarrow showed up with Ostin, the place was almost deserted, yet Tiny gave a dynamite performance. (6)

'In 1967 I was discovered in a little club in New York City called *Steve Paul's Scene*. It was an "in" club,' Tiny recalled, describing the night he was signed. 'They had very wealthy young girls who rang away from their mothers, 16-17 years old at that time. They would sit with good looking guys who were gigolos - guys like Jim Morrison (not him) but good looking guys of the day - 18-19 years old and they would go to them. They were rebelling against society at the time, and their parents had money. They liked me because I was different in sound, praise the Lord for his blessings!

'The very first song I sang was *Let A Smile be Your Umbrella,*' said Tiny. 'And he (Mo Ostin) started laughing. I sang *Tiptoe Through The Tulips* and then a duet, and immediately he called me over and asked how I'd like to sign with Warner Brothers. Not only did he ask me that, I heard a rare word in his sentence, he was going to *pay* me $750 to sign. Now that's more money than I ever saw!' (7)

More interested in fame than money, Tiny signed without reading the contract, a habit that always made him easy prey to unscrupulous promoters. Years of financial rip-offs followed, taking him on a roller-coaster ride from one of the highest earners in the business to being virtually destitute at certain periods of his life. Yet Tiny never regretted the moment, even advising young artists to simply sign – *sign! -* without reading a word. 'I signed and we sent off the contract. Boy I was sweating it out, cos he could change his mind the next day. It took me two weeks to get the contract from Hollywood, but praise the Lord I finally got it. My mother took it calmly, *Ahh, another of those things!* But I thank Jesus Christ it did happen.'

Tiny probably had more negotiating power than he thought. Frank Sinatra's Reprise label wasn't the only record company who wanted him. Kiki Hall still wanted a piece of Tiny. Bob Dylan, the Band, the Rolling Stones and the Beatles all liked him. And Richard Perry was somewhere in LA building his career on the cornerstone of three demos he had cut with Tiny Tim.

'One good thing in my favour is that another record company, ABC, also wanted to sign me - I had two companies interested, so Warner Bros moved. If he had that contract I would have signed it then and there on the spot. I don't care. I never give them a chance to think. A guy came over, a big guy, and he says *We'd like to sign you.* I said, *Right now, I'll sign.* I wouldn't care what they gave me. A lot of people make mistakes by trying to be too smart and they want more. They lose their break because they've made them think. When a big company comes over, don't make them think: *sign!* Never let a golden break go by! I'll tell you another thing, don't let anyone feed you the line *You should get more for that.* Forget it! If they're going to pay you well, who cares how slow, but just make sure you've got some royalties coming, that's the only thing.' (8)

In 1967, $750 was a lot of money. At the time of signing Tiny was earning $41 on a good week. It had been $20pw not so long before. And, virtually nothing during the 50s.

42

God Bless Tiny Tim

And so the Reprise Label (a subsidiary of Warner) decided to record an album of Tiny Tim songs and the executives needed to match him with a producer. Around this time Perry gained an interview with Warner Bros Records LA and brought in samples of his work, which were the three Tiny Tim demos. 'Oh, we just signed him!' they told Perry.

As Yarrow was a known Tiny Tim admirer and Peter Paul & Mary were big artists for the Warner Brothers, Perry assumed Peter Yarrow would be the natural choice of producer and that would be that. On the contrary, they told Perry, 'We're looking for a producer for Tiny'.

'So that's when I knew that fate had brought us together again', Perry continued. 'I think we called him on the phone right then and there. I knew that even if I didn't get the job I would have an opportunity to make the album with him I always dreamed about making.'

Richard Perry! Well, of course Tiny agreed to the choice of producer as well as the dates for the recording session! He caught a train from New York to Los Angeles because in those days Tiny was still afraid to fly, avoiding planes as much as possible.Perry's vision was genuinely farseeing and creatively, he had a lot of room to move. To date everything Tiny had achieved was with the solitary backing of his ukulele, whereas Perry's concept required the best musicians in the country and a full orchestra. Perry said, 'On the *God Bless Tiny Tim* album we did some country songs. One of them was maybe not written that way, but we did it as a country song, it was called *Then I'll Be Satisfied With Life.* The other was called, *Daddy Daddy What Is Heaven Like?* If you listen to the low voice that he sings in that, that's pure country. And we did a country song or two on the second album as well. Actually we did a song that I wrote called *Have You Seen My Little Sue?* That's an example of his ability to sing country music. It always fascinated how he came to know that music, because it wasn't something he would have been exposed to sitting in his apartment in New York.' (9)

Released in February 1968, the result was the magnificent and majestic *God Bless Tiny Tim* album that reached No 17 (June 1968) on the US album charts and spawned Tiny's best known song, *Tiptoe Through The Tulips* which peaked at No 7 and was remembered ever after. Cousins Hal and Bernie were proud of him, the older family members were perplexed. His mother was astonished, 'Who would have thought this would happen!' she bleated. (10)

This was really big time. *God Bless Tiny Tim* was an international hit. That was how we heard of him in Australia. Everyone was interested, especially Dan Rowan & Dick Martin who booked him in February 1968 for their *Laugh-In* TV show. Tiny stole the night and became a regular.

In early April, scouting for Johnny Carson, Craig Tennis spotted Tiny's act and briefed Carson, who booked him for his Tonight Show. Singing his trademark *Tiptoe Through the Tulips* - watch Tiny's first *Johnny Carson Show* appearance on youtube. Within 15 weeks, *God Bless Tiny Tim* sold 150,000 copies and attracted great reviews from every magazine in the country, as well as writer Albert Goldman, who might have been hard on Elvis but - like Lenny Bruce and Richard Perry - never lost his enthusiasm for Tiny Tim. (11)

Rowan & Martin and Carson also liked Tiny and in their own way. They made him a regular on their respective shows, and went in the bat for him when 'the career fell' (Tiny's expression). However, they positioned Tiny in the wrong slot. Tiny Tim was a singer, not a comedian and he should never have *been* the joke! Where Rowan and Martin were often plain silly, Perry went on to organise elegant Tiny Tim concerts with full orchestral backing.

Best Of Everything

Tiny said, 'When you make it after 20 years, you sit in a room and you see beautiful trays of food – the best of everything, and you're looking back at the years of many people who never made it. You're looking back at the years I walked night after night, early morning. The ridicule I got for years and years, especially with the long hair going back to 1954. All those years, you back at those things and all of a sudden it's over. One out of a million made it and I look in the mirror and I'm one of them, thank God through Christ. It's a great feeling. *Time* magazine and you're on the cover or inside. *Newsweek!* Everything you have ever wanted is suddenly there. The world is seeing you. Some people like me, some people don't, that's not important. The point is, I made it over the hurdle the same as Elvis Presley and the rest of them, for the one time in my life'. (12)

He was being offered a cornucopia of drugs that he never took and women were throwing themselves at him. This had unexpected complications. Any other star would have simply partied hard, that wasn't Tiny. Sure, he got into a few compromising situations but he turned them down - most of the time. This approach-avoidance sexual conflict frustrated his management who could never quite get it right for him. On one hand Tiny seemed to want to entice beautiful young women, to whom he would dedicate songs and give 13 trophies between 1963-69, while on the other he didn't want to engage in premarital sex.

There are stories of Tiny walking through the most decadent Hollywood parties, heading to his room, reading his Bible and praying. There are recollections of naked girls staking him out in his room with Tiny averting his eyes and saying, 'Go home to your mother!' There are also other tales - not many - where he 'slipped'. He had a bit of a tryst with a girl in his dressing room in May, the morning before flying home from Los Angeles to New York with Richard Perry and manager Ron DeBlasio. Things were getting complicated.

To Herbert from Hubert

In June 1968 Tiny met two of his great heroes. The first was Irving Kaufman, whom Tiny met at Kaufman's Los Angeles home when Kaufman was 78-years old. He appreciated Tiny's effusive adulation. When Tiny sang his songs, it brought tears to his eyes. Kaufman taught Tiny one of his own songs, *Down Virginia Way*. Tiny insisted on singing it on his second album, which was about to be recorded. Perry disagreed, but Tiny had his way.

Rudy Vallee was less elderly (about to turn 67) and more difficult. He scarcely believed his eyes when they met. Tiny had based sections of his act on Vallee – but look at him, with long hair, face powder, the *thank-God- through-Christ* routine and a shopping bag carrying his ukulele and an alarm clock!

Vallee settled down enough to be extremely impressed with Tiny's renditions of his own songs. He was also pleased with what Tiny had said about him in the press, whenever journalists asked Tiny to talk about music – which was less and less now. They all seemed to want him to talk about his religious views, the number of times he washed per day and especially his attitudes to sex. It made good copy in an age of free love. Before parting, Vallee, whose real name was Hubert, signed an autograph to Tiny, 'To Herbert from Hubert'.

At the end of the year, while working at the Fountainbleau Miami, Tiny received a call from Vallee, wanting to record with Tiny. Tiny saw immense potential for the project, as well as taking it as a great honour. It was entirely appropriate, the old master and the new. It was a perfect chance for both to cement their places in the history of music – Vallee by making a late-in-life comeback while endorsing Tiny's place among the crooning greats in the way that Larry Love had always dreamed!

Just one little detail. Now that he was under contract, Tiny was no longer free to sing with whomever he liked. Managers DeBlasio and Silver refused, leaving Tiny disappointed and embarrassed and Vallee angry and badmouthing Tiny. 'When they let in Tiny Tim, they let in the Hunchback of Notre Dame!' Vallee bitterly exploded.

Holy Freak

In June 1968, about the time he met Kaufman and Vallee, Tiny played his first big concert with a 30-piece orchestra. It was produced by Richard Perry, who was rapidly attracting the adjective 'genius'.

Staged by Roy Silver, whose vision too should not be underestimated, the concert was held at the San Monica Civic Auditorium, San Francisco where Tiny delivered a first class performance. (13)

It was the first time Tiny had performed live with a full orchestra, and – as Perry correctly anticipated – the impact was phenomenal. Repeated in Vancouver Canada in September, this concept would reach its zenith at the Royal Albert Hall, London, before the year was out.

Meanwhile, the whole of America had discovered Tiny Tim, and it couldn't get enough. After seeing a 1968 performance, Albert Goldman writing for the *New York Times,* described Tiny Tim's act like this. 'Today, when Tiny Tim walks on stage, he still gets a lot of laughs, lots of tittering and elbow-in-the-ribs condescension: but that's just the flotsam on a great rolling wave of love that breaks over his head with his first kisses and curtsies. Even those who can't understand him have to admit that he really gets under their cuticle.

'Tiny Tim is really a holy freak; how splendid that today the word should be a term of endearment and unabashed admiration. For bizarreness is an essential part of his tradition; that exaggeration of style that borders on the grotesque and demands an answering contortion of personality that is the performers equivalent of the submissive self-abnegation of the saint. Like all holy men, Tiny Tim is inviolable.

'Even in the mocking arena of the *Tonight* show, he behaved with the perfect freedom from inhibition, with the absolute imperviousness to ridicule that must have been the style of the ancient Christians in the Roman amphitheatre. He reduced Johnny Carson to his straight man with a few childlike answers, Carson, his radar scanning the house, realised immediately that Tiny Tim's obvious vulnerability made him untouchable. Asked to do an encore, Tiny Tim didn't even bother to raise from the guests' chair; he cocked up his uke, lifted his mad face in the air and went into a soprano fantasia on *The Birds Are Coming* that was as finely focused, as technically flawless as the carefully insulated products of the recording studio.' (14)

Mr Harrison & Mr Sinatra

It is rumoured that around this time – via Frank Sinatra's Reprise label – Tiny Tim slipped into Mafia control. Rowan & Martin's national tour and Bob Hope's approach to Tiny to appear in one of his films were turned down in favour of gambling joints in Las Vegas, like *Caesar's Palace* where Tiny always felt uncomfortable and was paid $50,000 for just one week, that he never saw.

Throughout the 60s the Beatles annually recorded a special disk for Beatles Fan Club members. In December, shortly after the release of his *Tiny Tim's 2nd Album,* Tiny appeared on the Beatles 1968 Christmas record. The Tiny Tim segment was a George Harrison initiative.

George Harrison's fascination for the uke possibly dates back to this 1968 recording with Tiny in the New York hotel where George and Patti Harrison were staying. Everyone who has seen *Concert For George* (2002) will have noted many references to Harrison's fascination with the uke. Buyers of his *Brainwashed* album will have enjoyed his ukulele song, *Between the Devil and the Deep Blue Sea.*

For his fans, Harrison recorded Tiny on his hand held tape recorder. He began upbeat, 'Hello this is Merry Christmas…' slowing to Harrison singing a composed-on-the-spot Christmas song, *Happy Christmas, Happy New Year, all the best to you from here…'.* White noise. Sped up *Helter Skelter.* Lennon talks about two balloons called Jock and Yono, quite bitter, but funny. Harrison again, followed by *At the third stroke it will be…*Ringo Starr! More Lennon - 'Once upon a pool table there lived a shorthaired butcher's boy…'.

Abrupt cut to George: *We have a special guest here this evening Mr Tiny Tim, I'd like to ask him to say a few words.*

'Oh, hello to you nice people – oh!'
Would you like to sing us a little song?

Tiny sings *Nowhere Man* in the high voice, enhanced with clicks, gasps and soft applause from George, Patti and the others who were in the room.

Thank you Tiny, God bless you Tiny. Orchestral exit. Every Beatles fan club member in the world received that record. (15)

After this, George and Tiny dropped in on a Sinatra recording session. Sinatra was being 'Cranky Franky' until Tiny expressed how much he loved Mr Sinatra's music, recalling how he had cued up all those years ago, to see him exit the back door to screaming fans.

'Ah Tiny, those were the days,' said Frank, clearly mollified by Tiny's patter. From those sessions, Sinatra published a photograph of Tiny on the back cover of his *Circles* album.

Unforgettable Times

What follows are two stellar events which most people believe confirm Tiny Tim in the Hall of Fame – the marriage to Miss Vicki, watched by more people than the Moonwalk and the Isle of Wight Concert, listed among the Top 10 live performances ever in 2004 by *Q Magazine* - up there with Bob Dylan and Nirvana.

Nevertheless, his performance at the Royal Albert Hall on 30 October 1968 eclipsed even these unbelievable moments. Fortunately in 2000 Richard Perry, who orchestrated the concert, released the tapes on CD on the Warner Archives label. It is the San Monica Concert made perfect.

'He was definitely one of the greatest, certainly the most unique,' said Perry. 'I loved his theatrical potential. I was into very theatrical records and he was the perfect artist to do that with. I liked the many different spirits that lived within him. I'm a great admirer of variety, and nobody incorporated variety in their vocal abilities like Tiny. They were unforgettable times.' (16)

Footnotes:

1. Eric Olsen, Paul Verna, Carlo Wolff, *The Encyclopedia of Record Producers,* pp. 622-623, Billboard Books, New York.
2. The history of *The Escorts* by Stephen Bennett can be found on www.doowopcaferadio.com/Escorts.html
3. Richard Perry, interview with Lowell Tarling, 1 April 2002.
4. Ernie Clark, interview with Tiny Tim, 1993.
5. Tiny Tim, interview with Lowell Tarling, 6 September 1983. Tiny told this story often, most famously at the Royal Albert Hall Concert, which has been released on CD by Rhino/Warner Archives. Further information: www.rhinohandmade.com Tiny makes this story seem as if they were meeting as strangers, yet Bob Dylan's *Chronicles Volume One* reveals they have known each other well since 1963. Also, Ernie Clark, interview with Tiny Tim, 1993.
6. Sue Khaury, *Memories of My Husband Tiny Tim,* 1998 unpublished.
7. Tiny Tim, interview with Lowell Tarling, 6 September 1983. Also, Tiny Tim interview with Lowell Tarling, 4 April 1992.
8. Tiny Tim, interview with Lowell Tarling, 6 September 1983.
9. Richard Perry, interview with Lowell Tarling, 1 April 2002.
10. Tiny Tim, interview with Lowell Tarling, 4 April 1992.
11. Albert Goldman, letters to Martin Sharp dated 7 February 1982 and 20 April 1982.
12. Tiny Tim, interview with Lowell Tarling, 6 September 1983.
13. Bootleg CDs of *Live at the San Monica Civic Centre* and *Live in Vancouver* are available, possibly online. In 2009, as part of the extended package accompanying his *Together Through Life* CD, Bob Dylan released *The Lost Interview,* a DVD of Roy Silver talking. Although not about Tiny, it paints a good portrait of Silver himself.
14. Albert Goldman, *New York Times,* 1968.
15. Beatles Flexidisc for fans only, Christmas 1967.
16. Richard Perry, interview with Lowell Tarling, 1 April 2002.

5

Royal Albert Hall, 30 October 1968

I had the great pleasure of hearing that the Rolling Stones and the Beatles are here.
Tiny Tim

Everyone is here, Marianne Faithful, two Rolling Stones, two Beatles, possibly Princess Margaret (photographed with Tiny around this time). And so on. Peter Starstedt, Joe Cocker and the Bonzo Dog Doo Dah Band are on the same bill, but nobody talks about them. It's all Tiny.

Under the baton of Richard Perry, dressed in white tails, are 10 violins, four violas, four cellos, one bass guitar, two guitarists, banjo and Hawaiian guitar, one harpist, one pianist, five trumpets, three trombones, sax/flute/oboe/clarinet, bassoon and Cor Anglaise, percussion and the respected drummer Andy White, with a connection to the Beatles.

The lights are dimmed and the *God Bless Tiny Tim Overture* floods the concert hall. The lush *Tiptoe Through the Tulips* fanfare comes across as a statement of intent, quickly followed by *On The Old Front Porch* a dance-banter between brass and strings. Tense violins lead to the orchestral sounds of *As Time Goes By*. Before the audience can relax, the musicians skip their way through *I'm A Nut*. Surprise now, a waltz that Perry whips into the whirlwind apocalypse of *The Icecaps Are Melting*. It builds and builds turns into circus music, and feeds into a second fanfare, even more majestic than the first. And then. And then. Perry lifts his 30-piece National Concert Orchestra into the song everyone has been waiting for, the magnificent hit record that everybody knows - *Tiptoe Through The Tulips*.

And then, Tiny Tim walks on.

There is resounding applause as Tiny approaches the microphone. He is dressed in a fawn-brown Carnaby Street checked jacket, which clashes nicely with his pink checked shirt and yellow-lime green tie.

Outside the theatre, the billboards are huge. In London, no one has ever seen nor heard anyone like this before, but *vive la difference* is a catchphrase of the times.

Onstage with the stateliness of the Royal Albert Hall and a full orchestra behind him, Tiny looks like a gift from the gods - the Human Canary, who trills like a bird, sings like Russ Colombo, encompasses all boundaries of popular song, switching roles between entertainer and music history lecturer.

Tiny starts with 'Welcome to my dream...' an invitation into his gentle world. *Will you be there long, or just passing through?* Close your eyes and you're transported into a Heaven of flowers, camp innocence and that fairy princess. '*So glad you got here, and I hope you can stay, but welcome to my dream – anyway'*. Surreal orchestral meld for 38 seconds, half of which is layered with applause.

After welcoming his audience, Tiny skips through *Living in the Sunlight, Loving in the Moonlight* in the high voice, 'I'm so happy – aha – happy-go-lucky me...!' The rhythm section creeps in, followed by the brass and a pecking piano. Huge ovation. Cut to Tiny with no orchestra now, nothing to hold him up, he's strumming his ukulele and singing about being as 'free an any daughter'. The orchestra rejoins, the audience gasps and he trills into an even higher register. With perfect control Richard Perry watches Tiny, raises his arms and wraps up the song.

'Thank you, thank you so much, thank you so much, ' says Tiny. 'It's a thrill being here tonight at this great Royal Albert Hall. I hope I can do it justice. I want to thank you all for being so wonderful. I want to say this next number was a number done in 1913 by Mr Billy Murray and Miss Ada Jones in the old vaudeville houses before the war'. *On The Old Front Porch,* is a love-duet where he flirts with himself as the lover and the beloved. *Well kisses do excite me, but gee you tried to bite me!*

After meeting Tiny at London's Speakeasy Club, Martin gave him a full page in London OZ magazine, which I see as an 'announcement' by Martin, that a great artist has arrived.

'In 1916 way before he made *Mame,* way before he made *Swanee,* Mr Jolson came out on the stage of the Palais Theatre with this song recorded on the Columbia label 6754…'. The band opens the song with a shuffle, and Tiny enters it in a light baritone, asking the audience if they've seen his 'sweet' because she's a gal you 'stop and stare at coming down the street'. Then he lists all the things about her – the pretty dress, the look of happiness, the great big motorcar – *I Gave Her That.*

'Thank you so much, thank you. 1929 as we all know was the start of the Depression. It was a great disaster when the stockmarket fell – we were all there lookin'. A little ole song came out of the radio, Mr Crosby sang it (and so many others) on CBS…'. Strings introduce *Brother, Can You Spare Me A Dime,* an important song made famous by Rudy Vallee as well as Crosby. It featured on Tiny's *Chameleon* (1982) album and in many concerts over the years. Of course, as the years passed and history evolved, each rendition gained a new meaning. Thunderous applause tonight.

'One of the first soft singers, before Mr Vallee, was a gentleman named Mr Gene Austin, and in 1927 he made this song famous on the old Victor Record label…'. Tiny delivers *Save Your Sorrows For Tomorrow* in a piercing falsetto.

'One of my rare numbers, when I used to be known as Texarkana Tex, in the days when I handled that hat…' Tiny strums the opening bars and sings in a deeper register, the song *Love Is No Excuse,* with a message that is very much in line with what Tiny would tell journalists when they later asked about his sex life. *Love is no excuse for what we're doing…sure we love each other, and it could be so nice, not if someone else has gotta pay, our love for each other looks good in the night but our love could never see the light of day…*

The song closes with a band sting, and Tiny says, 'Thank you my dear friends. In 1929…' the piano tinkles and someone yells out. 'I beg your pardon?' He corrects the date to '31. The audience laughs, and Tiny introduces his warm rendition of *As Time Goes By,* an outstanding track on his *Second Album.* 'Mr Rudy Vallee, the first swooner-crooner, made this song famous, but it was revived again in 43. At that time, there I was strollin' the streets, reading them comic books.' He sings it in a high croon, as did Vallee.

Under Richard Perry's masterly baton the orchestra swells and breaks like the ocean, retreating then soaring. The audience cannot believe such a beautiful song is coming from someone who only moments before was Texarkana Tex. And then, in case they've closed their eyes and forgotten this is still Tiny Tim, he clicks his tongue on the final words, '…as time (click click)…goes by'. The orchestra crashes down the closing chords. The audience goes wild.

A Little Smile Will Go A Long Long Way is sung with zest. Tiny appears to be having fun with this song, closing in the high falsetto. If Tiny had any misgivings about the grandeur of performing at the Royal Albert Hall, they were dispelled three songs back. Before this welcoming audience, he can now do anything he likes. And so he takes them back to the *Page Three* and sings what he describes as 'a little duet with myself', announced in a risqué voice, which makes the audience snigger. The song *I've Got You Babe* has always been a core song in Tiny's repertoire. Never more so than tonight.

He opens with a few strums on his ukulele, then 'ah-ha ah-ha' in a falsetto, 'la-la la-la' as the deep response – Tiny finds his note – peaks – cradles the high note - then he begins the song in fluttering falsetto, answering himself in a flat Sonny Bono voice that surprises the audience into laughter. There is a tense silence as he works his way through the next verse, the middle eight, and then he jolts us on the line, 'some people say your hair's too long', holding the word 'hairrrrrrrrrr' on a piercing stratospheric high note for a full 14 seconds – and only moving on when the audience breaks into spontaneous applause. Talk about shrill! Tiny ends with a call-and-answer routine from high to low. The applause is deafening and continues for almost 30 seconds after the close of the song.

Says Tiny, 'Memories…in 1902 Mr George M Cohen wrote this number and I've got it gathering dust in my music collection.' *I'll Be Satisfied With Life* is a song from *God Bless Tiny Tim,* one that Richard Perry likes because of its Country feel. The song lists all the material things one might want, including staying 16 forever, and the classic rhyme 'if Tuesday Weld would only be my wife – then I'll be satisfied with life'. Tiny hits his straps in the second verse, omitting his LP reference to Tuesday Weld.

'In 1910, Mr Billy Williams – great English star of his day – did this number, and it's the only time it's been done outside the States since that time'. The song is called *Where Does Daddy Go When He Goes Out?* which Tiny performs on ukulele and sings by himself, even vocally filling in a few orchestral notes here and there, before the orchestra wraps up the final note with a sting that jolts you right up the spinal cord, even if you're listening to it on CD.

You Call It Madness, I Call It Love is a warm ballad sung as Larry Love, in a voice of which Rudy Vallee would have been proud. The orchestra creates a bedrock of sound punctuated by a gorgeous lonely trumpet over which Tiny overlays dulcet tones.

Tick-tick-tick-tick-tick-tick on the edge of the snare. Enter a muted brass section before Tiny enters the song in his John Barrymore ('Darling, how depressed I am') voice. 'One eye is brown, the other is brown, I am the fish, I swim around...' Piercing strings. 'You say I'm lost, I disagree. The map has changed, and with it me'. Gong. 'Gliding through the seaweed what strange things I see below...nowhere else to go!' To which the orchestra breaks into a Titanic waltz, as Tiny chirps that the icecaps are melting - as if it's the end of the world on a ship of fools, the humiliations of which Tiny – the fish – has escaped and turned to advantage. It is an unusual Bill Dorsey song that the audience recognises from the *God Bless* album.

'What does it mean?' is a frequent question over the years. Is this tsunami song about the environment? Is it a precursor of the Apocalypse? Is it a Jeremiad on existing society? Is it the Tiny Tim story encapsulated? From all accounts neither Tiny nor Richard Perry seemed to have a 'thing' about the song. It was included on the *God Bless* albums because it was casually suggested by someone sitting in on the session. They tried it and it worked. It may not have meant much at the time yet every time Tiny sings it, it is absolutely poignant.

'All the world is drowning to wash away the sin...!' sings Tiny, breaking into high-pitched eerie laugher which morphs into ghoulish sinister laughter, then yelps of 'Ah! Ah!'

Tick-tick-tick-tick-tick-tick on the edge of the snare drum and that tense muted brass section, as Tiny starts breathing hard and goes 'Ooh!' as if delighted by a lover. And before the audience can think, he's John Barrymore again. 'The seagulls fly, in search of land, the children hide, beneath the sand. Floating toys, come crashing down, I play the fish, I swim around'. Gong. Huge finale, as the icecaps melt, the world drowns in a sea of orchestral circus music, above which Tiny says in the highest possible spoken voice, 'My friends, I don't care where you are, you can be sitting there on that seat, you can be in that car...just watch out for those melting icecaps! They're coming down! Look at them, look at them come! I see em, I see em, Who-ho! Ho-ho!' leading to another gigantic close and 30 seconds of applause with people yelling 'More! More!'

Then Tiny is alone again with his little ukulele in his hand. He snorts four times into the microphone, makes a gasping noise, and everybody laughs. We're back at the *Page Three*, as Tiny pretends to look into a mirror and sings, 'You're the one I care for...' applause, laughter, 'You're the one I'm there for, I know you care for me...'. This one is called *I Love Me,* sung in the high voice. 'It's grand when I look in the glass and know I'm all mine...' leading to, 'I take me to a quiet place, I put me arm around my waist, if me gets fresh me slaps me face, I'm wild about myself!'

'Thank you...' and he snorts once more. Then keeps strumming, continuing in the same persona, breaking into *I Wonder How I Look When I'm Asleep.* Orchestral wrap-up.

'Mr Cab Calloway in 1936, at the Heidi-Ho Club in Harlem made this song famous...'. Rat-a-tat-tat drum entry, big brass, and it's the big band song, *Frisco Flo* performed flawlessly leading to a zippy ending, with howling trumpets riding over the applause.

Back to the *Page Three*. First, a delightful rendition of *I'm Glad I'm A Boy* leading to *My Hero* followed by a Tom Lehrer song, recorded in 1953. Tiny – unusually – doesn't announce the recording details. It is a macabre song called *I Hold Your Hand In Mine,* the hand being severed from the body. 'But still I keep your hand as a precious souvenir', to which the audience again starts yelling for 'More!'

Without hesitation the electric guitar starts clicking in the opening chords of the only Rock song in the show, *Earth Angel* at which point Tiny reveals his complete mastery of popular song, from the turn of the century to Elvis. (He is about to deliver on the Beatles, the Rolling Stones and Bob Dylan, in a most personal way.) Richard Perry's cleverly structured presentation of Tiny is paying off in spades. Like the opening of a flower, he has revealed more and more about Tiny, the deeper we get into the concert the more Perry is pulling back the orchestra, leaving Tiny more and more to 'go it alone' with his trademark uke.

'Thank you. You know my dear friends, I had one of the greatest thrills. I have visited Mr Dylan in his house, wonderful people. I remember doing a song, I said, "You know Mr Dylan, it's a great thrill meeting you". He said, "Mr Tim, a great pleasure meeting you". I did one of his numbers. I said, "You know Mr Dylan, you are today what Mr Vallee was in nineteen hundred and twenty nine". He said to me, "How was Mr Vallee?"'. Audience laughter. 'I said, "Well, you know I remember when he was the first swooner crooner, he had em all in the aisles, they were swooning over him. Same way with you. Now, today you can write and sing songs in a way no one else can do, for instance when Mr Vallee came out, he would do something like this...' and Tiny plays *The Maine Stein Song,* which involves some vocal acrobatics in the chorus. 'And of course he sang...' *Vagabond Lover',* which Tiny delivers in Vallee's feathery vocal style.

'And he said to me, "Well, he sounded pretty interesting". I said, "You know how would he sound if he sang one of your numbers? Supposing he was in his heyday today, how would he sound doing this one?' Tiny sings *Like A Rolling Stone* in the Rudy Vallee voice. 'And he said, "That's mighty interesting." And I said, "Mr Dylan, supposing you were alive in nineteen hundred and twenty nine, now how would you sound doing his number, *My Time Is Your Time?'* with which Tiny launches into the Vallee song in a Dylan voice. To which Tiny receives an ovation on the word 'har-moan-ize'.

'He said, *Good night, would you like a banana?'* Band sting, laughter.

Continuing now, unaccompanied. 'Thank you, I don't know how many people are here tonight. I had the great pleasure of hearing that the Rolling Stones and the Beatles were here. Whether or not they are – I remember doing one number in 1966 in a little ole place in California...', and he breaks into a high voice rendition of *Satisfaction* complete with 'oohs' and 'ahhs' as he 'tried', and he *tried*, and he *TRIED* upwards and into the high voice! Before the audience can applaud he snaps into, 'You know I had the pleasure of meeting the Rolling Stones in 1964 when they came to New York, at a little party. At that time I was strolling around the Village, someone invited me to Mr Crew's party. They just came over, I had the thrill of meeting them and they did *Time Is On My Side* which is of course their first really big hit. And I was singing there and somebody asked me to do *Time Is On My Side* to the Rolling Stones, and that was a great thrill and it went something like this...'. He sings it in the high voice complete with clock noises. 'Time is on my side, yes it is/no it isn't'. Tick-tick-tock.

'Really, with them and the Beatles, I think you've got the two greatest groups in the world today...' rousing applause. 'And I'd like to sing this number, because this number is very very dear to me. In 1966, while I was struggling along, I first sang it to Miss Jill and then I continued it, because she liked it. Now she's gone, but the song remains!' Laughter. High-pitched *Nowhere Man* which is eerily serious until he breaks it down like this: 'Nowhere man...*yes*. Take your time – *oh ho!* – don't worry. Nowhere man, the world is at your command!' Big moment. Laughter. Applause. 'Thank you, thank you...' and the song continues, ending on a big high note.

'Thank you so much,' says Tiny. 'I want to thank everyone here, the wonderful Keystone Charity Fund, everyone here in England, believe me I think it's a real great city – town – country – and I love every minute of it. I want to thank Mr Richard Perry, my wonderful record producer…' crashing applause, '…this great wonderful orchestra, who played so great at such short notice…', crashing applause again.

'I want to thank Mr Nick Lucas for making the song what it was then and for you all, making it what it is today…' and he strums the opening bars of his legendary hit, *Tiptoe Through The Tulips.* As soon as he sings the word, 'tiptoe' the audience breaks into warm applause. They express their *'love'* - if you like - the word of the times. 'Thank you, thank you' says Tiny, blowing kisses and continuing only accompanied by his uke. The orchestra doesn't creep in until the second verse. In the middle eight, Perry brings in strings for 'knee deep'. Tiny clicks his tongue in the 'tap dance' section. Beautiful soaring heights. *Tiptoe Through The Tulips* amidst the dignity of the Albert Hall, with its magnificent ceiling and all that history, since its opening in 1871 by Queen Victoria. The song snaps to its end, received with urgent cries of 'More!' There are whistles, stamping feet and a full 60 seconds of applause, hoping that Tiny Tim won't leave the stage.

'This is really a great thrill,' Tiny continues. 'I want to thank Mr John Stevens for his wonderful store in Carnaby Street. I want to thank Mr Mick and Miss Marianne. I want to thank you all, I want to thank you all for everything. Thank you.' Huge applause.

'And I think this number is an appropriate one.' The gorgeous balance/finale to his opening welcome - to his dream - this one is entitled *I'll See You Again,* which of course he does, at the Isle of Wight Concert, where Tiny Tim will once again leave his audience begging for more.

More! More! More!

Big band ending. Full strings, full voice, full everything, high voice, tender voice – the final note is the word *goodbye* as he exits to a crashing orchestra which couldn't be bigger - trumpet fanfare, screaming audience, non-stop clapping, cymbals and a passionate Mr Perry whipping his musicians up to bigger heights, again and again – whipping them up in a cascade of notes which culminates as high and sharp as possible. (1)

Tonight, Tiny Tim is the talk of the town.

Footnotes:

(1) Tiny Tim, *Live At the Royal Albert Hall,* CD. Original recording, Richard Perry, compilation produced by Roland Worthington Hand, curator The Rhino Handmade Institute of Petromusicology, Rhino Handmade, Warner Brothers Records.

6

Human Canary, Caged

I thank the Lord mostly humbly for making me a star.
People come up to me, they don't even know what I do,
they're in awe with the name.
Tiny Tim

Guitarist extraordinaire and co-founder of Cream, Eric Clapton was living at a place known as The Pheasantry in London's Chelsea with several creative Australians. He had a special rapport with his artist-flatmate Phillippe Mora and Martin Sharp. Mora would make an *avant-garde* film funded by Clapton. And Martin had written the words to *Tales of Brave Ulysses* that Clapton had set to music for Cream's new LP, from which the friendship and interchange of ideas developed.

Martin's covers design for Cream's second album, *Disraeli Gears,* is among the best known album cover in Rock history. He also designed the cover/s to its *Wheels of Fire* follow-up. That Clapton introduced Martin to the music of Tiny Tim is less well known. It happened like this. Cream toured America unrelentingly throughout 1966-1968 during which period Clapton absorbed everything new and American. This was when Tiny's stars were on the ascendant and Clapton caught his act at Steve Paul's Scene. When Cream came home for a 10-day break, Clapton noticed Martin's musical preferences tended towards the Rudy Vallee, Al Jolson and Bing Crosby-style. 'You should go see this Tiny Tim guy,' Clapton urged, 'he plays all those old songs you like.' (1)

And so in October 1968, Martin, accompanied by Richard Neville and Louise Ferrier – stalwarts of *Oz Magazine* - attended Tiny Tim's Albert Hall Concert, where Martin had an epiphany - there onstage was the 'perfect' artist, the Leonardo of Popular Song, an artist equal to Vincent Van Gogh, the artist he would most like to work with. But Tiny was in a different league. He was too famous, too illustrious and unapproachable.

Martin explained, 'The Beatles had something to do with Tiny being in England – that show at the Albert Hall was for a big showbiz charity called *Keystone* and boy it was packed.

'I'd never heard him sing a word until the Albert Hall, that's why he blew me away because I thought, 'Boy – this guy just *knows!*' And *Brother Can You Spare A Dime* was a song I'd heard just a snatch of on an Al Bowly album, just two lines of it, then Tiny sang it at the Albert Hall and I was amazed. That's when I thought I'd love to work with Tiny. I thought I could do something for his staging or that whole Paper Moon world of popular songs. I thought he would be the absolute heart of show business. Uncontactable! I didn't even try, I didn't even go backstage, I thought, "This guy is enormous!"'

Back at the Pheasantry, Sharp wrote diary notes under a heading, 'First Impressions'. He penned, 'Did you tiptoe through the tulips with Tiny Tim? To see his only London concert was a revelation. He is the "Spirit of Popular Music", an anthropologist, a mystic, the wise man disguised as a fool. He spans the whole of Pop with such grace and eloquence. He transcends the "campness" of his image and becomes a truly great entertainer (a compliment which cannot be paid to many of our contemporary pop "stars").

'I did see Tiny Tim backed by the London Philharmonic give, really GIVE, a performance that was great, not "groovy" not "gas man" but GREAT!! He was generous and he loves music and he told me so in such an articulate, honest and open way that I felt the beauty. He sang me the songs that my grandparents were turned on by when they were my age, and he sang me the songs my parents loved, and he made me love them too – and he destroyed my prejudice and created the link between all music and showed me that it is one river of soul and sound and love and pain.' (2)

Tiny was a star indeed, the 'Douanier Rousseau' of Pop. As far as his mass audience was concerned, he had managed to transcend age, convention and style starting with his 1929 Nick Lucas song, which he'd kept singing from all those years ago.

Million Dollar Baby

Around this time Ron DeBlasio and Mo Ostin from the Reprise Label sent the firm Campbell, Silver & Cosby (Bruce Campbell, Roy Silver and Bill Cosby) an acetate of *God Bless Tiny Tim* and asked them to handle the management side of his career. Things went well at first, though in time both Cosby and Tiny became increasingly disenchanted.

Demand came in thick and fast – TV shows, live appearances, radio, publishing and probably all sorts of merchandising. For a comprehensive gig guide, you'll have to find a more detailed biography than mine.

Before 1968, the most Tiny had earned in a single week for all 34 years of his life was $51. Now, his total 1968 gross earnings were around $1 million, including $25,000 per week for a two-week booking at the College Inn, Sherman House. Also $60,000 for a 10-night engagement at the Fontainbleau Miami. He filled San Francisco's Fillmore West Theatre, sat with his beloved Dodgers in their dugout during a game and went to parties with actors like Zsa Zsa Gabor and Warren Beatty.

Tiny also hung out with Alan Alda's son Robert, Eric Clapton's girlfriend Catherine James, and Charles Laughton's wife, Elsa. Liberace attended Tiny's concert and congratulated him backstage. When Tiny opened in Las Vegas, he got 'good luck' telegrams from Rudy Vallee and Elvis Presley.

Tiny should not have played Las Vegas, it was an artless, cynical booking and a monumental career mistake. His managers made $50,000 in one week, while Tiny received pocket money. Apparently Tiny didn't care, although around this time he had developed a serious gratuity habit by tipping big all bellboys who pressed a lift button for him or helped him with his bags. This habit never left him, not even when he was poor. He could part with $100 simply walking through a hotel lobby and getting into an awaiting cab. I saw it.

Rowan & Martin

Tiny was also snapped up by Rowan & Martin for the television show, *Laugh-In* where audience didn't quite know what to make of him. No matter, he upstaged the best of them with his self-effacing coy and campy act. Said Tiny on the show, 'Before I was a big star people used to point on the street at me and laugh, now I am a big star, people point to me on the street…and laugh'. And laugh they did, though at a big cost to Tiny's artistry.

A five minute segment on television was not an ideal medium for such a complex performer and the exposure might not have been good for the artistic side of his career. As far as the medium of television was concerned, his excellent singing would become secondary to his ability to draw laughs. Was he a singer or a comedian? A compilation of Tiny's *Laugh In* skits (1968-1971) can be viewed on youtube as one document. He had an excellent relationship with Dan Rowan & Dick Martin. They wanted to book him for a national tour. Despite the drawbacks, it might have been a better idea than sending him to Vegas.

Constant Sexual Pressure

Tiny was now a target for groupies, which he tried to avoid because of his religious beliefs. The Plaster Casters even called by. (The Plaster Casters made plaster casts of rock star penises and breasts. Tiny did not acquiesce.)

He no longer lived at home, but in a series of hotel rooms in whatever city he was performing. He was a magnet for girls, women and fans. There was constant pressure virtually every night, and sometimes he 'slipped' - incidents he described in too way much detail to journalists.

What is equally well documented are the times when he turned them down, for example Tiny's third wife Miss Sue recounts, 'Tiny told me this funny story once about one of his managers who was a playboy and had this big mansion where there was this wild stuff going on, a lot of drinking, drugs and wild sex happenings, and part of the deal was that Tiny would stay there and that was part of his pay. And he'd walk through these rooms with all this debauchery in this place and walk through to his room. One time his manager sent this young girl to him. This young girl was maybe 19 and she said, "I've been sent up here to make you happy" and Tiny said to her, "What are you doing here? What are you doing with these people? How old are you?" And she said, "Are you sure you don't want me?" And he said, "No, go away honey".' (3)

In her tell-all book, *I'm With The Band,* celebrity groupie Pamela Des Barres describes a sexual encounter with Tiny. He hid in the shower. 'After about half an hour he emerged. He was scared out of his wits and drawing long shuddering breaths, he peeked at us behind his fingers'. After trying to entice him for about an hour, the girls gave up and went to Frank Zappa's room instead. (4)

Tiny went to extremes to put an end to these 'temptations'. He hired the services of a bodyguard of sorts, Gary Greene, who was paid $100 per week to keep the girls away. Sometimes Tiny worked against Greene and secretly smuggled girls into his room. But notwithstanding all this, and until his marriage to Miss Vicki Budinger 18 months later, Tiny remained a virgin, which puzzled both his management and road crew. In fact, it drove them crazy.

Says Tiny, 'I would go to an airport and there would be a thousand people waiting for me to come in. They were all waiting for me, and not one of them smiled when I walked in, like they were waiting for a creature from out of space, so I learned never to speak unless spoken to. But as soon as one had the nerve to come over and ask for an autograph, they all followed suit.' These were high times indeed for Tiny, who could do no wrong. People bought his records, loved his concerts and laughed at his humour.

At this time, in Minneapolis, Miss Sue Gardner – to be Tiny's third wife - was watching a television show and fell in love with him on the spot. Tiny was the first guy she ever had a crush on. She had 55 posters of him on her bedroom wall. *God Bless Tiny Tim* was the first album she'd ever bought. (5)

Mr Crosby

Tiny's met another of his idols when he shared a bill with Bing Crosby at the Hollywood Palace. Crosby, the all-American male, was initially quite cynical about the persona of Tiny Tim. This was quickly dispelled when Tiny engaged him – on camera – on the subject of Crosby's own changing career-voice. Crosby was amazed that Tiny could mimic his 'early voice' followed by his 'later voice'. Crosby was astonished to realise he was in the presence of a dedicated fan.

Tiny said, 'I remember doing the Hollywood Palace with him and he didn't know what to expect. Then when we started reading the script we were meant to do it during rehearsal, he was singing in the voice he's got now and I was supposed to sing another song from his early years. Of course, his voice faded. He sang one song and I wanted to, even for a second, get his high voice, feel his spirit, just a little bit – never as great as he was – just to thrill him the way he thrilled me, that's all I wanted to see.

'I was looking at his face when he did the following song, *Oh Please*. When he heard that he said, "Give that guy a box of Snickers" and nobody laughed, no one in that studio laughed. Then he did another song and I did this one, *Learn To Croon*. Then I looked at his face and I knew he didn't understand but maybe that was just my opinion. Then he said, "Give that boy another box of Snickers" and no one laughed, the stage crew didn't laugh. I personally think that he was so surprised. He couldn't believe that from this young long-haired thing that he couldn't understand – to see this – but in a sense, to hear his own youth.

'Finally I did this one for him, *June In January*. He went (Tiny sings the last words of the song in the later Crosby voice) then we switched, he was singing the lower part to a modern number like *Cool Of The Evening* and I went in my high voice, a triplet duet with Bobbie Gentry – they were doing the low voice and I was doing the high voice.' (6)

The TV spot initially went perfectly – and very 1940s - until Tiny was required to sing his final number. This time Tiny switched gears from Crosby to Jerry Lee Lewis' *Great Balls of Fire,* which he performed with too much zest for Crosby's tastes. Tiny ripped off his jacket and clawed at his clothes, against a backing of a full-tilt Rock band. Crosby stood in the aisles shaking his head, unable to comprehend how Tiny could switch from Crosby to *this?*

Tiny Tim's Long-Awaited *Second Album*

Problems with *Tiny Tim's Second Album* delayed its release until January 1969. He dedicated it to his septuagenarian parents. The album should have been another triumph, but there were unforeseen problems. Tiny was arguing with Richard Perry about the selection and treatment of some of the songs.

There was another problem too, the waters were muddied by the release of *Concert In Fairyland* the previous August, an album cobbled together from an under-produced demo session recorded by Tiny as Darry Dover in 1962 and released by Richard Perry's father-in-law - of all people!

Fans who bought it thought it was Tiny's follow-up to *God Bless* and were disappointed by this scrappy bootleg. Attempting to stave off the damage that *Fairyland* had done, a couple of quick singles were released, *Bring Back Those Rock-A-Bye Baby Days* (July) followed by *Be My Love/Hello Hello*. They didn't impact. To make matters worse Tiny had argued so much with Richard Perry that Perry (whose reputation was now established) no longer wanted to work with him. (7)

All this brought urgency to the second album, which was delayed because Tiny was in such demand as a performer that his management couldn't get him into a studio. And when they did, they realised they had miscued, the *Second Album* failed to sell as quickly as the first, despite Tiny's now massive fame. The powerful Jerry Lee Lewis song *Great Balls Of Fire* was released as a single. It charted, though not in the Top 20.

But what was he famous for? Pundits debated the question 'is this guy for real?' The public found his personality sexually ambiguous and wondered how much of this was orchestrated? Journalists dug deep, only to find this was the real thing. Tiny's fame suddenly switched to the public concentrating on irrelevancies like the alarm clock in his shopping bag, that he ate pumpkin seeds, took lots of showers and talked frenetically about Jesus Christ.

His great talent, evidenced at the Royal Albert Hall Concert, was not known by the majority of people who tuned into *Laugh-In* where Tiny was usually required to flutter a bit before singing something silly. Rather than cementing his reputation with his young audience, the promoters seemed content with the gimmicky image before eventually dropping him and blaming him.

Superstar

Tiny was a superstar now. No longer could he walk the streets of New York and catch a subway. he could not even visit to his roots, the small clubs, street musicians, friends from the *Page Three* and *Hubert's Flea Circus.* In 1969, we're talking *traffic jam* crowds, too many to manage. His managers locked him away in a suite, often with Ron DeBlasio and his wife in the second bedroom. The only fans/friends he met were at signing sessions. This is how he met young Mark Mitchell who remained a friend for life.

Mitchell said, 'The day I met him, he was so gracious – he signed my diary and he gave me a big poster of himself and we had a friendship from the minute we met. And back in those days, he was playing the Playboy Club Boston, which is no longer there, but those were the days when a celebrity like Tiny, when they wanted something, they got what they wanted. And he got me into the Playboy Club.

'Everywhere he went, he made sure I was there. And of course, we could have gotten into trouble for having a minor in there even though I wasn't caught drinking or anything, but the bunnies were walking around. I wasn't interested in any of that, I just wanted to see Tiny sing. Later, I remember sharing a candy bar with Miss Vicki, who I thought at the time was a lot older but in reality she was only about five years older than me.' (8) Coincidentally, Tiny also met Jim Foley on the same day, another friend for life.

At this stage of Tiny's career people like Mitchell and Foley were part of the passing parade. Such friendships were only sealed with the passage of time. After each signing session or public appearance Tiny was whisked away by his management and closeted to safety. The Human Canary had become a caged bird. The world was at his feet yet he was locked away and untouchable. Tiny now had everything he had ever dreamed of – way beyond his wildest dreams. He had met Kaufman, Vallee and Crosby. He had justified himself to his parents and made Aunt Leah's prediction come true. Cousin Hal was clearly proud of him now. But younger Cousin Bernie missed him, not understanding the impact of fame and why Herbie never called him any more?

DeBlasio and Silver probably did what they could to keep Tiny happy. He wasn't like any other star. Certainly every other Rock star in town wanted sex and drugs, not Tiny. He wanted food.

Although earning – for example - $30,000 for a series of mid-west concerts in January and $5000 on 2 February for a concert at Waterloo Iowa, plus $320 for an appearance on the *Mike Douglas Show,* etc, etc, in this period Tiny never saw money. Convinced that he was being 'robbed' he figured the only way for him to take advantage of his earnings was to spend what he could by putting it on the tab. He started with mail order items and bought the most expensive Martin guitar through a catalogue, had it sent to the room, then set about buying something else – like, a $100 ukulele. After this he worked his way through the menu. By this time Tiny was treating DeBlasio like a warden, while DeBlasio was trying to figure out what Tiny was going to do next.

Since the age of 12 Tiny seldom ate in public, and so – alone with his Bible, ukulele and pulp magazines - he ordered excessive amounts of food to be sent to his room, so much that the word spread amongst the hotel staff that 'Tiny Tim was having a food orgy'. When DeBlasio came to his room he hid the pizzas and other foodstuffs under the bed, on top of the cupboards, everywhere he could. When DeBlasio left the suite, Tiny gradually worked his way around all the plates of food. And so his body shape began to change, from the skeletal Tiny Tim to someone who was slightly chubby. (9)

Tiny's managers took care of all Tiny's business. They gave him $100 per week and free room service, that's all. That was probably the $100 he gave Greene to keep the girls away. (10) Yet he was capable of filling the palace of Rock the Fillmore West Stadium in San Francisco. He even calmed the Hell's Angels on one occasion when he balladeered them.

When asked why he ate so much. Tiny said, 'When it was food or guitars I knew they were robbing me. I don't like to make blame, I don't want to bear false witness but I did make more than $1 million, almost $2 million. I'm talking 1968 up to the end of 1969 and there was no one counting it. They used to put their hand on the salary and have me sign the contract without seeing it because they did not want me telling the press what I was making, and so I never saw the amount I was making for all those little jobs I had when I was hot in 1968 and 1969.

'The big jobs, I know what I made. I know I made $50,000 that week at Caesar's Palace and then they held me over for another two days for another $7500 – that's $57,000 for that job alone. And then I made another $65,000 that same year in Florida a few month's later. Those two jobs alone, not counting 20 engagements I had in summertime of at least $5000 an engagement – that's $100,000 for the two months of summer. And we're not even talking royalties from the sales of the album. The album came No 7 on the charts during that year and the single *Tiptoe* hit No 17.' (11)

Locked away, wanting/not wanting women, annoying his management with a string of unexpected problems, Tiny had a whole different set of requirements from the usual Rock star - some to do with his religious beliefs, and lots to do with Miss-This and Miss-That. Furthermore, he wasn't toeing the line when talking to the press. He infuriated DeBlasio and Silver when he told his fans on-air that his newest single, *America, I Love You* was 'junk'. Mo Ostin tuned in to that program, turned incandescent at what he heard and cancelled Tiny's contract on the spot!

In March he was signed up by Americana Hotels for a multi-city deal, a coup for DeBlasio, so things were good again. But that all changed when Tiny was being whisked away from the media crying out, 'Help! Help! They're holding me captive!'

Although it surely sounds like the lonely tale of a popular star closeted away by his management, Tiny always didn't see it that way. 'Mr DeBlasio is a fine man,' he said. As for the unhappy trappings of fame, Tiny felt they were glorious, and would not have had things any other way. He said, 'When you make it after 20 years, you sit down in a room and you see beautiful trays of food – the best of everything – and you're looking back at the years of many people who never made it. You're looking back at the years when I walked night after night, early morning. The ridicule I got – naturally – in the daytime for years and years, especially with the long hair going back to 1954. All those years – you look back, and all of a sudden it's over. One out of a million made it, and I look in the mirror and I'm one of them. Thank God through Christ!' (12)

In April De Blasio was tired of handling Tiny. Another change followed in May when Bill Cosby pulled out of Campbell, Silver & Cosby.

Favourite Pioneer Recording Artists

In May, while at a Sherman Inn engagement in Chicago, Tiny met Jim Walsh in the audience. Walsh was the editor of a magazine called *Favorite Pioneer Recording Artists,* which had a fascination for the history of popular song.

At this stage Tiny had a backing line-up of Peter Palmer's Orchestra as well as a girl singing-dancing group known as the *Gold Diggers,* who were regularly used by Dean Martin on the *Dean Martin Show*. As the editor of a magazine that was dedicated to singers like Henry Burr, Irving Kaufman and Russ Conway, Walsh was fascinated by Tiny's knowledge of the period. They met and Tiny gave a great interview about the recording artists he loved, to someone who knew what he was talking about.

People often ask the question, 'What was Tiny Tim like?' This interview is very much what he was like - someone who enjoyed talking about the history of music, especially the pre-vinyl era. In the mid-late stages of his life Tiny had a reputation for being a 'walking encyclopaedia' on the history of music. This was not generally recognised by the media at this stage of his career.

Most Fascinating Face In Showbusiness

At this time, Tiny's image was making a significant shift – from virtuoso singer to TV comic. He was no longer stick insect thin, the public was repeatedly told the number of times he showered per day and the press now described him as 'weird', rather than something kinder like 'touchingly naïve'. He was also cruelly described as 'ugly'. Sometimes he spoke of himself like that - though in truth he is no more ugly than any of his Rock contemporaries – say Mick Jagger, Frank Zappa. Ringo Starr…so what?

Tiny dates the backlash coming as early as May 1968 when the *Los Angeles Times* editorial opened up with, 'A low boo to Tiny Tim. What's happened to American civilisation?' From this came a gradual groundswell of criticism and lazy journalism that within two years refused to depict Tiny as anything other than a freak. What would now follow was Tiny's vertiginous fall from grace. (13)

Presley's biographer, Allan Goldman never thought him ugly. Rather than calling him 'the celery stalk with a soul', 'a Quasimodo to the middle classes' or 'America's curio in residence' he described him in 1968 as having 'the most fascinating face in show business'. Why did this ugly stuff happen? *Sick* magazine put a ferocious drawing of Tiny on the cover and inside published an uncomplimentary chart of the devolution of man, from ape to Tiny Tim. *Mad* magazine also gave him a serve. In *People* magazine 3 July 1992, Tiny reflected on common adjectives that have been used to describe him. He listed: perverted, queer, sick, an ugly duckling, pathetic, a tragedy, a curiosity, a boy only a mother could love. He concluded with, 'But they don't know me. God knows me, and that's a comfort'.

The *Washington Post* described him as a 'sartorial blunder'. *Newsweek* said he had, 'the face of a vampire and the mannerisms of a music hall diva'. It was nasty and undeservedly vindictive, which Tiny seemed to encourage, believing as he did all his life, that – as Oscar Wilde put it – 'The only thing worse than being talked about is not being talked about'.

For a better description see, Albert Goldman, *New York Times,* 1968. He describes Tiny like this, 'He has the most fascinating face in show business – a Janus face that flicks with the allegory of evil and innocence that underlies all his art, all those confrontations between melodramatic villains and helpless quivering maidens. Sometimes he looks like Fagin, with his long kinky hair, enormous hooked beak and long white white's teeth; then he reaches into his paper shopping bag, removes his ukulele, wrapped carefully in an old cardigan, and suddenly he's everybody's Jewish grandmother.' (14)

Footnotes:

1.   Eric Clapton, talking to Lowell Tarling about Martin Sharp/Tiny Tim, 11 November 1984. 'I never thought I would have started all this,' said Eric after seeing the complete footage of *Street of Dreams* at Sharp's house. (Lowell Tarling's 1984 diary notes.)

2.   Richard Neville, Hippie Hippie Shake, p. 126, William Heinemann Australia. Also, Martin Sharp, interview with Lowell Tarling, 6 September 1982. Sharp said, 'I've been given a particular insight, especially seeing the Albert Hall Concert which was the first time I'd ever heard him, so there was never any need to convince myself. I needed re-convincing in a way every now and then, which the tapes do, because I listen to them. Martin Sharp, interview with Lowell Tarling, 31 July 2003. Also, Martin Sharp, 1968 diary notes, 'First Impressions'.

3.   Sue Khaury, interview with Lowell Tarling and Michael Wilkinson, 30 March 2002.

4.   Pamela Des Barres, *I'm With The Band*.

5.   Sue Khaury, interview with Lowell Tarling and Michael Wilkinson, 30 March 2002.

6.   Tiny Tim, taped by Martin Sharp, *Wirian*, 1 June 1976.

7.   Bootleg recording, *Concert In Fairyland*, Bouquet Label. The tracks are: *Oh How I Miss You Tonight, Let me Call You Sweetheart, On The Good Ship Lollipop, Secret Love, Animal Crackers, Indian Love Call, Don't Take Your Love from me, If I Didn't Care, You Make me Feel so Young, I Got A Pain In My Sawdust, Be My Love, Toot-Toot-Tootsie*.

8.   Mark Mitchell, interview with Lowell Tarling, 30 March 2002.

9.   Tiny Tim, interview with Lowell Tarling, 6 September 1983. Tiny describes food excesses. He also says that he has never touched drugs, though he is not offended by other people's drug use 'Only for their health', that's all that bothers him.

10. Sue Khaury, *Memories of My Husband, Tiny Tim,* (unpublished document) 1998.

11. Tiny Tim, interview with Lowell Tarling dated 6 September 1983.

12. Tiny Tim, interview with Lowell Tarling dated 6 September 1983. Tiny describes the high life.

13. Tiny Tim, interviewed by Caroline Jones, *ABC Radio*, 25 October 1978.

14. *Sick,* November No. 63. Also *Mad*, April 1970, *People,* 3 July 1992. We could continue by turning this into an impossibly long list of derision and insults.

Martin celebrated Miss Vicki in London OZ magazine. Said Tiny, 'I'll be honest with you Mr Tarlin, I didn't know she was a virgin when I married her. She said she was. I know I never touched her until marriage. Even in marriage I didn't have a relationship with her until three days later. On the honeymoon, there was no intercourse, as far as I can remember, until three days later. I'll tell you why - I did it for the glory of God.'

Tiny Tim, 6 September 1983

7

Miss Vicki

I need someone to create for, a heart to sing to, a trophy to give!
Tiny Tim

Tiny was in love with love. He always claimed to be 'looking for a certain face'. He said, 'I need someone to create for, a heart to sing to, a trophy to give'. He spoke of going to strip clubs, sex joints, flicking through girlie magazines, not to look at bodies but in a never-ending search for 'that certain face'. (1)

He found it when he met pixie-ish Victoria Mae Budinger at a book signing session. He chose well. Briefly in the spotlight, Miss Vicki has been frequently listed in magazines of the time as an icon amongst 'Swinging Chicks of the 60s'. Miss Vicki's style has been acknowledged as influential on the period. She was a cross between London's Mary Quant and 99 in the hit TV show *Get Smart*. Here's how they met.

Beautiful Thoughts

On 2 June 1969 Tiny began a 16-day promotional tour for Doubleday Books to promote his delightful little book, *Beautiful Thoughts*. It is Tiny's 'take' on Norman Vincent Peale's *The Power of Positive Thinking*. The artwork by Frazier-Hauge is somewhat in the vein of the Beatles' *Yellow Submarine* and the slim volume comprises 40 Tiny Tim one-liners, one per page.

For example, Tiny writes: 'Darry Dover? Larry Love? Texarkana Tex? Judas K Foxglove? Vernon Castle? Emmett Swink? If your name isn't helping you…change it'. An extraordinary truism when you know his biography.

There are also lots of baseball references, the lyrics to a Stewart Jackson song of 1917, risqué humour like 'Sometimes a nice long shower will straighten you out', a collage featuring Bing Crosby, Rudy Vallee, Tuesday Weld, Shirley Temple and Don Drysdale. We also read: 'Romance is the main objective in life' followed by the poem to Miss Elizabeth Taylor that Tiny wrote in 1947.

Tiny signs out *Beautiful Thoughts* with, 'Don't be discouraged. Tiny Tim made it. Thank you and goodbye'. (1)

On 3 June 1969, the first day of the book's promotional tour, at Wanamaker's Department Store Philadelphia, there was a queue waiting to get their book signed.

Victoria Budinger was in that queue. Immediately he clapped eyes on her, Tiny shed a tear, which he caught in an envelope and kept in his ukulele. He told her this. It went down very well indeed. Miss Vicki had been a fan since the age of 15. She had his posters on her walls, had attended his concerts, now she had his autograph. And he had kept his tear.

'I saw her face and couldn't get it out of my mind', he explained. Four days later he arranged to see her again back in Philadelphia. They spent the next two months courting by phone.

And so, Miss Vicki and Tiny Tim fell in love. He was a famous attractive guy, definitely in love with her. She was fresh out of school and about to be bounced onto international television. *Why not?*

Approach-Avoidance

Everyone wanted a fairytale wedding and to keep it perfect Tiny should have – could have - courted Miss Vicki without a hitch. It could have all been swoon, croon and tulips. Instead Tiny was actually freaked out. He was approaching 40 and still a virgin. This relationship with Miss Vicki had upped the stakes.

Within days of captivating Miss Vicki, Tiny began a strong flirtation with Miss Jan Gianopolis. He also allowed himself to be distracted by other girls that crossed his path and in this way the run-up to the marriage was full of bumps and inconsistencies. The truth is, Tiny was genuinely scared of what he was getting into. He hadn't yet dealt with sex. And he certainly had never set up a home. Looking back over those years Tiny reckons he had 'an infantile mind'.

In his panic, Tiny entered a deeply religious period from which he emerged with a set of rules and sexual restraints 'for the glory of God'. Hardly any of these can be found in the Bible (like a period of abstinence between marriage and consummation) but Tiny spoke of them as his 'beliefs'.

One month before their engagement Tiny called Miss Vicki and said, 'These are my beliefs - we can't have sex just for pleasure unless kids are to be had. I said, "You don't have to marry me, but if we're going to get married that's how it should be. I know you're 17 – but you know how to read and write when you're 17 and you can understand this".' I guess, Miss Vicki went along with it. (3)

And then of course there were rules regarding cleanliness, which required separate bathrooms. Tiny had a complete aversion to all bodily emissions, especially blood. He went through three marriages without ever acknowledging the female menstrual cycle. He told me, 'I never saw any of that'.

Furthermore, Tiny was afraid of all animals, down to small lap dogs. Unwashed and even washed glasses never touched his lips. He never drank from glasses but 'straight out of the bottle'. He avoided being kissed on the mouth, even when greeted by celebrities. He was fascinated by skin care products. And he shook hands with his left hand. I guess Miss Vicki went along with all that too. It all must have seemed all right, him being so famous, and famous people being known for eccentricities.

Tiny formally asked Mr and Mrs Budinger for their daughter, Vicki's hand in marriage. Should the parents of either party disapprove, the wedding would be off. The Budingers agreed, Butros was pleased and Tilly was probably relieved. The boy would be wed.

The public got to know about it when Tiny proposed to Miss Vicki on-air on 17 September. She accepted. Now, Miss Vicki was elevated to stardom too. She made her debut on the *Ed Sullivan Show* with Tiny. This was followed by her appearance on the *Carson Show* where Tiny announced the engagement. Then Carson asked Tiny if he'd like to have the wedding ceremony live on the show, Tiny agreed and the date was set for December. 'Tiny accepted without considering how Vicki felt about it,' said Miss Sue commenting on Miss Vicki's burst of fame, whether she wanted it or not. 'The publicity machine was already rolling and she couldn't back out.' (4)

Tiny went on to propose to two other girls shortly after announcing his engagement (Miss Iris and Miss Marilyn). He continued seeing Miss Jan Gianopolis and had what he called, a 'honey affair' with Miss Toni. All this he confessed in full to Miss Vicki during these tense months of the engagement.

Tiny Tim had lost his nerve. But he regained it in time to give the world the wedding it had been waiting for. Orchestrated by the master of the deadpan one-liner, Johnny Carson, Tiny was so famous that it might as well have been a Royal wedding.

40 Million TV Viewers

And so it came to pass that on 17 December, Tiny Tim and 17-year old Vicki Budinger were wed on the *Johnny Carson Show* before the biggest televised audience in history. NBC estimates 35 million viewers, some say 40 million, others reckon 45. Either way, this television viewing record would not be eclipsed until the Moonwalk.

In New York alone, 84% of the population watched Tiny Tim and a helluva cute Miss Vicki exchange vows.

Cousin Hal was there with bells on! His sons Adrian and Haddon (aged 5 and 8) were Miss Vicki's trainbearers. Tillie and Buttros were there too! It was certainly a triumph, and not Tiny's last.

Nervous, cautious, shy, sincere, smartly-dressed in a frock coat, smelling nice, carrying a ukulele under his right arm and nothing like a Human Canary, Tiny Tim stood at the altar and awaited his bride.

Coy, trusting, apprehensive, with sober dignity and flashing her pixie beauty, Miss Vicki walked to his side.

The pastor who converted Tiny to Jesus Christ back in 1951, Rev Jack Wersten, was an officiate. The adjectives chosen for the vows were: sweet, gentle, kind, patient, not puffed up, charitable, slow to and anger and swift to forgive. Rings were exchanged.

You can watch it all on youtube. What you'll see is about seven minutes of Tiny and Miss Vicki's backs. You'll probably feel an enormous sincerity coming from the bride and groom. You'll see Tiny turn to kiss his bride. He cups his hands on Miss Vicki's cheeks, gently holds her and places a most delicate kiss on her lips.

All done now, the couple turn and face the cameras. A bridesmaid hands Miss Vicki a bouquet and the new Mr & Mrs Herbert Khaury walk out with great dignity to the applause of guests. The ceremony featured a seven-foot tall cake and 10,000 tulips specially imported from Holland. Thieves crashed the party and the wedding gifts stolen. (5)

It was a beautiful wedding. The world was astounded. But there was a problem. Tiny Tim was suddenly 'normal'. No one had seen this Tiny Tim before.

Rudy Vallee wasn't there, Tiny's management said he'd be only be welcome if he paid his own fare. Tiny's idol, treated like that! When he heard about it, Tiny hit the roof, 'He only wanted to feel *wanted!*' he exclaimed. But as far as Vallee was concerned, the omission was all Tiny's fault. Disgruntled, he went on to moan to the press.

What's Consummated?

Never having slept a night the same bed as anyone else in his life, Tiny opted for privacy on his honeymoon. At Tiny's behest, he and Miss Vicki spent the first three days of married life in separate rooms, in the most opulent hotel in town. They kept apart 17-20 December 'for the glory of God', so Tiny explained.

The couple was then whisked to the Bahamas where I guess Tiny lost his virginity, at last.

Tiny explained, 'Even in marriage I didn't have a relationship with Miss Vicki until three days later. On the honeymoon there was no intercourse, as far as I can remember, until three days. For the first three days I was in my room alone, she was in her room alone. We couldn't see each other.

'This is 1969 and it happened in the Bahamas. I had a 12-day vacation, four days for the honeymoon (12 days work, but they call it a 'vacation'). I did it for the glory of God. Marriage is not for sex alone but first to admire God for the great sanctity for having the joy of a woman and to remember that belongs to Him. I just worked for the glory of God so that he would bless the marriage. We'd have children only for the glory of Him and not touch each other for three days, like a Sanctuary. Now even if the marriage went astray it doesn't mean God was unhappy. He respects what we do for him. She knew this was going to happen before we were married. She was alone and I was alone. I was in the dark most of the time. In the daytime I just waited and I'd think of the Good Lord all day. I'd have my shower in my room alone, saw nobody, and just alone for three days - two nights and three days.

'The fourth night she came into the room and how it happened was - now I might have slightly cheated, I don't know. I don't remember everything. It's possible I might have tried something just before that and held off. I think that might have happened, but I can assure you it wasn't much. But I know the fourth day...' (6)

To-and-from the Bahamas, the press loved them. Everywhere they went Miss Vicki was pelted with questions.

'How do you like being married to Tiny Tim?'

'He's wonderful.'

'What do you call him?'

'I call him Herbie. Sometimes I call him dear'.

'Has your marriage been consummated?'

'What does that mean?' (7)

After this they flew to Brooklyn where they lived in the $650 per month apartment from which Tiny would be evicted in five years time.

For All My Little Friends

By the time Warner Brothers got around to Tiny's third album, *For All My Little Friends,* Perry had grown into a recognised recording genius. He'd produced Theodore Bikel, Captain Beefheart, Ella Fitzgerald. But not Tiny. Not any more.

In marrying Miss Vicki, something of Tiny's mystery was gone. He wasn't really weird - he was a husband. And with it, he lost something of the sexual ambiguity on which his stage and television persona traded. This caused a hiccough in the Warners marketing department. Then someone thought of something. What do husbands do? They father children.

Tiny's third LP was to be a collection of children songs. Warners wanted to re-position him as a children's act.

A kid's act? Just because he *knew* children's songs, from the old days with his cousins, didn't mean that was his choice of material. Tiny always balked at children's gigs. He was more relaxed with transsexuals!

Tiny's managers had seriously miscued. Hadn't the concert at the Royal Albert Hall defined Tiny at his best? That was Richard Perry's vision, but Richard Perry wasn't around any more. Perhaps this kid's album was a counter to *Concert In Fairyland* – though the managers surely can't have felt so threatened as to respond to such a feckless bootleg recording?

Instead of building on Tiny's strengths the third recording had the full flavour of a contractual obligation album. After this, Warners dropped Tiny. He was never again signed to a major recording label.

Even though the fans didn't buy it, in 1969 *For All My Little Friends* was nominated for a Grammy Award. (8)

Small Clubs

On 21 February Tiny played the Troubadour, Hollywood, the first small club appearance he'd played in a long time. Things were on a slide. Tiny's management looked for new ways to 'save' his career. Building on *For All My Little Friends* they came up with an idea for a kid's show, which interested Warners at first, but thankfully didn't come off.

But something had to come off. Things were going wrong. Tiny was in a car that was involved in an accident en route to Burbank to tape an appearance on the Andy Williams Show, followed by a stage accident while taping the Red Skelton Show.

In April, at the Freemont Hotel Las Vegas, Tiny made a choice that was to affect the musical rise of feminism when he inadvertently launched the career of Australian singer Helen Reddy, who went onto a smash hit with *I Am Woman*. It happened this way.

Reddy was married to DeBlasio's partner Jeff Wald. They were handling one of Tiny's shows, to be opened by an Australian act who cancelled at the last minute. DeBlasio asked Tiny who he'd like to fill the vacant spot on the bill? adding - 'How about Helen Reddy?'

Tiny thought about it briefly, only feeling uneasy because she was so closely linked to his management, then he said, 'Sure, let's use her.'

Tiny liked her act, described her as a 'wonderful singer' but was distressed to be told that this unknown singer was paid $7500 per week out of Tiny's earnings! 'That was unheard of!' he exclaimed, now totally disenchanted with his management.

The fights with DeBlasio continued. Tiny described DeBlasio and Silver as bad cop/good cop. DeBlasio reckoned he was trying to maintain Tiny's stage image and he did the screaming. Tiny never could take being yelled at. Silver did the '*there-there- there...*' stuff.

So, he holed up in his room, usually with Miss Vicki, who travelled with him and witnessed all this, though she has never spoken about it to the press. Alone in his room with the telephone, Tiny spent hours ringing out under various pseudonyms. The phone bill did not impress DeBlasio. Tiny wasn't impressed that no matter how much he earned, he never saw any money. Tiny dealt with it by spending big on his *per diem* account. But he had a wife now, who was similarly disenchanted with the management/money question. Vicki was asking direct questions. She was his wife and equal partner. She wasn't interested in running up the daily account, she was interested in running a marriage. *Show us the money!*

No doubt this was the start of Tiny's respective managers constantly bad-mouthing Miss Vicki as a 'gold digger' (over years) which simply ain't quite fair. She was actually Tiny's wife with every right to question what he earned. What if they should start a family?

Tiny's family was feeling the same way. So Butros, accompanied by Cousin Hal – who was now professionally equipped to understand balance sheets - flew to Los Angeles to figure out how it was possible that after earning so much money, Tiny was actually in debt!

Meanwhile the fights between Tiny and DeBlasio never abated. One time when DeBlasio was going to Los Angeles, Tiny asked him to pick up a megaphone ('bullhorn') for him, as his current one was broken. Even though he took $750 from the till to make the purchase, DeBlasio returned without it.

Tiny was livid, feeling the megaphone was integral to the old time sound he strove to create. Tiny threw an ashtray at Wald, who was in the room, and he fired DeBlasio on the spot. (10)

DeBlasio didn't care. He was also managing George Carlin, Helen Reddy and the Turtles. He picked up Tiny's season ticket for the Dodgers and the megaphone that had precipitated the crisis, found Tiny backstage at the Freemont, handed him the stuff and responded with, 'Here, I'm firing *you!*' Thus ended a productive two-and-a-half year relationship.

DeBlasio had started out as Silver's chief lieutenant, serving as Tiny's manager-bodyguard-confessor. Earlier in their relationship Tiny had given him a plaque that read, 'To Mr Ron DeBlasio, my favourite manager. Thank you for all you have put up with in my behalf. You certainly deserve this, 1968. Tiny Tim.'

Jim & Joe Cappy

After a series of managerial changes, Tiny's father Butros took over for a brief stint, until Tiny signed with Jim Cappy and brother Joe. Joe was a former construction worker who became Tiny's bodyguard and confidant for the next few years. A good guy, yes, but these guys were tough. They weren't in there for the art. (11)

Looking back, a Reprise release of *Tiny Tim at the Royal Albert Hall* would have been absolutely timely right now. It would have restored his stature as an extraordinary voice.

Tiny was less of a drawcard now. The Love Generation was over. 1971 was a bleaker world. Flowers were passé. Beautiful thoughts were no longer fashionable. It was all about Charlie Manson, Altamont, dead Jim, dead Janis, dead Jimi, dead Brian Jones. Tiny played smaller venues. And, as he travelled with his wife, he required two suites for separate bathrooms, which doubled the expenses.

Struggling for a hit record was difficult, but Tiny could still rely on his television appeal. That had not waned and in May – with Miss Vicki on the show too – Carson paid tribute to Tiny's staying power, after two years as a regular on the *Johnny Carson Show*.

Throughout this period, Tiny and Miss Vicki were continually hosted by famous stars, who invited them to their homes socially and while doing a TV shows together. Tiny said, 'I was doing a TV show in 1970. I met Mr Mickey Rooney. He invited me out to his house in the Valley, a nice little house. He talked to me about his waiting around and biding his time, waiting for the opening that would take him to the top, and now 10 years later he's got *Sugar Babies* and he's back on top.' (11)

There are lots and lots of anecdotes of Tiny meeting famous people. Readers should chase them down in Justin Martell's biography and Ernie Clark's Tiny Tim website, www.tinytim.com.org.

Exploration Of Punctuation

Meanwhile, Martin Sharp never forgot Tiny. He had featured him in the London underground magazine *OZ*, for which Martin was artistic director. Having designed two influential album covers and also working as Artistic Adviser for Mick Jagger's acting debut film *Performance*, Martin had quite a few Rock and film contacts, all of whom he tried to persuade into making a film about this *Leonardo da Vinci of Popular Song*. A couple of filmmakers reckoned they were more interested in Martin's fascination with Tiny than with Tiny Tim. This did not help the cause. (12)

Shortly after this Tiny came to England and, although they had previously met briefly at London's *Speakeasy Club,* Martin determined to go all-out and meet him properly.

He hired a car, and along with Richard Neville and Louise Ferrier (who had accompanied Sharp to the Albert Hall Concert) they drove to Caesar's Palace, a Working Men's Club in Luton. Martin hung around the stage door after the show and met Tiny. Martin felt this was a most significant meeting. Martin was working in visual collage and Tiny was working in musical collage.

Martin explains the connection, he says, 'I was working about the same time doing those collages, and Tiny was doing it with songs - transposing styles - the Bob Dylan/Rudy Vallee dialogue. He was doing with songs what I was doing with images. That's why I clicked with him.

People talk of great artists - Vincent Van Gogh comes immediately in my mind, and the other one is Tiny. Equal magnitudes, different mediums. So - when you meet a real one, you do what you can because you understand the danger of their lives'. (13)

On meeting Tiny, Martin was effusive with his praise and he asked Neville to 'get the gift' that was in the car – a huge painting from Martin's *Exploration of Punctuation* period. After a long silence Tiny shook his head and said, 'Oh what a shame Mr Sharp, it doesn't fit in my shopping bag!' (14)

In 1970 the cassette tape recorder was state-of-the-art technology. Martin bought one and started taping everything Tiny said and sang, as he would do throughout in their relationship. In an attempt to generate interest in Tiny's flagging career Martin gave his earliest tape to Pete Townshend. If it still exists at all, it is somewhere among Townshend's tapes.

Isle of Wight Music Festival

As Tiny's 'flagging career' was on everyone's lips, the unexpected happened. Tiny was invited to perform at the Isle of Wight Concert on 30 August 1970 at Afton Farm – the year after Bob Dylan's return to form at the same venue.

In the light of Woodstock, English promoters saw a copycat opportunity of putting on a music festival in a paddock as a quick financial scoop. But the 600,000-strong hippie audience was into Love not Money. They wanted a free concert/Be-In, which put the audience at loggerheads with promoters before a note was played.

The mood of the Isle of Wight Festival was bleak. So was the weather. The stadium was cramped, the sound was appalling, performers were not in full view and the toilets were disgusting. Ironically, the acoustics were best the non-paying area, a hill known as *Desolation Row* which overlooked the concert. Many of the paying audience moved back there, while the front of the stage turned ugly.

And aggro. A news tower in the VIP enclosure reports copped a ferocious hail of soft drink cans. Then a guy from the White Panthers demanded that Pepsi and Birds Eye donate their entire on-site warehouse to the crowd in return for a favourable mention in his speech. An insurrection followed, led by French Anarchists. Thousands walked out. Compère, Ricky Farr bleeted from the stage, 'Why are you doing this to us? We've given you this festival in peace and love, now you're breaking down our shops, you're breaking down our fences'.

The menace did not dispel. Joni Mitchell took the stage. *Boring! Boring!*

'Give me some respect – I'm an artist!' she screamed. They chucked cans at her.

Next, Jimi Hendrix came on late, had equipment problems and played badly. His band, the *Experience* kept stopping. He re-started songs, apologised and thanked the crowd for their patience. Miles Davis found the Isle of Wight experience pointless. Donovan and Ralph McTell might as well not have been there. Although Altamont was yet to come (the nadir of open air Rock) this Isle of Wight Concert was clearly an awful gig.

And then, like a ray of sunshine, there appeared the man they said was all washed up – Tiny Tim!

Tiny didn't want a Rock backing. He performed with two musicians, Jack Richards on drums and Cas Caswell on double bass. Said Caswell, ' If you play in front of 50 people you're pretty nervous, if you play in front of half a million people you're more nervous. But because it stretched over the horizon suddenly there was no nerves at all, because it was totally meaningless. There was this ocean of people. There was no part of the landscape you couldn't see full of people. The MD said, here's the dots lads and off we went'. (15)

What followed has consistently been lauded as one of the greatest gigs ever. It was included in the Top 10 live performances by *Q Magazine,* 2004. By the time Tiny got to sing, *Rule Brittania* and *There's Always Be An England* (see on youtube) he had the whole mass swaying in time and singing along with him. It was a peak performance - and his first medley. The medley idea stuck.

Tiny Tim turned into a triumph where Mitchell, Hendrix, Davies, Donovan and McTell had failed!

Biggest TV viewing audience to date…$megabucks in Vegas…Top 10 hit/s…now upstaging Hendrix.

People have forgotten all that.

The Medley

Then back to the clubs.

What have we got?

We've got a proven 'weird looking' singer who can throw his voice almost everywhere and a wife not yet 20 years old. She was probably frustrated by ageism, sexism and fast-talking promoters. So was Tiny.

His backing no longer had the class of Britain's National Concert Orchestra, as in the Royal Albert Hall. He was now doing it tough on the road.

After performing a difficult gig in Washington in 1970 and fearing the audience response, Tiny decided to override the derision by singing through it. Says Tiny, 'I couldn't stand the show I was doing. I started to sing without stopping and apparently that helped'.

The medley began as Tiny's defence mechanism against audience hostility. This, Tiny turned into an art. The medley gave him the opportunity to capitalise on his knowledge of popular song dating back to 1890. It also allowed him to perform his huge repertoire. Tiny discovered a vehicle that enabled him to sing – say – nine songs inside eight minutes – *It's A Long Way To Tipperary, Pack Up Your Troubles In Your Old Kit Bag, Bless Them All, Lili Marlene, There'll Be Bluebirds Over (The White Cliffs Of Dover), I've Got A Loverly Bunch Of Coconuts, Down At The Old Bull & Bush, Roll Out The Barrel, When Irish Eyes Are Smiling.* A collage of song.

The medley suggested possibilities that might also satisfy the missionary zeal that Tiny has always had about all eras of popular song.

It - RIP

Miss Vicki was with child within weeks of marriage. Her labour pains started in Houston when she was six and a half months pregnant. Tiny was working at the Cork Club and she was alone in her hotel room. She called for the hotel doctor who said it was nothing more than indigestion. He gave her painkiller tablets. By the time she was finally taken to hospital – hours later – the baby was stillborn.

Miss Vicki was crushed though, as she recalls, Tiny switched off emotionally. He returned to New York and continued working. He even had the thrill of meeting singer Gene Austin at the Cork Club on the day of the miscarriage. 'I was still in hospital. I begged him to please stay with me. I didn't want to be alone for a week in a strange city,' said Miss Vicki. 'But he just said *business is business* and flew off with his entourage. It was then that I decided to try for another baby!'

They had a tombstone made for the still-born child, which reads: *It, child of Mr & Mrs Herbert Khaury'.*

Grief is sometimes too much to bear. Sometimes disassociation helps, which seems what Tiny attempted. Mostly, he pulled it off. Not so when he and Miss Vicki appeared on the *Carson Show*. Instead of camping it up, being funny and upbeat, Tiny Tim (Miss Vicki by his side) became someone his viewers didn't recognise. They were parents who had lost their baby boy. It was, as they say, 'bad TV'. The year closed with Tiny writing magazine articles. He wrote an article for *Esquire Magazine* titled, 'The Perfect Mother'. (16)

More significantly, he also wrote for *Playboy* an article about the history of popular song from Thomas Alva Edison's invention of the phonograph through to the 1930s. Tiny wrote about the lives and songs of singers Byron G Harlan, Henry Burr, Arthur Fields, Irving Kaufman, Billy Murray, Ada Jones, Al Jolson, Russ Colombo and Rudy Vallee. (17) And he recorded *The Spaceship Song,* written eight years before for Miss Snooky at the *Page Three.*

Footnotes:

1. Tiny Tim, interview with Lowell Tarling, 22 August 1982.
2. Tiny Tim, *Beautiful Thoughts,* Doubleday & Company, Garden City New York, 1969.
3. Tiny Tim, interview with Lowell Tarling, 30 August 1983.
4. Sue Khaury, *Memories of My Husband, Tiny Tim,* (unpublished document) 1998.
5. Sue Khaury, *Memories of My Husband, Tiny Tim,* (unpublished document) 1998.
6. Tiny Tim, interview with Lowell Tarling, 6 September 1983.
7. Lloyd Shearer, *Sunday Bulletin (Philadelphia),* 1 March, 1970.
8. Tiny Tim, *For All My Little Friends,* record album, 1969. Tracks: *On The Good Ship Lollipop, Sunshine Cake, Mickey The Monkey, Hot And Cold Water, Two Times A Day, Chickery Chick, Oliphant The Eliphant, I'm A Lonesome Little Raindrop, They Always Pick On Me, Aren't You Glad You're You, Sadie The Seal, The Viper, Bill The Buffalo, Remember Your Name And Address, What The World Needs Now Is Love.*
9. Harold Stein, interview with Lowell Tarling, 1 April 2002. Also, Harry Stein, *Tiny Tim,* Playboy Press 1976, p. 9.
10. Harry Stein, *Tiny Tim,* Playboy Press 1976.
11. Scott Eyman, *Calendar,* 1 March 1981.
12. Martin Sharp, interview with Lowell Tarling, interview 13 April 1983.
13. Martin Sharp, interview with Lowell Tarling, interview 6 September 1982.
14. Richard Neville, *Hippie Hippie Shake,* William Heinemann Australia, 1995, pp.170-171.
15. Cas Caswell, interviewed by Vic King, Mike Plumbley and Pete Turner, Picnic in the Park, Cowes, August 1996.
16. Tiny Tim, 'The Perfect Mother', *Esquire,* December 1970, pp. 144-145.
17. Tiny Tim, 'The Great Crooners' *Playboy.*

8

Isadore Fertel
& Other Extraordinary Musical Projects

I know he was a warm person, I know he was a kind person.
Eccentric would be a way to describe him.
Miss Tulip, daughter

Being married made a huge difference to how Tiny's public saw him. That Miss Vicki happened to be tranquil, charming and attractive certainly prolonged television interest.

Tiny Tim had lost his innocence because there is something fundamentally un-weird about married people. Tiny's deportment was no big deal, compared to some. Like, Elvis who would pull out a handgun and shoot out TV screens. Sid Barrett, of Pink Floyd, who had become incomprehensible on stage. Brian Wilson, of the Beach Boys who was supposedly nuts. Several Rock stars who drove cars into swimming pools, smashed up hotel rooms and had unreasonable sexual demands. Maybe Tiny Tim wasn't so weird, after all? He didn't eat in public. Neither did Leslie West, the big guitarist in Jack Bruce's new superband *WBL* (ie. West, Bruce, Laing). Tiny took lots of showers. So might you if *you* were constantly locked up in hotel rooms with a shower, TV, bed, and little else. Tiny had an approach-avoidance to sex. Not uncommon. He had a mother fixation. Who hasn't? With jug band music making a comeback, even the ukulele was losing its weird, back in 1971.

To describe her father, Tulip prefers the word 'eccentric'. She said, 'I can't pinpoint his personality. I know he was a warm person, I know he was a kind person, but … I was never really close to him, so it's hard for me to define him or describe him. *Eccentric* would be a way to describe him.' (1)

Miss Tulip

Tiny and Miss Vicki's one and only 'blessed event' happened on 10 May 1971 when Tulip Victoria Khaury (Miss Tulip) was born. It was a 24-minute birth, which Tiny described as a 'blessing from God'. However, Tiny (who idealized parenthood) didn't understand fatherhood. He simply didn't know what to do, except work.

His income was all 'family money' now – and where was it?

Every major Rock star from this period has complained about being exploited by their management. Jimi Hendrix, the Rolling Stones, Eric Burdon, John Lennon, Cream, Bob Dylan, Pink Floyd, the Who, and more, all of whom looked to the Courts for justice. Contracts were written by sharp lawyers who put as much distance as they could between the artists and a proper accounting of their earnings. This ensured the artists remained in hock to their record companies for as long as possible. Exploitation was rife, and the Cappys stuck to the conventions of their industry. Miss Vicki saw through it and she didn't like what she saw. Tiny's management didn't like her. Miss Vicki was getting cross with Tiny as well. And that was another thing, Tiny hated – *hated* – being barked at. He simply couldn't take it.

Said Tiny, 'She would talk to me like this. (I'm not putting you on.) This is the way she talked to me (sweet voice), *Oh dearie, do you think I'm pretty?* I said, *Oh my darling, you know you're beautiful.* She had a cute voice. She'd put it on but I liked it. You shoulda heard her when she got angry!'

Of course Tiny knew his money was disappearing into management bank accounts, but to him, the fame was more important. Not so Miss Vicki, she couldn't stand Joe Cappy and couldn't afford more children. She now had a child to support and was finding her voice. Taking the Pill was anathema to Tiny's religious beliefs, but she took it anyway. Tiny found the packet and declared, 'Now that I know, I can't allow it'.

'That's fine by me!' she retorted, from which time they slept in separate beds and, according to Miss Vicki, had no more sex.

Tiny said, 'With Miss Vicki I wanted separate bedrooms. Maybe I'm wrong. When we got married I had a little bit more money then, we had 4-5 rooms: two bedrooms, one for Miss Tulip and one big bedroom with a gigantic king-size bed. Even then I slept at the other end - remember when I was with Miss Vicki, she was 17! I would get up at 4.00 in the morning. I couldn't sleep. I went into the bathroom and tried to rehearse the voice and get new sounds - always stick to my guns. The only reason I slept with her was there was no other room there and I didn't want to sleep on the couch. I never want to sleep with a woman in bed in marriage. I'll tell you why:

'I'm very fussy about cleanliness. No 1 - I hate to get up in the morning with bad breath. And No 2 - I always go to bed shaved, most of the time. My face is always cleansed with night creams. I can't take no body odours. I don't like men and women sharing the same bathrooms. We had different bathrooms in that house. She went to hers and I went to mine. Hers was in the outside room. I was in my own room. We slept in the same room, but my bathroom had a closed door. In order to go to the bathroom, she went out of the room and to the one in the main room. When we went on the road, 1971, 72, 73, most of the time let's say in the Holiday Inn – we'd get two separate rooms. One room was completely empty for the bathroom. So really, if the room was $50 we were paying $100, and nothing would go on in the other room except I put my stuff in that bathroom'. (2)

Opposite to Popular Culture

During this period Tiny certainly kept himself busy. He recorded a diverse range of 21 singles including a raunchy take on *Great Balls Of Fire,* a cowboy rendition of *Have You Seen My Little Sue?* the effete *Mickey The Monkey* and the childlike *On The Good Ship Lollipop.* From her childhood, Miss Tulip remembers *On The Good Ship Lollipop* best, because her grandma had the record. (3)

Ever 'different', in the post-hippie era, Tiny's patriotic take on the pro-conscription WW1 song, *What Kind Of An American Are You?* cut against the grain. With the Vietnam War a big issue at that time, this song came across like a poke at draft dodgers. Tiny's position was unclear – irony was not usually associated with Tiny Tim. Then, to keep everyone guessing, he would medley a pro-conscription song with an anti-conscription song from the same musical period. One example is, *I Didn't Raise My Boy To Be A Soldier*, an anti-war song that he would sing side-by-side pro-war numbers. From the time he parted his hair the opposite way to Valentino all those years ago, Tiny deliberately took an opposite position to popular culture. The 70s were about Dave Bowie, Glam, Punk, Kraftwerk, Dance, Techno, etc…while Tiny Tim continually dug deeper into the 40s, 30s, as far back as he could. This was really his thing: he was a transporter of songs from the past.

Grandpa Tim

Constantly seeking the unexpected, Tiny then recorded in an old-time studio in New York. There he laid down a dozen songs, some of which he wrote himself. Like a tribute to Jimi Hendrix, Janis Joplin and Jim Morrison titled, *Why Did They Have To Die So Young?*

Under the pseudonym Grandpa Tim he also recorded a couple of songs using what he called his 'Byron G Harlan old man's voice'. The first was *Delilah* and the second *My Way,* which Tiny described at the time as 'one of the best things I ever did'. He would revisit the song in 1982 and prove that point again. He also recorded *The Happy Wanderer/Juanita Banana* as Tiny Tim in 1972.

Next, Tiny and Miss Vicki formed a partnership, the aptly named Vic-Tim label (that flagged the words 'Jesus Saves') as well as the less attractively named Toilet Records ('sit and listen'). All Tiny needed now was a protégé. He found one.

Tiny proclaimed, 'The most important thing I did as head of Toilet Records was discover a new talent – Isadore Fertel. I paid him $100 to cut two songs for me'.

John Carmen

Fertel wasn't a problem for Miss Vicki. Her husband's so-called best friend and manager – Joe Cappy – was. It was an explosive situation against a vacillating backdrop of plenty money/no money. Miss Vicki dug her heels in about the money, when that didn't work she announced that she never wanted Cappy to set foot in her house again.

Bored and probably dead cynical about the whole recording industry, Miss Vicki began a relationship with model/actor John Carmen whom she had met at a New York television studio where Tiny was doing a show. Carmen was 18 at the time, one year younger than Miss Vicki.

It wasn't a difficult affair to manage, Tiny being away 90 per cent of the time. After this, the Tiny Tim-Miss Vicki marriage was all over.

Rock Around The Clock, In Yiddish

Enter - Isadore Fertel, someone so unusual that even Tiny giggled whenever he talked about him. 'I always wanted to be Larry Love' Tiny once said. Well, Isadore wanted to be Tiny Tim.

Fertel was short, bald and wore thick spectacles that made his eyes seem huge. He had an enormous smile. He talked with a lisp. And if you hadn't already picked it, within seconds of meeting he'd make sure you knew he was Jewish. A Jewish *woman*, in fact. Fertel was an outspoken feminist and card-carrying member of the National Organisation of Woman (NOW). He said things like, 'If I were a woman – and how I wish I were – I'd probably be a lethbian myself'.

Like Tiny, he was reluctant to wed and even slower than Tiny to have sex. His marriage remained unconsummated for months until Fertel's sister-in-law had enough. When cajoling didn't work, she tried insistence. When that didn't work, she took charge and supervised the whole thing. Still, this extraordinary marriage seemed to work. Fertel explains his relationship to his mother-in-law like this, 'On Father's Days, ath a treat her mother would get me a dress, do my nails and make me up'.

Plus he had a thing about blizzards. He loved them, talked incessantly about them, and travelled distances to see them. 'Thank goodneth winter ith coming! That makes it all worthwhile,' Fertel told Tiny's first biographer, Harry Stein. 'Oh yeth, every year I come up north in the fall. If I went home I'd find out they had a snowthorm here and I'd scream and yell cauth I mithed it. I hope it'll be a real severe winter thith year, otherwise I'm wasting my time, money and aggravation in New York'.

Tiny, who equated eccentricity with talent, felt he had discovered a great star in Isadore Fertel.

At Tiny's urging Fertel took to the amateur club circuit, reliving Tiny's own life (he even became a messenger boy). Fertel notched up good success at the Upper East Side club Catch A Falling Star where he appeared in a dress and sang *I Am Woman*. Tiny was sufficiently impressed to release the song on Toilet Records. Tiny also admired Fertel's version of *Rock Around The Clock* in Yiddish. (4)

Tiny got Fertel a TV spot on the Stanley Siegel Show in 1976. He later appeared with him – with Tiny as the straight man, providing the ukulele backing for Fertel's own compositions. These included *The Reagan-Begin Song*, about international leaders, Ronald Reagan and Menachem Begin. His song *Susan B* is a feminist call to equal rights in the home. (See it for yourself, on youtube.)

Tough Times For Tiny

Things were going wrong, his baby daughter wasn't getting enough attention, relationships with management were hostile, Richard Perry had moved on, records weren't selling, Tiny was playing smaller venues. Warner Bros was losing interest and Tiny's Dad, Butros was seriously ill with diabetes. Tiny's wife was rebelling, so was his protégé. Thank God–through-Christ for the Johnny Carson Show!

In October, with Miss Tulip only five months old, Miss Vicki confronted Tiny and announced the marriage was on the rocks. Fertel got involved, backing Miss Vicki all the way, because – as a woman and a feminist – he couldn't bear Tiny's attitudes to Miss Vicki, conception and the Pill. 'When any woman ith oppressed,' said Fertel crossly, 'I am oppressed. I thought the way he treated her, she should have left long ago'. And so Fertel entered the realm of opinion, after which Tiny didn't speak to him for nearly 12 months. (4)

In December – among his many bookings - Tiny performed at the *Playboy Club.* He also appeared on the *Carson Show* in the same month. Tiny described Carson's gig as a 'charity booking' because Carson always liked him and felt sorry for him. The press snapped that one up too and depicted Tiny as being on the skids, out of work, bankrupt and a loser. They never relented.

It's simply untrue. Sure, times were sometimes tough. Sure, he never again saw the big pay cheques. But - having been King for a Day - throughout his life Tiny always played medium-sized clubs, always had a famous name, always continued recording, always kept company with famous people and sometimes played packed auditoriums to enthusiastic receptions.

Miss Vicki too had become irrevocably famous, a burden she would never lose, being the other half of the most watched event in television history (to date). As a late-60s icon she is remembered for her style, beauty and fashion-sense. Miss Vicki made numerous television appearances and even shared the vocals with Tiny on studio recordings, including the song *Why?* She was growing in confidence and, having given up minding Tiny's interests, she looked after her own.

Miss Vicki ran off with John Carmen in Tiny's absence. They drew lots of attention, partying hard at New York's trendiest clubs. In later discussions about this period, Tiny seemed more concerned about his wife's 'sin' than being jilted. Sadly, this was also the year that Butros Khaury died.

After four months apart Miss Vicki returned to Tiny who, of course, took her back. Shortly afterwards the happily reunited family - Tiny, Miss Vicki and Miss Tulip appeared on national television, on the *Mike Douglas Show.*

They remained together for a while, both trying to make the marriage work in their own way, having tasted both parenthood and separation. This was probably the only time both parents played Mum and Dad to Miss Tulip. She said, 'I don't really have many memories because my mother and he split when I was two, so I really didn't spend that much time with him'. (5)

Tiny's third wife, Miss Sue explains the situation like this, 'Vicki was not easily led at all. She talked in a little girl voice and seemed that she would be very easy to convince of this or that but in fact she's a very strong-willed person and they didn't get on at all. And of course, Tiny was just an impossible husband for Vicki.

'She could be impetuous like a child too and at one point she wanted to turn off the News that he was watching. She goes, "I don't want to watch this man talking," and Tiny said something like, "I'm watching this, I'm interested in it". She just hauled off and slapped him across the face. And he had a horror of physical violence - he'd been beaten by his Dad. He got up and said, "If you ever hit me again you can go out that door and I don't care where you go". I think this happened early in the marriage. *Very* early in the marriage. So things were rocky between them.' (6)

Heart Attack At the Wheel

While on an eight-week tour of the British provinces, Tiny experienced the danger of being on the road. With Jim Cappy at the wheel, a car came out of nowhere, careened across the road, slid through a paddock and smashed into a couple of cars.

Tiny and Miss Vicki were in one of those cars. Miss Vicki and Cappy both broke their collarbones, Tiny was okay, and but the driver of the offending vehicle was dead – probably from the heart attack, which caused his car to blast off the road in the first place.

Within the month, on the same tour, Miss Vicki took a shine to the minibus driver, Amos Levy. So that had consequences. After a gruelling tour, everyone returned to America in December.

Art Book

In January 1974, during Tiny's three-week tour of Australia, Martin again connected with Tiny. This time in a club in the provincial town of Newcastle NSW, where Tiny was performing. Says Martin, 'It was like he was waiting for someone to come.'

Martin had previously met Tiny at the Speakeasy Club in London, and again in a worker's club in Luton. Martin described the meeting like this, 'The first time I made a tape was in England at Caesar's Palace Luton 1969-70. I was hoping to inspire someone with the material, but I held the microphone too close to Tiny and it all came out blurred. We got on very well. That was our first meeting.'

*

Either way, the intervening years had been kinder to Martin than to Tiny. Having tasted international success through his work with the band Cream, Martin came home to an inheritance and a burst of creative energy that established him as the darling of Sydney. Martin wrote Tiny a letter, which said, 'I really love what you're doing. Anything I can do to help…?' And Martin was in a position to help.

He said, 'Tiny got to know me in Australia. He was doing a gig in Newcastle in the clubs and I went up there and got talking with him and recording. I spent a lot of time with him in January 1974 in Newcastle.

'I dragged myself up there, I wasn't feeling too fantastic at the time. I had met him – he didn't really know me at that stage but I got a fantastic welcome. I got to sing with him on the first song I recorded there, *Miss You More Than I Can Say*, I just picked up the melody. It was like the audience meeting the singer again.' (7)

He presented Tiny a copy of his newly published *Art Book,* which depicted a series classic artworks juxtaposed upon each other to create a new meaning. Martin had created 38 fine art collage images combining paintings by Van Gogh/Bonnard, Magritte/Duchamp, De Chirico/Ernst and more. (8) Tiny flicked to the Hamilton image of a brown-hued negative of Bing Crosby against a surreal De Chirico street corner, looked at Mr Sharp knowingly and exclaimed, 'Oh, it's Mr Crosby!' The connection was made.

Martin explained, 'About the same time I was doing collages Tiny was doing with songs what I was doing with images, that's why I clicked with him. I understood scientifically that he was really on an edge. And Tiny could get into the book, which was interesting because he doesn't know fine art.'

As a visual artist, Martin had a film in mind, though initially not one that he intended to make himself, but an idea that he could offer to a major studio and offer his services as Artistic Adviser to the Director. Martin had experience in this role, first with the film *Performance* and now having worked on the Peter Weir film, *Picnic at Hanging Rock.*

Confident that Tiny had the support of 'Pop people' like Pete Townshend and Eric Clapton, the idea for the film came to Sharp while travelling on the metro in Paris. (9)

In the early 1970s Martin and a team of artists, created the Yellow House, a live-in art gallery in Sydney Australia. Among Martin's contributions was a collage book (kinda like Magic Theatre OZ). It was known as the 'Catalog'. Martin included Tiny alongside other heroes - Rene Magritte, Vincent Van Gogh…alongside lots of cut-ups from the Eadweard Muybridge book, 'The Human Figure in Motion'.

Leonardo Da Vinci of Popular Song

At this stage of Tiny's career his critics were keen to point out that he never really settled down – he had many voices which included a piercing falsetto, light falsetto, resonant baritone, an old man's voice, a Rock yowl, a Country ring, a milky romantic tone as well as the outrageous camp squeals for which he became so famous. He was criticised for his refusal to settle into a niche, which was *precisely* what Martin liked about him.

Says Martin, 'He's probably got the fastest throat around. He's the Leonardo Da Vinci of Popular Song. He's like Vincent Van Gogh, only he's a singer. Pete Townshend has always had a very soft spot for Tiny. I think he felt guilty when they appeared together at The Scene in New York and Tiny had to follow The Who between major acts. Pete Townshend promised to introduce him with a big flourish but the boys in the band wanted to get on with the show and pushed Pete into another direction. He neglected it and he always remembered that as the time he let Tiny down. He did a lot to transfer early Tiny tapes in his studio. He probably has the mintest copies.

'I started looking through scripts like *The Jazz Singer*. I came up with a Tin Pan Alley version of *Orpheus and Eurydice,* and that became a feature film idea. I was getting the idea on the metro in Paris. The idea became real though in a documentary way, the film we actually made. I also spoke to Eric Clapton about him and Eric said he didn't like the tremolo in his voice because it frightened him. (10)

'He never stopped being famous. He was famous for being a failure. The dream of Miss Vicki - well that collapsed and his career collapsed very much at the same time. He reckons it was already on the slide by the time of the Albert Hall Concert – which I see as a swansong in a way, on the grand stage. And the grand stage was removed from him, the records deals were removed and he was exiled to the very outer suburbs of show business, which is where I saw him in 1974, in a Leagues Club.' (11)

In this way, the start of a new relationship began.

Footnotes:

1. Tulip Stewart, interview with Lowell Tarling, 2 April 2002.
2. Tiny Tim, interview with Lowell Tarling, 6 September 1983.
3. Tulip Stewart, interview with Lowell Tarling, 2 April 2002.
4. Harry Stein, *Tiny Tim,* Playboy Press 1976.
5. Tulip Stewart, interview with Lowell Tarling, 2 April 2002.
6. Sue Khaury, interview with Lowell Tarling and Michael Wilkinson, 1 April 2002.
7. Martin Sharp, interview with Lowell Tarling, 1 February 1983.
8. Martin Sharp, *Art Book,* Mathews Miller Dunbar, London 1972.
9. Martin Sharp, interview with Lowell Tarling, 6 September 1982.
10. Martin Sharp, interview with Lowell Tarling, 13 April 1983.
11. Martin Sharp, interview with Lowell Tarling, 29 December 1990. Also, Martin Sharp, interview with Lowell Tarling, 24 January 1997.

Martin, Lowell and Jane, with the 1983 version of Martin's 'Film Script' painting in the background.

Photo credit: Peter Jensen

9

1975-1979

I went back home to mother for two weeks,
back to that dingy apartment where I came from.
Tiny Tim

On 23 January 1974 - the very day Tiny returned home from his Australian tour - Miss Vicki confronted him for the final time. She said, 'The last time I left you, I did it when you were gone. This time I'm telling you to your face!' She left, taking Miss Tulip with her. Now, having to support herself and Miss Tulip, Miss Vicki first took a sales job in a department store.

Tiny explained the reason for the failure of his marriage, 'I got tired of Miss Vicki and she got tired of me. It's a natural function. I expected it before I married. When two people know Jesus Christ, it's better - but when one only knows him or has a more powerful sway over the other one in error…? When I got tired I said, *O Lord I'm tired of Miss Vicki, but help me renew my tiredness,* and he did. But her God was the god of the world and she left.'

To Australian radio presenter Caroline Jones, Tiny explained in 1978, 'I was to blame with Miss Vicki because I didn't want to marry and it was very difficult. I was getting into trouble with girls - it was the only reason I married. I don't blame her because at least she evened up the score.' (1)

However much he shrugged off his broken marriage in interviews, Tiny was genuinely devastated. He worried that bone for years. Though by March he didn't appear too worried. He had re-established contact with Miss Jan Gianopolis, the fan – now friend - with whom he had flirted outrageously in the lead-up to the wedding. Later, Miss Vicki told the press that she believed Tiny never loved her. Even if that were true, he certainly never forgot her and neither did the public. Tiny and Miss Vicki had been ground on the same anvil.

Throughout his life Tiny continued to phone Miss Vicki for advice, sometimes desperately, especially concerning his love life. In press interviews, Tiny frequently spoke about his concern (love?) for Miss Vicki. For years he told reporters and friends that he would take her back again (if she had a blood test). Though in reality, he knew the marriage side of their relationship was well and truly and irrevocably over.

Miss Vicki's parents had separated around the same time as their breakup, so she conveniently moved in with her mother until she got re-established. Then she quit her sales job and took a spot at Minnie's Lounge in Camden New Jersey. After all, she was 'Miss Vicki' and still a celebrity in her own right. She traded on this (a bit) and continued working as a Go-Go dancer for a time. Life had given her a big break – international fame. Should she capitalise on it or not?

The press had a field day of course, beating up whatever Miss Vicki said about Tiny, especially his lack of sexual prowess. However, there is no reason to believe this is true – after all, he did father a child! Nor is there any reason to believe Miss Vicki necessarily said those things in the way they were sensationalised. But Tiny didn't fight the accusations. He blamed himself for the collapse of the marriage and admitted all sexual inadequacies. In fact, he boldly continued the theme, startling reporters with way too much detail. So did Miss Vicki, when she sold her story *My Insufferable Marriage To Tiny Tim* to London's *Sunday Mirror* for a reputed $15,000.

Stayin' Alive

Advocates of peace & love have always been kind to Tiny, but for about a decade (say, 1969-1979) a fair percentage of his audience suddenly went feral. The peace & love people bought acreages in the country, renounced capitalism and electricity, and opted for self-sufficiency. This, fused with a few other factors, destroyed Tiny's record sales. During the 70s, the big record sales went to city folk who were into Glam Rock, Soft Rock and the kind of Disco Music about to be codified in falsetto in the *Saturday Night Fever* film.

The falsetto voice has been a standard element of Rock music since the Doo-Wop bands. Quartet singers like The Diamonds soared into the upper registers on hits like *Little Darlin'*. Frankie Valli made ample use of falsetto in his early 60s hits with the Four Seasons. Brian Wilson used it in Beach Boys songs like *Surfer Girl*. The Newbeats gave it a Brit-pop feel with their hit, *Bread and Butter*. Mick Jagger ooo-ed in falsetto through the Rolling Stones hit *Miss You*. But during their mid-70s *Night Fever* period, the Bee Gees probably derived their squeak more from R&B bands like the Stylistics and the Delphonics. Despite all that it is Tiny – not Brian Wilson, Barry Gibb or Mick Jagger – who is remembered for the high voice. Having famously restored the falsetto to the Top 10 in 1968 with *Tiptoe*, by the late-70s Tiny was performing the Bee Gees' hit *Stayin' Alive* in his live repertoire. Tiny earthed it with his deeper register. It was the Bee Gees who sang it in falsetto.

Talk Of The Town, Illinois

On the rebound from Miss Vicki, Tiny found solace in Miss Jan Gianopolis. He saw her again in October at the Holiday Inn in Torrance California. On the basis of his religious beliefs, Tiny suddenly cut the potential affair before leaving for another Holiday Inn booking at the close of 1974 - this one in Decatur, Illinois.

Decatur is where Tiny ran into Harry Stein, his first biographer (son of librettist Joseph Stein, who wrote *Fiddler on the Roof* and not to be confused with Tiny's cousin, Harold [Hal] Stein.). Stein based his biography on a series of 20 taped interviews with Tiny and others close to him, in which Stein presented Tiny as happy, positive, kinky, kooky but definitely down on his luck. Through the tapes, Stein's bio bears the unmistakable authenticity of Tiny's own voice.

Stein followed Tiny around a bit. He saw the low points and some high points too. Like the time just eight people showed up to hear Tiny perform at the *Talk of the Town*. The opening set included the songs *Blue Suede Shoes, Make Believe* and *Tiptoe Through the Tulips* with a vocal back-up called the 'Tulips' and a band called the 'Timmies'. Ha ha ha. Jim Cappy was still Tiny's manager. Cappy – described by Stein as 'an endlessly patient little guy in a flowered silk shirt and shades' – told Stein, 'I see a place like this, and I wish the night were over. This is the worst ever, the lowest'.

Then everything suddenly turned around. Tiny's singing voice carried into the public area. The people heard him and started pouring in. The room gradually filled. Two hundred people jammed the performance for the second set. The applause got thunderous and everyone sang along. Tiny's closing medley included, *Roll Out The Barrel, Oh Susanna* and *Grand Old Flag,* and the audience was belting it out with him. When he finished there was bedlam, screams for another encore! As Tiny briskly left the stage the owner of the place caught Cappy by the arm and said, 'He can come back any time!' Cappy smiled and mumbled under his breath, 'Fat chance'. Meanwhile, Tiny was besieged with requests for autographs and small talk. As he walked out of the room, a big meaty guy slapped Tiny hard on the back and drunkenly told him he was terrific, just great. 'What a really nice guy,' said Tiny sitting in a Chevrolet, 'You meet such nice people out here in the grass roots'. (2)

Eviction

Beseiged for autographs, as famous as anybody in the world, the Tiny Tim show paid good money, but not great money. These gigs were not enough to pay the bills. The press said that he was down to his last $20 and therefore bankrupt. Perhaps 'technically' bankrupt, but Tiny was certainly bringing money in. Unfortunately, the turnover was not reflected in the profit.

In September 1975, Tiny was evicted from the apartment in Brooklyn where he had lived with Miss Vicki and Miss Tulip. After countless squabbles over money, Tiny's management now refused to continue paying his rent. It was a tough time. He moved in with his mother for two weeks before moving to the Golden Gate Motel. Tiny said, 'My manager refused to pay the hotel bills and I went back home to mother for two weeks, back to that dingy apartment where I came from, with nothing but loud noises from outside all the time. I didn't dare go down because I was too ashamed.' (3)

He also admitted hiding from creditors. Tiny was experiencing a discrepancy between his income and his fame. He did not generate enough income to protect himself from his fame. Everywhere he went, everyone – *everyone* - knew who he was. He had no anonymity.

Tiny In Texas

From the early-1960s was Tiny always in demand, though not necessarily in the right way. The problem wasn't finding gigs, it was finding good ones. Poor Tiny. He was lugging it now. He went on to play terrible venues, like a four-night booking in a trailer park bar in Texas, redolent of the *Rawhide* scene from the Blues Brothers film. The stage looked like a jail cell, it was protected by steel wire. Armed only with his little ukulele, Tiny sang bravely and way too melodically for a rough crowd of Good Ole Boys, who gulped Millers and Budweiser beers, then pelted their empties at the human canary in the cage. Doggedly Tiny performed the second night, hoping to win over this hellhole crowd but alas he was greeted with even greater hostility. Chairs were thrown at him, a table hit the wire. The whole show was pointless, so Tiny suggested that he should quit and be paid off. 'Naw boy,' the Good Ole proprietor replied (probably spitting on the ground as he spoke) 'Yr booked til Sat-dee, you play til Sat-dee'. The third night was even worse. Word had got around that Tiny Tim was performing and rednecks travelled great distances to pelt things at him. The crowd got bigger and wilder. Once more Tiny asked to be paid off, but again the owner said nope. Not til Sat-dee night. But when Tiny showed up on the Saturday night, everything – *everything* - was gone. The pre-fab beer barn building had been lifted onto a truck and moved elsewhere, leaving Tiny unpaid and somewhere in Texas. (4)

Soldier Of Showbiz

It was awful, but Tiny never cracked. He never stopped carrying himself as a star. And he never publicly reverted to Herbert Khaury. When questioned, Tiny always held the line, feeding the press a range of sometimes startling stories, often about hygiene, sex and religion. It was Tiny's fans, friends, family and admirers who wanted Tiny's press coverage to be handled with more dignity, not Tiny himself. No matter what they wrote about him, Tiny was never happier than to see himself in the *National Enquirer*. Later in life he spoke about the importance of 'keeping the image' and why he tolerated – sometimes enjoyed - being the subject of journalistic trash.

He said, 'The reason I allow the press to do that is very simple. First of all the name of the game is *show* business. It's not a private business. This is a public business. The very fascination of seeing a character on the screen, magnifies their charisma. Most people in the world will never be on television. A lot of people in the world cry for a minute, they scream to their neighbours, *Did you see me? Did you see me?* So in a business where *show* is the business, why do I tell them about my showers and everything? I'm always saying that because I know that people want to know about it. They also want to know what goes on in the private life. They should know. Show business is not a private life. If I wanted a private life then I should have been anything but in show business. If I'm a stockbroker or if I'm working in a business, I have a good right to say, *What I do in my private life with Miss Vicki, or whoever I'm with, I'm sorry I can't tell you.* Stars love to get the applause. They love to bring the house down. They feel great when they get great reviews. They feel great when they marry a beautiful woman - Nicole Kidman - so they always want their crazy public feats to be magnified. They have to remember: *we are soldiers of show business and show business is a public business.* They can call me tomorrow with a booking and I can answer them. It's braver if I go and better for the business if I go, because even though I may have to be the sheep for the night, when it passes they can say, *That man was nasty but he kept his composure and he kept the image.* But if I whinge about it and somebody says, *Aaah ya can't sing!* It's better if I say, *Well, that's your opinion. I'm sorry if you feel like that.* Of course, everyone will look - a guilt complex - and you get the victory. In fact if I keep quiet about it, become nice about it, it takes some ammunition away from him and I live up to my image. But if I answer, *I can't sing because your Mother gave me birth!* I get the crowd's applause and I win the battle. But I've lost…because he made a star come down from - you know what. He's moved the star of it.' (5)

Tiny was cleverer than people thought. He certainly kept himself in the public eye throughout the 70s to the point where in the early 80s – after not having had a hit record for more than 12 years – Tiny Tim was voted the fifth most identifiable face in the world after Mickey Mouse, the Pope, the President of the United States and Elvis Presley. A similar survey conducted in the early 90s came up with a similar result, with Tiny again in the top five.

Second Car Accident

Then, another disaster. While heading to play a concert at Huntsville Alabama, Tiny was involved in a second fatal road accident with remarkable similarities to the one that had happened in England. In this second collision, driver, 62-year old Paul Croop, was killed after ploughing into a car which was carrying Tiny, manager/driver James Cappeliuzzo (Cappy), and two young musicians - Abe Mason and Robin Winters - both of whom suffered mainly cuts and bruises. The 55-year old wife of the dead driver, Marjorie Croop was critically injured from mass injuries. Tiny suffered chest and ankle injuries and, when interviewed, had no memory of the crash. But Tiny, typically, was unfazed and positive. He had new ideas. Much had happened to Tiny's stage act over the past 10 years. He had gone from strumming his solo ukulele to being backed by the world's finest orchestras and back to solo uke again. In 1975 he was 42 years old and his voice was changing. So too was his act. Tiny's falsetto was becoming reedier while his bass-baritone was becoming much more forceful.

Nude Centrefold

In October 1975 Miss Vicki posed for a centrespread spread for the nudie *Oui* magazine. The cheeky sub-heading read, *Tiny Tim Doesn't Tiptoe Through Her Tulips Any More.* The text followed the course of Miss Vicki's life - a 15-year old with a 'terrible crush' on Tiny, she had pictures of him on her bedroom wall, went to his concerts, they met, courted, then married on Johnny Carson's *Tonight Show* with a record-breaking viewing audience. 'When we finally did have sex, it turned out that he was not the answer to a maiden's prayer,' she complained, followed by admissions like, 'I drank a lot and went out with a lot of men. I couldn't keep track of them'.
As for the photographs, readers saw the lot. Alluring, in a girlie – rather than womanly - sort of way. (6)

When facing the press, Tiny could not have been more horrified, describing the photos as '…shocking, shocking, *shocking!*' pictures. Privately though, he said to me, darkly, 'I knew why she did it…'. In 1991, when I visited his apartment at the Olcott Hotel in New York, the first thing Tiny showed me in his bedroom was the *Oui* centrespread of Miss Vicki which – after all those years - he still kept in the top drawer beside his bed. The telephone, uke, Bible and rosary beads were also close to hand.

'How can you do that?' I asked, 'Have the Bible in the same drawer as soft porn?'

'You can look but you mustn't touch, Mr Tarlin,' he replied.

Miss Tulip

'Mum never really cared for my Dad,' said Miss Tulip. 'And growing up with her I guess I always had negative feedback when it came to my Dad. It kinda left a negative impression on me. All these good things people tell me about my Dad - I never heard that side - so it's kinda hard to put those two things together because I never knew that side of him. I always knew all the bad things.

My Mum would say, *He never pays child support* and *He doesn't take care of you* and *He doesn't have anything to do with you*. She thought he was crazy and it was always negative. She always apologised to me, *I'm so sorry I married him* and *I'm so sorry I made him your father*. And as a kid, those things really stick and it made it very difficult for me because – I have to admit - I was almost embarrassed about my father because she made him look so bad in my eyes. I now almost find myself having to defend him to her – at least when he was alive I did – because I would always tell my Mum, *That's my <u>Dad</u> you're talking about. You might not like him, but he's still my Dad!* She couldn't relate to that because her father was always there for her.' (7)

Now, as an unmarried man, and albeit in a more 'knowing' way, Tiny returned to his pre-marriage crushes on film stars as well as a string of flutters – an endlessly succession of Miss This and Miss That. Maybe, inspired by Miss Vicki's foray into the edges of libidinous entertainment, in 1976 Tiny developed ideas for two erotic films in which he planned to feature – *The Seduction Of Mr T* (with Marilyn Chambers, famous for the mid-70s film *Insatiable)*. And another title, *The Man They Love To Hate.*

Hate? … The mid-70s must have been cruel to Tiny for him to come up with a title like that.

Marathon Ideas

In June/July 1976 Tiny toured Australia to a mixed reception. He was booed at an Essendon Hotel Melbourne but hugely welcomed at Martin's home, Wirian, in Sydney where a world of new opportunities opened up. Martin, who had always wanted to work with Tiny, expressed his enthusiasm for Tiny's music by writing a cover article for the socio-political *Quadrant* magazine and creating two new Tiny Tim images for the issue. (8)

In 1976 Sydneysiders were proud of their Martin Sharp and they really didn't want to lose him to Tiny. Martin had worked with artists Peter Kingston, Richard Liney, Tim Lewis and Garry Shead on Sydney's Luna Park funfair. He designed the face, the biggest piece of Pop Art in the Southern Hemisphere. Speaking for his peers, prominent Australian media/radio personality John Singleton (Singo) wanted more of that and less of Tiny. Encrypting the Australian art scene of the period, and with Tiny present at the restaurant table, Singo blustered at Martin in despair, 'In 1976 there was only Brett Whiteley and Martin Sharp…!' (9)

Nevertheless, Martin's fascination was non-negotiable and in July 1976 he began taping Tiny in earnest, leading to a collection of one thousand tapes over a 20-year period, and inspiring all other Tiny Tim tapists who were to come. (Like me, David Tibet, Johnny Pineapple, and others…) Tiny responded in full voice. He also shared many of his love-fantasies on tape. Like, his love for actress Miss Cybil Shepherd. Martin and Tiny also talked about doing some kind of project/s, together…

One achievement of this Australian tour was that the first footage of Martin's *Street of Dreams* film was shot when Tiny arrived at the airport, followed by more footage in Martin's legendary 'kitchen'.

Said Martin, 'I'm making the film so people can see him as I've seen him. Tiny is a difficult artist to understand, but there will come a time when certain people will understand more about him and that's why I'm making a film, because they don't have the access to him that I've had – that's why I'm here. That's why Carlos Castaneda was there - to record Don Juan – that sort of thing. So really Tiny is an absolute enigma and that's what's fascinating'. (10)

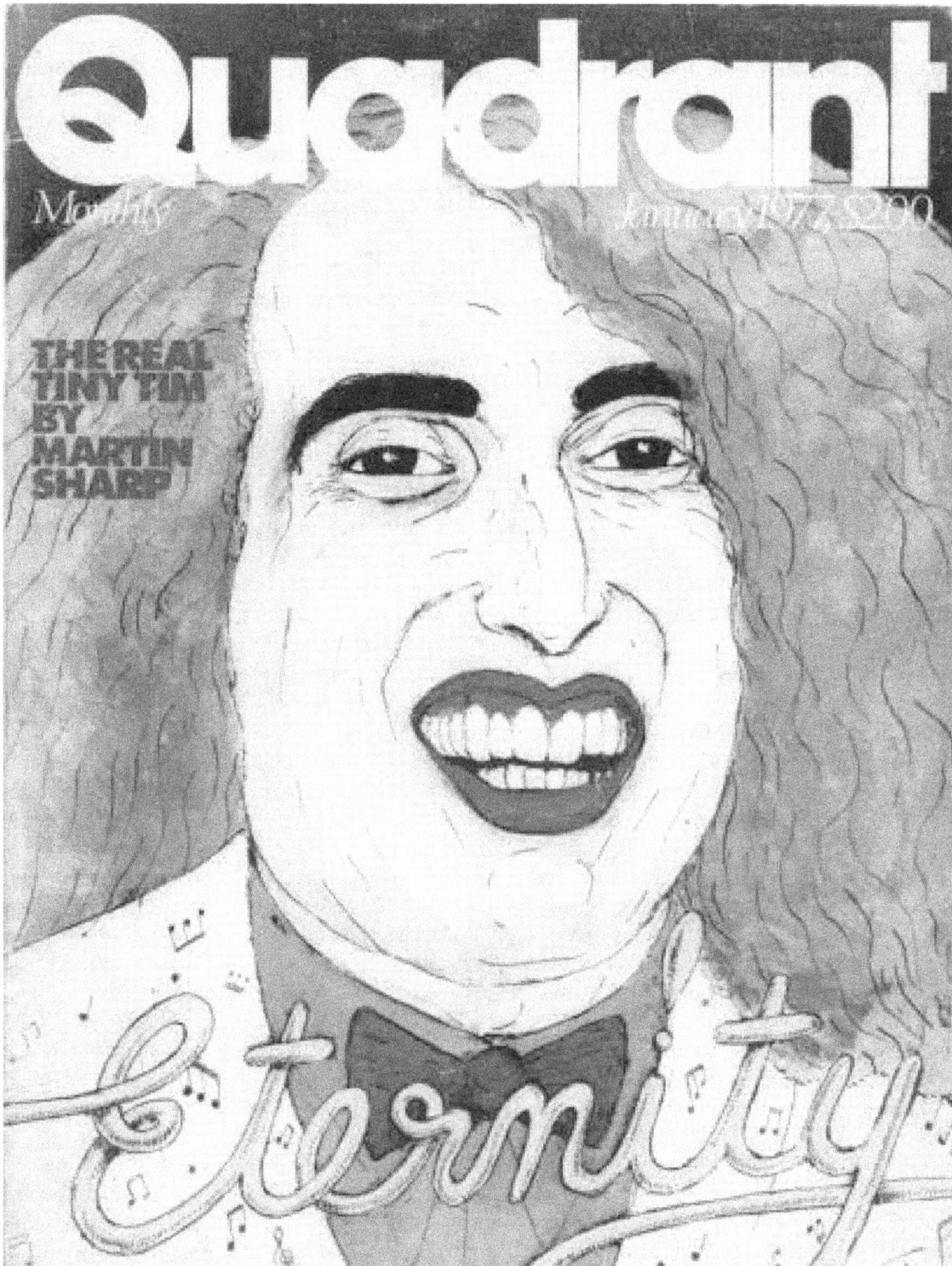

I'm going back to Newcastle where I left a note to Tiny saying, 'If there's anything I can do to help...'. That's why I wrote that piece for Quadrant a few years later, but it was based on that sort of material.

Martin Sharp, 16 October 2003

They shared other ideas. like recording a multi-volume *History Of Popular Song,* starting with Henry Burr, through Russ Colombo, Irving Kaufman, Rudy Vallee, Bing Crosby and into the modern period. The Bee Gees? Rod Stewart? Marvin Gaye? Sure - why not! As well as the film, another idea that stuck was a one-hour marathon to journey through the above trajectory of song.

Tiny discussed all this with Mr Cappy and Cappy was impressed. Tiny telegrammed Martin immediately, 'Dear Mr Sharp, Mr Joe Cappy is very enthused and very interested in doing your idea of the one hour song marathon. All that's required is the following three round trips first class airplane tickets to Australia three paid for rooms in a first class hotel and weekly allowances for me and the financial settlement feel free to call him if you can come up with this sincerely and thanks for everything, *Tiny Tim*'. (11)

The Playboy Press

Early in the same year Playboy Press had published Tiny's biography, *Tiny Tim* by Harry Stein. It was mostly welcomed by Tiny aficionados simply because there was nothing else on the market. The value of Stein's book is that he filled in the gaps from the early days through the famous days and he let Tiny do most of the telling. Unfortunately he allowed Tiny to distract him with sensational stories about lovemaking with honey and the like, which are largely irrelevant to Tiny's life as a man and as an artist. (12)

Stein also tried to talk to those who knew Tiny from the early days. 'He interviewed me on 42nd Street for about 15 minutes,' said cousin Harold, 'A good biography hasn't been done yet'. Tiny's great record producer, Richard Perry was another who Stein interviewed. About Tiny he said, 'Jesus Christ yeah! I would love to work with that guy again!' However, Isadore Fertel was a pretty lively interview for Stein. Fertel jumps out of the pages as a Jewish woman with a blizzard fetish. Nice trimmings, but Martin felt the book lacked something deep in its core. He said, 'Harry Stein is typical of those who have been drawn by the strange power of entertainers and yet been unable to come to terms with his real genius, which exists not in the realm of his personal behaviour, fascinating as this may be, but in the area of his greatest magic, his vocal virtuosity. He was fascinated by the man but he never listened to the singer'. (13)

Tiny probably like Stein's bio. He seemed to like everything written about him, especially if it appeared in his old favourite, the *National Enqurier*. Though in reality, by this time he probably realised that his real biographer was Mr Sharp, and the medium would not be pen on paper, but film and tape. (14)

Growing a Marathon

Tiny returned to Australia in 1978. That's when I first saw him. Tiny was the feature act at the opening of an inner-Sydney shopping centre. I was a schoolteacher at the time, and I probably got the word from 2 Double J Radio (now Triple J). So I told my wife Robbie, she gathered our two kids Amber (4) and Joel (2), and we headed to the shopping plaza to see Tiny - the guy whose first two albums I'd owned, as well as the sheet music to *Tiptoe*.

He was physically bigger than I expected, dressed in a multicoloured outfit, wearing a tie and carrying a shopping bag from which he extracted his Martin ukulele. Onstage with him was a small combo, who didn't do much at the start but worked themselves into a small frenzy for the encore. They mostly let Tiny strum his way through pre-40s covers until he closed with *Tiptoe*. Of course, the crowd yelled, clapped and demanded more. And then an amazing thing happened. Tiny placed his uke in his shopping bag, grabbed the mike with his left hand, gave a nod to the combo and they fired right up, Tiny's voice dropped about three octaves and the song was a rip-thru *Great Balls of Fire*.

The crowd went crazy. So did Tiny. *Goodness gracious, great balls of fire...*He tore off his jacket, then – as the song peaked – he lay on his back like a giant beetle, arms and legs flailing. Then whoosh. He was gone. Somewhere close to Leichhardt Sydney, my family had seen Tiny Tim for the first time.

'Where's Martin Sharp?' I asked someone who looked like they were a part of Tiny's retinue.

Street of Dreams

On 4 December 1978, Tiny and Cappy signed a contractual agreement with Martin's company *Street of Dreams* for Tiny to be an actor (playing himself) in a movie to be produced by Martin. The film was to be 'a portrait of Tiny' set around a marathon-medley. Martin described the marathon as 'the backbone of the film'. He also added, 'No more well-known person has ever appeared in an Australian feature'. (15)

Again Tiny returned to his theme of creating a Musical History Tour, describing to Martin how the marathon should be. Tiny said, 'I would like to take a shot and put on a non-stop continuous dance sing-along medley. Firstly you would have old numbers like *Babyface* and *Four Leaf Clover* and then complete Rock songs from the late-40s (of course the Blacks always had it with the Rhythm and Blues). And then up to the White-50s, and then up to Soul and the 60s, and up to the current time.

'This way several things happen: firstly you once more take what the public liked on stage and put it on record. In fact, the medley has already been proven successful on stage. I find my key thing in the medley are the styles of Harry Richmond, Henry Burr, Bill Murray and the other great artists shown to their best advantage. Secondly, it's never been done before in such a way. Thirdly, it goes on forever, they can dance to it without stopping, and they can sing to it. And if this works, then the doors are open because it's no more the *Tiptoe* image alone. It's got to be top musicians so that I don't have to struggle for the sound because the sound will automatically be there. Frankly, if this thing flops, I wouldn't know where to go because this is one of my pet projects. I don't believe these managers understand and of course it's hard to grasp unless you feel it, and I guess you do Mr Sharp - but this is where the direction lies'. (16)

This painting, titled 'Film Script' refers to Martin's film about Tiny. It is acrylic paint on paper, mounted on board 136 x 319 cm. So it's big. Started in 1976, Martin has constantly overpainted from 1976-2004. Elements of the essential image have changed over the years, as has the colour of Tiny's hair.

*

84

One Trick Pony

Martin's project was not Tiny's only film engagement of 1979. Around this time Paul Simon released his *One Trick Pony* album. Simon's film of the same name gave Tiny a cameo spot. Tiny said, 'I was thrilled to make the movie with him. They shot it at the Concorde Theatre in 1979.

'I was supposed to sing an old song and he was supposed to come into the kitchen, look at me and walk out. The song that I sang in that movie was, *There's a broken heart for every light on Broadway; A broken dream for every light I say...* that old Jolson number.

'I must have done 40 seconds of song in that movie, but he cut it down and you're lucky to see five seconds, 10 seconds. Anyway, some writer reviewed the movie and said - in 1980 this was - and he said the best part about the movie was Tiny Tim walking through and singing that song, and that was only five seconds. So you know how much he loved the movie! I've never heard from Mr Simon since.' (17)

Creative Burst

What would now follow is the most extended period of creativity in Tiny's entire career. The four days from 9-12 January 1979 were extraordinary. Tiny and Martin, and all the others involved must have been amazed at what they accomplished!

The overall musical director was the internationally-respected cellist, Nathan Waks. And Tiny's personal musical director was old-time pianist Marvin Lewis. A lot of the sessions' success was due to the rapport between Tiny and Lewis, both being familiar with vintage tunes - like *Love You Funny Thing* - and loving them. William Yang's photographs created a new-look 'louche' Tiny Tim album cover, consistent with his past and current image. And Martin clinched it with his *Chameleon* poster.

Martin was producer, artistic director and at times booking agent. He organised Sydney's best studio, EMI Studio 301, for the recording sessions, as well as the Floating Palais in Sydney's Luna Park as the venue for the World Non-Stop Singing Record.

Between them - Nathan Waks, Marvin Lewis and others - Martin and Tiny produced a grand trilogy of albums: *Chameleon, Wonderful World Of Romance* and *Keeping My Troubles To Myself.*

Martin gives all the credit to Tiny. Explaining the process. Martin said, '*Chameleon* was Tiny and Nathan Waks - and me being an absolute fan and saying, "Go for it". I suggested probably a few of the songs. Sometimes if you suggest them he'll do one, but really he can do what he wants.' (18)

Martin further organised a film crew to shoot whatever he could afford for the *Street of Dreams* film. Whenever Tiny was around, Martin also carried a hand held cassette recorder so that he could record all Tiny's instructions, thoughts, ideas and songs.

On 9 January 1979 Tiny recorded six tracks, four of which would feature on the *Chameleon* LP - *Staying Alive, My Way, Mickey Mouse Club March, It's A Long Way To Tipperary.* The tracks *St Louis Blues* and *Just A Gigolo* were held over. Some tracks have shades of Grandpa Tim, even the 'Tiny Tim' of *To All My Little Friends.* But for *Staying Alive* Tiny worked up his persona of 'the New York-style defacto man...' - which was actually himself at the time.

Next day, in Studio 301, with three key songs in the bag, the musos must have felt confident. They were then joined by Australian actor/musician David Gulpilil featured on didgeridoo on *Staying Alive* that they reworked. The band also recorded more tracks for *Chameleon.* The standout is *Brother Can You Spare a Dime* (two takes), which Tiny had done proud a decade before at the Royal Albert Hall. The *Chameleon* version is raunchier. Finally, on the third day, with Marvin Lewis on piano and no other musicians, Tiny recorded 13 tracks 'direct to disc' for an album called *Wonderful World of Romance.* As if cutting two albums in three days was not a marathon enough, on the following day - backed by Tiny Tim's Orchestra, The Time Machine - Tiny set the World Non-Stop Singing Record (for a professional singer) which was 2 hours, 15 minutes and seven seconds (about the time it takes a champion runner to run 42k) at Luna Park, Sydney. (19)

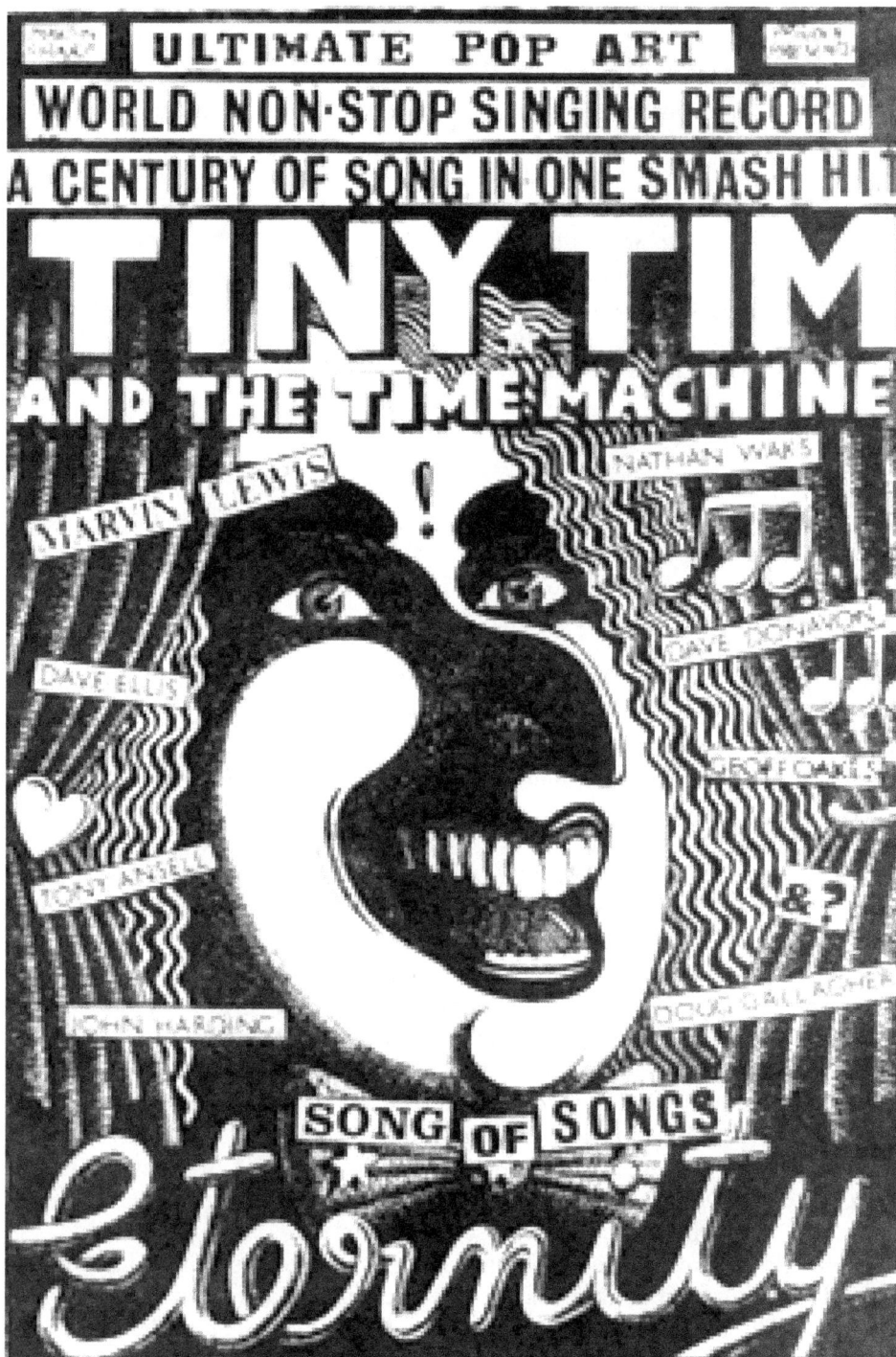

On 12 January 1979, Tiny Tim broke the World Non-Stop Singing Record (for a professional singer) at Luna Park, Sydney, Australia. He sang for 2 hours, 15 minutes and seven seconds. 'The World Professional Singing Record' is the backbone of Martin's film. On one level it's an athletic event - also it's a showcase for talent, singing ability, memory and composition. It's a musical tour de force. Two hours and fifteen minutes. And of course, he told a story in it as well.

Martin Sharp, 13 April 1983

Footnotes:

1. Tiny Tim, interview with Lowell Tarling dated 30 August 1983. Also, Tiny Tim, interviewed by Caroline Jones, *ABC Radio*, 25 October 1978.
2. Harry Stein, *Tiny Tim,* Playboy Press 1976.
3. Tiny Tim, interviewed by John Elder for *People* magazine, 3 June 1992. Also, Tiny Tim, interview with Martin Sharp, *Quadrant,* January 1997.
4. Jim White, 'The Strange Afterlife of Tiny Tim', *Night & Day,* 5 January 1997.
5. Tiny Tim, interview with Lowell Tarling dated 4 April 1992.
6. *Oui* magazine, October 1975.
7. Tulip Stewart, interview with Lowell Tarling, 2 April 2002.
8. Martin Sharp, interviewed by Lowell Tarling, 1 February 1983. See also, Martin Sharp, 'The Real Tiny Tim', *Quadrant,* January 1977.
9. Tiny Tim, Martin Sharp and John Singleton at *Eliza's Restaurant,* Woollahra, Sydney, 26 August 1982.
10. Martin Sharp, interview with Lowell Tarling, 6 September 1982.
11. Tiny Tim, telegram to Martin Sharp, dated 16 July 1986.
12. Harry Stein, *Tiny Tim,* Playboy Press 1976.
13. Harold Stein, interview with Lowell Tarling, April 2002. And, Martin Sharp, 'The Real Tiny Tim', *Quadrant,* January 1977.
14. John Elder, *People* magazine, 3 June 1992.
15. Tiny Tim, taped by Martin Sharp at the Cosmopolitan Motor Inn, Double Bay, Sydney, 4 December 1978, Tiny is taped reading and discussing the contract. Also, Martin Sharp, interview with Lowell Tarling, 13 April 1983.
16. Tiny Tim, interview with Martin Sharp, *Quadrant,* January 1997.
17. Tiny Tim, interview with Lowell Tarling dated 4 April 1992.
18. Martin Sharp, interviewed by Lowell Tarling, 1 February 1983. Also, Martin Sharp, interviewed by Lowell Tarling, 24 January 1997.
19. *Luna Park Marathon* is a handmade CD, not generally available. However, large sections of the Marathon can be viewed via youtube in Martin's film *Street of Dreams*.

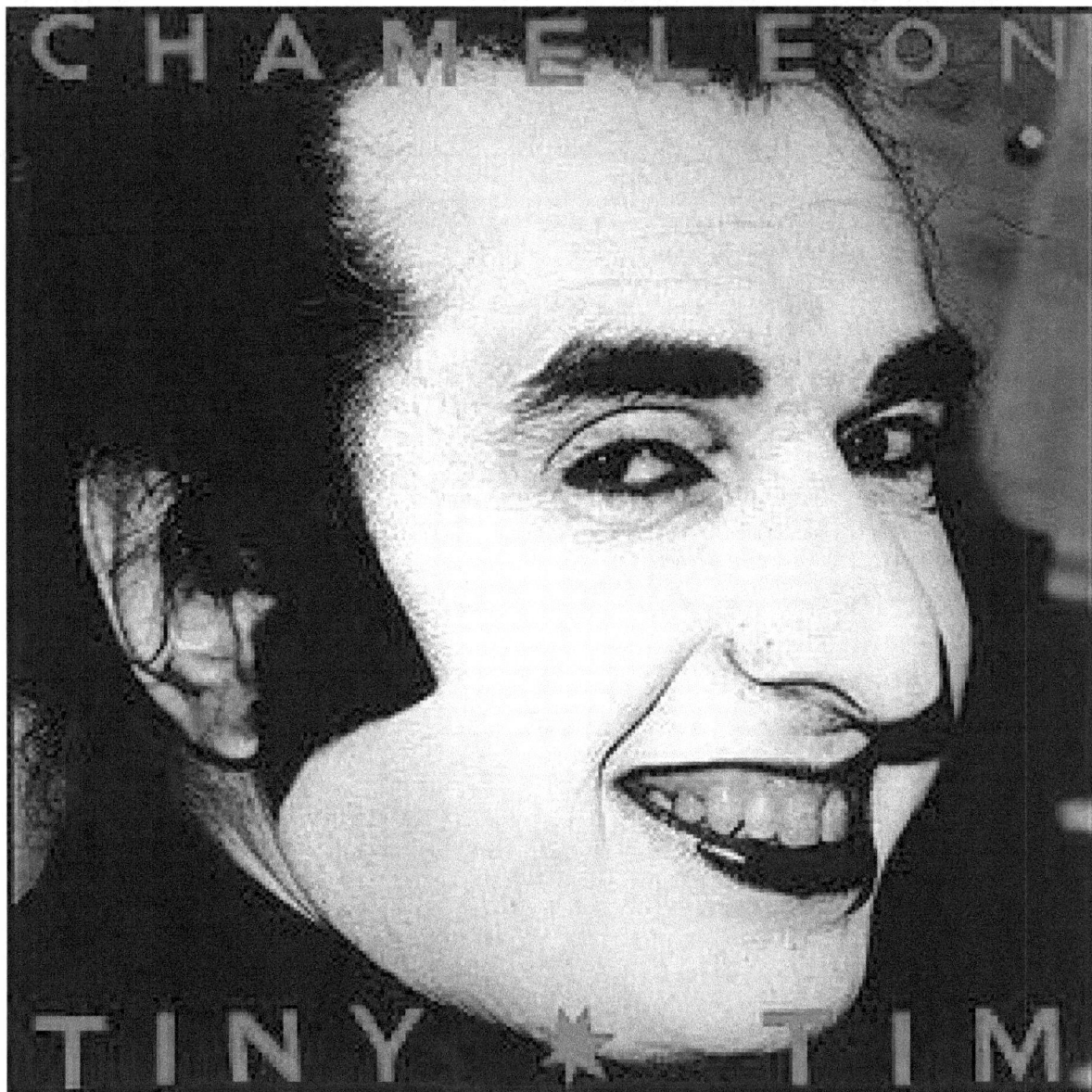

Ultimately it was Tiny who thought of the Chameleon concept. It was going to be called The Great Pretender. He really knows what he wants, but he's working with very primitive tools - like, someone like me who knows nothing about recording. Making this LP was a pretty ad lib situation and not the sort of circumstances I would ideally like to put him in. I think Tiny should have the best equipment at his command and every musician he wants.

Martin Sharp, 1 February 1983

10

World Non-Stop Professional Singing Record
12 January 1979

I always had the desire to bring Tiny and Luna Park together. I thought my role in it was to give him a bigger setting and to give him the opportunity to do what he most wanted to do.
Martin Sharp, artist

Almost shyly Tiny faces the press in the afternoon prior to the marathon. The press conference is held at Wirian in the room later known as the film editing room. 'Gentle persons from the press and media,' he calls them. 'I am still a great star in a small way.' (1)

'Have you been training this morning?' someone asks.

'No,' Tiny replies, pausing. 'I've been training for the last eight years,' he says, referencing the Isle of Wight when the mini-marathon became part of his act.

However, this is different. This is a full marathon. The longest Tiny had previously sung without a break was only recent - 90 minutes at the Queens Hotel in Brisbane. He tells the press he was 'scared' singing so long in public without a break. The press asks about the concept of a marathon, which by definition suggests a test of endurance. Tiny picks up the thought and says, 'The purpose of this marathon maybe has some athletic justification. The goal will be to go straight for at least two hours'. After the media conference, the journos leave and Tiny prepares to face his public and camera crew.

Tiny and his retinue approach Luna Park from the water. As he crosses Sydney Harbour, Tiny sings a snippet of *Harbour of Love,* which he abandons in favour of the Charles Harrison song, *Love's Ship.* Towards the close of the song, someone remarks on the size of the gathering, which Tiny dismisses by saying they are only there for the rides, and quips that free admission is what *he* needs to draw a crowd, 'If I didn't get them in then, I'd be in trouble!' he chuckles.

Joking with Martin, playing to the camera and blowing kisses to the people welcoming him from the shore, Tiny is given a hand to climb from the boat onto the pier. He enters the Floating Palais almost shyly, walks though a welcoming crowd and retires to his dressing room to change his clothes, powder his face and pray. Martin's first choice for Tiny's marathon medley was Sydney's historic State Theatre. He had also had other ideas - the elegant Regent Theatre perhaps? In the end the synchronicity of the Luna Park venue proved irresistible to Martin. 'He sprang from the carnival,' he explains, 'Tiny's first job was as the Human Canary in Hubert's Flea Circus on Times Square.' And so Martin brings Tiny back to the imagery that reflects some of his vital past.

The marathon-medley is held in the mad and marvellous Floating Palais. This old concrete barge is surmounted with an elegant timber pavilion, its corrugated cement roof is supported by imposing scissor trusses. Originally designed in 1935 by architect Sam Lipson, the Palais is considered an essential part of the character of Luna Park. It was lovingly restored in 1976 by Martin, Peter Kingston, Tim Lewis and Richard Liney. Liney painted the interior of the Floating Palais. He remodeled the bar and added a large mirror decorated with Suzie Wong against a Sydney Harbour background. Based on the original design, Liney also added the painted fences and lampposts to the harbour frontage.

In his dressing room Tiny kneels before the mirror and prays, expressing an attitude of gratitude for his past. To his Lord he proclaims, 'I sit here with my mirror, and mirrors are a reflection of the past. I think of how wonderful you've been to me for nine years, a man who didn't have to do all this, backing me up when I didn't have a cent. I owe you a lot, still you've been faithful to me and tonight's the night of the big concert'. And with a bemused Marvin Lewis watching, the 4-person crew is filming everything. Tiny dabs his cheek with powder for the last time and announces, 'Another puff, for all the great cosmeticians of the world'.

The booming voice of Adrian Rawlins announces that Tiny is about to come onstage, to an applauding audience who shortly before were treated to a 'mystery guest' the popular art-singer Jeannie Lewis, dressed as Pierrette. Rawlins continues, 'We are all here, as you know, to celebrate the centenary of recorded sound. In 1878 Thomas Alva Edison invented the phonograph and the world has been swinging ever since!'

Musical fanfare.

'Ladies and gentleman, guys and gals, welcome to the setting of the world non-stop professional singing record. Would you welcome to the stage America's Ambassador of Song, the Eternal Troubadour, the Human Lyrebird, the Superman of Song, Mr Tiny Tim!' Dressed in his comic strip suit Tiny emerges stage-left, blowing kisses, carrying a shopping bag and trying not to trip over the leads in his pathway to the microphone.

He stands towards the front of the stage close to his audience, holding the microphone not his uke. The crowd surges, they applaud, Tiny blows kisses, flutters his eyes, raises them upward, blows one final kiss to Heaven and starts singing where the compère left off - *Mr Phonograph* a turn-of-the-century tribute to Mr Edison. Red shirt, red lights, red hair, red stage. Red is the dominant colour of the comic strip suit, the colour of much of the Palais' sets and décor, and as if that isn't all red enough, there is a filter on the light, making Tiny's mop of normally burgundy-coloured hair positively glow.

Without a pause, Tiny launches into the up-tempo *Goody Goody*. Some people dance, but before they can settle into the song it changes to *It's A Good Day* then *Don't Sit Under The Apple Tree (With Anyone Else But Me)*. The pace slows, *Shine On Harvest Moon. Pennies From Heaven*. Now faster, *Coming In On A Wing And A Prayer, Don't Fence Me In* followed by the first song in the evening where Tiny uses his famous falsetto - *Cool Water. Swanee, For Me And My Gal, I Want A Girl Like The Girl That Married Dear Old Dad,* followed by a few songs which seem to relate to his estranged wife – *I Wonder Who's Kissing Her Now, After The Ball* and *Just One More Chance*. Strong audience response, many people waltz, leading to Tiny's *Just A Gigolo* fantasy, which he sings in firm voice. The pace quickens, *Accentuate The Positives,* followed by *The Chattanooga Choo Choo* a real tongue twister, which Tiny sings very fast. Everyone gets on the dance floor for *It's Gonna Be A Great Day*.

Through all of this, Tiny never misses a lyric, never plays his ukulele and rarely uses the high voice. His order of songs sometimes appears to have a storyline, as the songs flow with machinegun rapidity. One minute the audience is swaying, next they are dancing. Then they're at a standstill for an Al Jolson song they might have heard Grandma sing. *Mame, Praise The Lord And Pass The Ammunition, Give Me That Ole Time Religion, Bad Moon Rising, Blue Suede Shoes, I Don't Want To Set The World On Fire*. The audience senses that he's peaking. Tiny alters the mood once more, to the swaying rhythm of *He's Got The Whole World In His Hands* during which the two hour mark is acknowledged and the audience goes wild, Tiny responds with kisses and 'thank you, thank you' squeezed between phrases of song. The next song is *Michael Row The Boat Ashore*. He is now well clear of the two-hour mark. He has achieved what he set out to do and the record is set. Tiny is smiling. In his hands, an interminably long lyric sheet Tiny performs as his encore, a power rendition of *Staying Alive* – a mini-marathon in itself – 'stayin' alive, stayin' alive…'. People are now partying hard, cheering, clapping. After two hours, 15 minutes and seven seconds Tiny steps back from the mic, which passes to Rawlins who announces, 'I think we've witnessed a historic event – the new World Heavyweight Singing Champion, the one and only – Tiny Tim!'

Hoorah!

'Thank you, thank you,' responds Tiny. 'And God bless you all.' (2)

Footnotes:
1. *Sydney Morning Herald,* 9 January 1979.
2. Martin Sharp film, *Street Of Dreams,* 1998. The *Luna Park Marathon* is a handmade CD, not generally available.

11

Australian Connection

I never thought I would have started all this…
Eric Clapton (about Martin's *Street of Dreams* film)

At the start of 1970, Martin was known in Sydney for many things, most notably *The Yellow House,* a live-in art gallery at the bohemian end of town. He was also known for his cheeky collages and fabulous pictures. In the early to mid-70s Martin worked on the restoration of Luna Park with other artists, many of whom he had known from Australian OZ days and the Yellow House.

Through these years Tiny was the sub-plot for much of Martin's art, and after signing the contractual agreement with Tiny and his management, Tiny became Martin's central theme. His main work comprised posters and paintings of Tiny, album covers, tapes, photographs and the film, *Street Of Dreams.*

The Human Lyrebird

Martin had not intended to do everything himself. Optimistically he believed that having been properly exposed to Tiny, filmmakers and record producers would be keen to work on the film.

He was hoping to sell Street of Dreams to a major movie house, pitching for cult movie status. But the Australian Film Commission declined to fund the project, originally titled The Lyre Bird, Tiny Tim. So Martin privately approached producer Peter Weir with whom he had worked as art director for the film Picnic At Hanging Rock. But Weir was working on another project (The Last Wave) and had little interest in a film about Tiny. Likewise producer Bruce Beresford was busy. And although quite sympathetic, Jim Sharman, the man behind the Rocky Horror Picture Show, was doing other things too.

Although often charmed by the footage, the major movie houses did not throw their weight behind the project, leaving Martin to do everything himself, including the financing. And so Martin mortgaged his substantial house, Wirian, in order to finance the film, produce Tiny Tim albums and organise concerts in Australia, with the cooperation of Tiny's management and Australian promoters. Martin bore all major production responsibilities that he had hoped to share.

Nevertheless, Tiny must have been pleased to know that from this time on, and for the rest of his life, somewhere in the Antipodes was a small outpost constantly working on his music, taped conversations, film and visual images - the firstfruits of which were excellent.

After Tiny returned to the States, Martin and Tiny talked regularly on the phone about many projects. Martin's phone bill must have been astronomical! First, they had to finish *Chameleon,* after which Tiny felt they might release a definitive musical history, along the lines of a *Reader's Digest* compilation - only by one artist. Around this time it was estimated that Tiny probably knew 2000 songs off the top of his head, though with hindsight it appears this figure appears way understated.

Divorce

In accordance with US law, after a period of separation the State grants married partners a divorce without the partners suing and so 1979 marked the official end of Tiny's marriage to Miss Vicki.

Tiny often told the media that he would welcome her back, from which point Tiny would launching into his views on the Bible's teachings about b-r-e-a-s-t cancer, s-e-x and the contraception pill. Tiny also volunteered lots of information about his current crushes – though he would constantly return to talking about Miss Vicki, which frustrated his managers who wanted him to simply forget her.

In August 1979 Tiny surprised everyone at a performance at the *La Magnette* club with Miss Vicki joining him as a dancer. They continued together on-and-off professionally for the following five or six months, even making a joint-appearance on America's *Tomorrow Show.* (1)

Also in 1979 Tiny made his last appearance on the *Carson Show,* with the song *Tiptoe to the Gaspumps.* This was followed by an interview and a finale of *Do You Think I'm Sexy?* with Tiny falling to the floor, ripping off his suit, shirt and tie and throwing them into the amazed audience. (2)

Tiny then got himself a permanent place of residence, probably the only one he ever selected for himself, and where he would live for the next decade and a half. The Olcott Hotel is a 16-storey establishment, located on West 72nd Street in New York's Upper West Side. In 1980 all units had pantries or kitchenettes, and a one-bedroom apartment like Tiny's cost $400-$600 per month. The Olcott was located next door to the Dakota Hotel. At the time Tiny moved in, John Lennon lived there with wife Yoko Ono and their son Sean. 'I saw him once,' Tiny ruminated, 'but I didn't want to bother him'. (3)

Chameleon

Returning to Australia in 1980, Tiny – now with mulberry-coloured hair - again teamed up with Martin and under the musical direction of Nathan Waks, they completed the remaining tracks for *Chameleon* – ie. *Deep Night, Song Without A Name* and *My Song.*

To these 11 tracks was added *Country Queen* (recorded by Tiny in Nashville for True Records on the day of Elvis' death in 1977). Eight hundred copies of *Chameleon* were released by Martin's *Street of Dreams Productions*. Martin said, 'Nathan really produced that record. I suppose I was the financial producer and getting the people together, but he was the contact with the studio'. (4)

It was certainly well received by the small audience who heard it. Listeners who were expecting a Human Canary were amazed at the depth and richness of Tiny's baritone on tracks like *Brother Can You Spare A Dime? The Great Pretender* and *Staying Alive.* They were also amazed at the album's versatility, from the fragile rendition of *My Song* to the Islander sound of *The Hukilau.* However, without the support of a major recording label, and with limited airplay, this sensational record never got the exposure it deserved. (5)

Not so much was expected from the second Street of Dreams album. *Wonderful World of Romance* was recorded direct to disc at EMI Studio 301, and unofficially labelled, 'For Fans Only'. It was an unplugged style of album with Tiny singing old time favourites to the relaxed accompaniment of Marvin Lewis' piano. At the time, this record was mostly given away to friends and not released to CD until 2006. (6)

Roy Radin's Vaudeville Show

In 1981, Tiny joined *Roy Radin's Vaudeville Show*. Radin was a Long Island NY entrepreneur whose touring extravaganza featured legends of past eras. Radin is probably best remembered for his unsuccessful attempt to finance *The Cotton Club* film, which – through a series of underworld connections - led to his contract killing in 1983.

Radin made his fortune rekindling his audiences' past memories. He brought back stars like Milton Berle, Danny & the Juniors, the Shirelles and the Drifters. There was also comedian Georgie Jessel, star of a 1926 movie *Vesti da Giubba.* And so on.

In 1981, singer Eddie Fisher appeared on the same bill as Tiny. Fisher was once famous for having more consecutive chart hits than Elvis Presley. He was even more famous for marrying Elizabeth Taylor. Anyway, Tiny was part of that tour, which was wildly successful until Radin's interest waned.

This is how the press wrote about one of Tiny's performances, 'On a sparsely attended night in Cleveland Tiny Tim is fourth on the bill and his introduction by George Savalas – as surly and self-satisfied as his brother Telly, but with more hair – is met with generous applause. He immediately goes into *Tiptoe* but it is during *Great Balls Of Fire* that he begins to have a good time, his unwieldy body accentuating the beat, tossing his tie to the audience. During his finale, the old Rockabilly tune *Pledging My Love,* Tiny wins the heart of the audience.'

In this same article, Tiny describes himself as, 'Doing one-nighters, getting by. I don't want to just get by. I want to go back to Hollywood. Character actors, records, TV shots…I don't care, I wanna go back on top and I think I can'. (7)

Then, Tiny surprised everyone by appearing at the Nu Wave/No Wave *Rock Lounge* club in New York. The *Bulletin* reports Tiny as a punk rocker, 'packing them in'. They describe his appearance as 'crazy-coloured shoulder-length hair, bondage trousers, zips and safety pins'. I do wish I'd seen that! (8)

Tiny's stage costumes were becoming more extraordinary. In April, he appeared dressed in a comic strip suit to promote his new single *Comic Strip Man.* Back in Australia this was duly noted, leading to the creation of the famous Tiny Tim suits, which Martin gradually turned into an art form. Tiny had lots of other plans too, including making a television pilot with Jonathon Winters and honouring lots of bookings in New York State. Tiny was also lauding the talents of a Miss Louise Berger. He was priming her to join him on the vaudeville show. But the vaudeville show was coming apart, due to Radin's illicit personal habits and ultimately his killing.

Filming in New York

Meanwhile, Martin and his team continued working on the film, which had up to now mostly been filmed at Sydney's Luna Park and also around Wirian. These reels include the pre-marathon press conference, the marathon itself and Tiny declaiming the mighty talents of Miss Natasha, a transsexual dancer who performed for Tiny in Martin's film editing room.

In May 1981, Martin sent a camera crew to New York to film Tiny. The New York footage was essential to setting the Tiny's story in context. It featured a trip through Tiny's past, including a drive through New York with Tiny pointing out sites from the old neighbourhood, where he played curb ball, where he went to school, etc. It was all good historical footage.

Tiny's Mum, Tillie, was also interviewed. She showed the crew through the apartment, even taking them into Tiny's bedroom from early childhood until he became famous. The message *Jesus Saves* in Tiny's youthful writing was still visible on the peeling wall.

When asked whether she was proud of her son, Tillie replied (in her Yiddish accent), 'Why shouldn't I be?' Later, she ribbed Tiny on camera, reminding him that his cousin Harold was Promotional Manager for WKTU Disco 92. 'He got a better position that you!' she despaired.

One evening, on impulse, Tiny phoned the camera crew and told them to come to his room. They arrived to find an alcohol-fuelled Tiny in the company of someone called Pleasure Aims, a burlesque babe from New York's *Melody Burlesk Theatre.* Phew, that was unexpected.

As if on cue, she stripped to her underwear and the camera started rolling. Tiny chuckled a bit before expounding the wonderful attributes of champagne and also of his female companion. With the confidence of someone used to being in charge, Miss Pleasure teased Tiny into removing her bra. After baring her boobs on film, followed by a bit of innocent bed-play, Tiny quite suddenly switched gears and turned his attention onto the film crew.

Uncertain whether to keep filming, the cameraman said, 'Tell me Tiny, why did you bring us here tonight?'

'Well,' replied Tiny thoughtfully, 'You're making a film, and I thought you'd want to film this. *What did you expect to film?'* he asked, putting the voyeurism back into the mind of the viewers. (9)

Over the following weeks, Tiny teased the gossip magazines by telling them about footage of him with 'naked women'. His management was appalled! What was he saying? Tiny Tim - who talked so much about Jesus Christ - was here captured on film with a half-naked burlesque dancer. It was gratuitous! It wasn't even a paparazzi job!

Said Martin, who by this early stage had about 140 hours on celluloid, 'I showed some of the film to some of his connections in New York and they were all horrified. "What will his mother say? Children love him…" all that sort of stuff. I felt genuine opposition. These hardened guys were saying, *You can't show that!*' (10)

Deep Tongue

This was Tiny's 'sexy' period, I guess.

His next US single (1982) was the Rod Stewart song, *Do You Think I'm Sexy?* sung in Tiny's *Stayin' Alive* persona.

Tiny had enjoyed a few dalliances over the years. He was a virgin at the marriage altar. He'd been a faithful husband to Miss Vicki. But circumstance had projected him into now being 'the New York-style defacto man'. Always keen about appearing in movies, he revived his blue movie idea, *Deep Tongue*. Tiny was serious enough about this venture to discuss it with Martin and director Peter Weir, at Weir's Sydney home.

The morality of doing such a movie posed a problem. Tiny had to work through his religious convictions first, which he explained to Martin and Weir, 'Getting involved in a blue movie is of deep concern. I don't mind making the public angry – I'd love to – but would it disgrace God? Would *He* understand?' (11)

Then Tiny met Miss Dixie, and moved on.

Miss Dixie

Tiny met her on 13 March 1982 while travelling on a cruise ship the S.S Norway. Miss Dixie was 25, part Indian/Irish/Polish. She was a widow whose father was a Hells Angel known as Chief. What started as a flirtatious relationship extended into a physical relationship. This played on Tiny's conscience. He found the physical side of this relationship compelling and presented Miss Dixie with a trophy – his 16th.

Marriage was on the cards, but it had certain drawbacks. Miss Dixie's husband had been killed in a 1978 construction accident, leaving her with a $200,000-plus pension, which would be terminated on re-marriage. Tiny wasn't making enough money to support her and he wouldn't risk closing off her independent income stream. But for the sake of righteous sex, marry her - he must.

Finally he hit on an idea, a loophole in God's Laws, which he described as a 'spiritual marriage'. This clandestine ritual required kneeling in prayer and pledging their vows before the presence of the Lord in the privacy of their hotel room. Only then could Tiny enjoy the sex (apparently he did) with a more-or-less clear conscience. Tiny described his spiritual marriage to Miss Dixie, 'When I committed sins with her I said, *O Lord I have wronged.* But you know, at least we got married in a mock-way - but it still doesn't make it right. *I want to marry this woman, help me out of this.* And sure enough, he did, because even though I married Miss Dixie in a mock-marriage last year (ed: 1982) in her room in Florida when she came to visit me at the Holiday Inn - we got down on our knees and I held her hand and I said, *O Lord you know that I can't finance her now and she'll lose her compensation if she marries me and it's not right to go into bed with her, but you know how much I love her. You know she's the most important woman to me that I've ever met. Yet your laws are still superb.* I'm holding her hand, I'm down on my knees. I want to marry her in a mock-way. *I don't suggest anyone else do it, nor do I consider myself right in your grace, because I can't presume on your mercy. I met her because of thy grace, which is not by accident. You know the feelings in the heart, you see it now. Yet I cannot sleep with her outside of marriage. I cannot marry her. What am I to do?* She came to visit me with her daughter in the Holiday Inn while I'm playing in this club for four weeks. So he knows the heart. We got married under his eyes in a mock-way without putting pressure on her. This was my idea, so she's not really involved from her end. Still it's wrong and I got back into my room and thought, *O Lord no matter what I did, just help me out in the right way.* Her tubes are tied. She can't have any kids. So by praying for the right thing, realising, prostrating myself that no matter how right it seems to me, it's not right with him. I can't fight the physical and the spiritual end of his laws.' (12)

Still, the relationship continued. Back in New York they shared a room at the Olcott Hotel. The room was three stories below his regular room, where his mother had moved in after the death of Boutros. Said Cousin Bernie, 'Tiny looked after his Mum. He was really good about that. I don't know if she appreciated or not what he did'. (13) Tiny and Miss Dixie stayed in bed for hours, Tiny barely ate so that he needn't share a lavatory. After that, he had to face his mum. She really berated him. He said, 'My mother was hitting the ceiling – hoh! hoh! wow! – God bless her sweetly, she knew I was down there with her. She said, You're a no good tramp! You and her are the same way! She's using you! She's dreaming you out!' (14) Miss Dixie was very much on his mind when he returned to Australia in August-September for a six-week tour. (15)

Australian entrepreneur, Peter Connyngham had booked a series of club gigs for Tiny, as well as lots of media. In collaboration with Connyngham, Martin extended Tiny's stay to work on various projects as well as staging a spectacular concert at the Sydney Opera House.

In August 1982, one of the first things Tiny did on arrival was to sit with Martin and look through the rushes of the *Street Of Dreams* movie. Tiny enjoyed what he saw, which was a slight change of emphasis. Martin had become analytical about the Luna Park fire and incorporated it into the plot. The fire occurred 9 June 1979, barely five months after Tiny's marathon. It spread from the Ghost Train and killed six children and one adult. Martin had spliced this news footage alongside footage of Tiny singing.

Tiny spent the next day with Connygnham, going through various booking arrangements, then he spent more time with Martin in preparation for the Sydney Opera House Concert. Tiny was really flat out. He appeared at a Beauty Show at the Chevron Hotel, performed the Bexley North RSL Club, did a radio interview with John Singleton, a press interview with the *Daily Telegraph,* performed the Campbelltown RSL Club, then another radio interview, this time with comedy actor-cum-radio presenter, Lex Marinos. After all that, he took time out to meet musicians Mic and Jim Conway, with whom he would be performing the following Saturday night at the Masquerade Ball at the Paddington Town Hall. This was followed by another radio interview, with comic presenter, Jonathon Coleman - prior to playing a gig at the Strata nightclub, where he won over a tough audience. Tiny's commitments just went on and on. The promoters never took their foot off the pedal.

Dave Newland & me

The following day, I interviewed Tiny for the paper I wrote for, *The Southern Flyer,* which is how we met. By 1982, I was three years out of school teaching and working as a freelance writer. The *Southern Flyer* was an independently owned part-arty and part-regional tabloid magazine.

It was editor Steve Elias' idea, not mine. Twelve days before, he commissioned me to interview Tiny for his magazine. 'You're weird enough…!' he laughed. So I phoned Martin right out of the blue. He gave me Mr Bill Hollander's number – Tiny's manager. While I had Martin on the line, I quickly squeezed in a question about Tiny's alter ego?

'He does have one…' Martin replied, '…but I'll let you find it'.

On 24 August, Dave Newland and I sauntered through the door of the Cosmopolitan Hotel with instructions from Steve to photograph everything and write as many words as possible. I'd talked Hollander into giving me an hour. He said okay and told Dave and me to wait on the verandah deck, while Tiny was finishing another interview inside. So Dave and I sat around until Tiny emerged, dressed in a frilly shirt and mauve suit with black trim. Before we got started, he asked me to send him my article, 'good or bad'. It shocked me a little, to think he would bother to spend an hour with someone who might write something bad about him.

The Paddo Masquerade Ball, held at the Paddington Town Hall featured Tiny and the Conway Brothers Band.

I clicked on my cassette player, fully aware that after years of practice, Tiny would have his patter all figured out. My guess was that Tiny would probably more or less reiterate what he had just given the *Daily Telegraph* journalist. And that's probably what happened at the start - Tiny ran through his patter about birth control, abortions, cancers and hysterectomies. Intending to somehow break his rhythm, I jumped in with a question about Miss Tulip, which he brushed aside, babbling on about Miss Dixie. I jumped in again, asking whether he saw Miss Tulip much?

'I do keep in touch with her...' was all he said, moving to the Biblical take on divorce.

'What does Miss Tulip think of you as her Dad?' I insisted.

'I don't think she knows what she thinks of me yet', he replied, slightly reluctantly. 'I think...I'm just a wonderment, a curiosity, and I think that one day – God willing – we will be together. I'm fond of her, there's no doubt about it'.

Not wanting to be a pain in the arse, I backed off. He'd given my question all he could and probably wanted to get back to being Tiny Tim, which was the business of the day. But I did break his patter, and I did let him know there was something different about me. I spent the next 55 minutes playing along – and getting along – with him. I followed with a lollipop question about Miss Dixie. Tiny clapped his hands, threw back his head and laughed. 'I'll show you a picture!' he enthused, 'the latest one from New York!'

Then we moved through a short history of popular song, Tiny dropping names I'd not heard of, like John McCormick, Enrico Caruso, Billy Murray, Irving Kaufman, Arthur Fields and the music of the 1910s. He explained the impact of the microphone, the Charleston, songs of WW2. He walked me through all this, while Dave had unrestricted access with his camera. The cover of this book (front and back) is taken from this session, Tiny gaily talking about romance, Miss Dixie, and Martin's forthcoming film.

He said, 'Mr Sharp took the film to New York and plus there were some scenes with...er...you know...?' Tiny feigned embarrassment and said, '...naked women in it.

'I go to topless, bottomless bars...'. Then a sudden switch, 'Not any more since Miss Dixie! But before I used to go to topless, bottomless bars. Believe it or not, not aroused, not to look at their bodies, but I was looking for a certain face. I need someone to create for, a heart to sing to again! A trophy to give!'

Before our hour was up, Dave had snapped a roll of b/w film, Tiny confessed to my tape recorder that he'd had an inferiority complex when he was young. He then pulled the uke from his shopping bag and broke into *Carolina Moon* for a couple of fans who had spotted us.

'Well Dave', I said, as we drove the short distance to Martin's house to pick up a couple of posters, 'We had a good time, but I don't think we got the story. He was toying with us'.

'I think we did', he replied.

'What about all that fake religious stuff?' I insisted.

'He meant it.'

'I doubt that very much. Let's see what Martin has to say?'

Well, Martin didn't say much. He was busy with a phone call to his mother. He gave us a *Chameleon* poster each, granted Dave permission to take a few shots of him and that was it.

Tiny Tim for Tiny Prices

Two days later, and feeling I hadn't scratched the surface of Tiny Tim, I called on Martin at 9.30am. Even though he didn't know me, he was most hospitable, giving me a bowl of black coffee and telling me that Tiny is a genius, in the same way that Vincent van Gogh is a genius.

Boldly I suggested that Tiny is a sex creep. Martin squared me in the eyes and replied, 'Tiny would never do anything unethical'. And, religion? Martin said, 'I've seen Tiny walk into a motel and the first thing he's looked for is a Bible'. (Okay Dave, you win.) Martin reckoned that if I jumped in the car right now and drove to Miranda Fair – a shopping centre in Sydney's southern suburbs – I'd catch another performance. As it turned out, it wasn't a performance at all. I found Tiny in the menswear section of the Grace Brothers department store. His entourage had wandered off and left Tiny by himself in the underwear section where he was about to perform. People walked by and pointed at him. I hurried over and shook his hand. He seemed relieved. 'Mr Tarlin, what a pleasant surprise!'

Next, a salesperson wearing a blue bow tie guided Tiny to a tacky gold-painted throne, sat him down and spruiked, 'Tiny Tim for tiny prices. Underpants reduced to 99 cents…but only while Tiny Tim is in the store!'

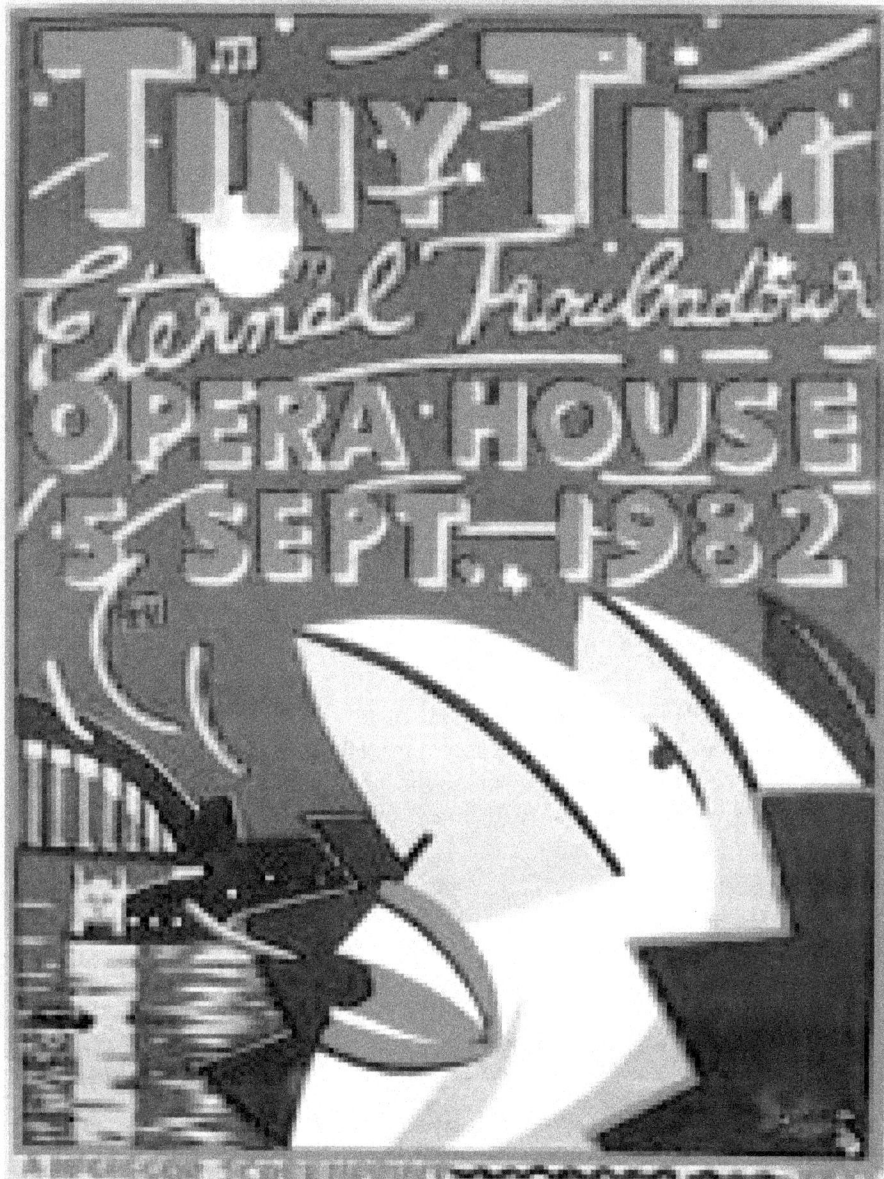

'Tiny was going to pull the Opera House concert because Miss Dixie hadn't rung, and that's because she was the muse - to project this great love out in song. I think Tiny is a real champion of the outsiders, the long shots, the Ugly Ducklings. They let the greatest beauty through, they couldn't believe it!'

Martin Sharp, 24 January 1994

'We didn't know it'd be like this when we left the States,' Hollander whispered to me, 'We'd have never agreed to this!' The spruiker wrapped up after about 10 minutes and invited the audience to come up and say hi to Tiny. All of a sudden Tiny was swamped with people wanting him to sign things. Joining the queue, I asked an elderly woman whether or not she liked him? 'Not particularly', she replied - though she still queued for the autograph. When she reached him, he pulled out his uke, gave *Smile Awhile* a short burst and she sang along with him!

Mr Hollander then invited me to join them for a luncheon provided by Grace Brothers store. There were about eight of us including the Australian promoter, store manager, a couple of people representing Martin, a couple of people representing the department store and Tiny at the far end of the table. No one really spoke to him. I also noticed that he didn't eat. Instead he drank an enormous quantity of tomato juice mixed with Tabasco sauce. 'If you gave him another jug, he'd do it again...' Hollander explained, going on to discuss Tiny's unhealthy eating habits and propensity for having a flutter on the horses.

'But you haven't really seen Tiny in full flight. Instead of driving home, why don't you catch him tonight at Sylvania Waters?'

I'm glad I declined. It was a bad night. There was an audience of six people. However, I did agree to come back within the week, bringing my wife Robbie to see Tiny perform at the Sydney Opera House on 5 September.

Sydney Opera House Concert

Martin designed a spectacular poster for this event, with Tiny's face as the Opera House itself and Luna Park peeping through the background. This collector's piece gave the concert great art credentials and plenty of publicity. It was the place to be if you were in Sydney that night. The Concert Hall was quite full. The audience comprised the cream of Sydney's glitterati, actors, celebrities, artists and bohemians.

Tiny opened with the song *Street of Dreams*, with beautiful cello accompaniment from Nathan Waks, who was also musical director. After a huge applause, Tiny moved to *My Song*, again from the *Chameleon* LP. Third song was Tiny's composition *Forever Miss Dixie*, a waltz. Then a reprise of *My Song*, after which Tiny thanked each band member by name.

Tiny was on stage for almost two hours and the concert moved through many phrases. Sometimes it mirrored the Albert Hall Concert, other times it mirrored the marathon. What a pleasure it was being there! He peaked with a couple of Aussie songs, *Waltzing Mathilda* and – significantly - the *Luna Park Song*...'Take me back to Luna Park, just for fun!' Before leaving the country, Tiny went back to the EMI studio with Martin and recorded four tracks with musicians who were perfect for what Tiny and Martin had in mind. The four songs on this extended 45 recording were, *The Bible My Mother Left For Me, Forever Miss Dixie, Keeping My Troubles To Myself* and *The Last Mile Of The Way*. Played in sequence, the four tracks read like Tiny's mini-autobiography. (16)

This wonderful EP record touched many people. The title song *Keeping My Troubles To Myself* featured a monologue, 'You only liked me best when I was playing the jester, my smile's not to deceive, I only give what you want to receive...' which reminded listeners of Tiny's career. However, it was the religious content that really spoke to Martin. After this recording he said, 'I would say that religiously he is the most powerful person I've met and it was unexpected because it was initially a musical interest, and then another side emerged.'

As for the sexual content of Tiny's conversations, which bothered me at the start, Martin said, 'It's his weakness and his strength, it's very paradoxical. You don't find many religious leaders prepared to talk about sex. It's the total frankness of that area which is fantastic and why I understand his insistence that I record that. He said, "Got your tape recorder on? Come over, I'm going to tell you about my sexual fantasies" and I thought, *Good God, what's this guy doing?*' (17)

Goodbye Miss Dixie

One hangover from Tiny's 1982 Australian tour was that the host of the *Tonight Show,* Don Lane, offered Tiny and Miss Dixie another TV wedding, which included a $10,000 wedding dress and a splendid 10-day honeymoon at Queensland's Great Barrier Reef. Miss Dixie was not impressed.

When he dared broach the subject, Tiny said, 'Her personality changed from white to black, like Joan Crawford in *Mildred Pierce. You want to turn me into another Miss Vicki!'* she exclaimed.

He said, 'I sent Miss Dixie about 52 cards, poems and letters and telephone calls and presents and she was so happy and as soon as I came to visit her I was supposed to stay a week at her place from September 21st til the 28th. First day I came in I mentioned the so-called marriage that was supposed to take place and – boom - she hit the stairway and we had an argument and broke it all up. She was so anxious to see me, but the first day I walked through that door, it started right then and there and it made the whole Australian trip that I had – which was so great last year – just explode. It was as if I never should have left her, I couldn't believe what happened. It all worked for the best but it was really a tough thing to overcome and then I had to come back to New York, it was like coming back into a black storm.' (18)

So ended that romance and Tiny continued gigging. Americana Hotels signed him to a multi-city deal that began in March 1983. He continued to play bars, clubs and vaudeville. (19)

One lovely moment was at the Tulip Festival, held in the Hershey Gardens, Toronto, Canada, a park opposite a factory with 80,000 tulips where they named a path the *Tiny Tim Tiptoe Trail* and got Tiny himself to make the impressions of his feet in the concrete, like stepping stones.

Footnotes:

1. *Sunday Telegraph,* 12 August 1979.
2. Ernie Clark, interview with Lowell Tarling 30 March 2002. Tiny's version of *Do You Think I'm Sexy* is on youtube.
3. Tiny Tim, interview with Lowell Tarling, 4 April 1992.
4. Martin Sharp, interview with Lowell Tarling, 1 February 1983. On this tape Sharp talks about the recording of the album, of which 800 were initially pressed.
5. Tiny Tim, *Chameleon,* Street of Dreams Productions. The tracks are: *Brother Can You Spare A Dime? It's A Long Way To Tipperary, Deep Night, The Song Without A Name, The Hukilau, The Great Pretender, My Song, Street Of Dreams, Country Queen, Mickey Mouse Club March, Staying Alive, My Way.* Released in 2006 on CD by Zero Communications, Japan. Check out *Stayin Alive* on youtube!
6. Tiny Tim, *Wonderful World Of Romance,* Street of Dreams Productions. The tracks are: *Wonderful World of Romance, She's A New Kind Of Old-Fashioned Girl, Love You Funny Thing, Million Dollar Baby, Prisoner Of Love, As You Desire Me, Auf Wiedershen My Dear, Goodnight Sweetheart, Stand Up And Sing For Your Father, Memories Of France, When You Look In The Heart Of A Rose, That Wonderful Mother Of Mine, For The Sake Of Auld Lang Syne.* Released in 2006 on CD by Zero Communications, Japan.
7. Scott Eyman, *Calendar,* 1 March 1981.
8. *The Bulletin,* 10 March 1981.
9. Martin Sharp film, *Street Of Dreams,* 1998.
10. Martin Sharp, interview with Lowell Tarling, 1 February 1983.
11. Tiny Tim, taped by Martin Sharp, Meridian Lodge, 27 October 1978. Tiny discusses making a porn movie with Martin Sharp and Jon Lewis. Tiny Tim, taped by Martin Sharp, at the home of film-maker Peter Weir, 27 October 1978.
12. Tiny Tim, interview with Lowell Tarling, 30 August 1983. Also interview with Lowell Tarling, 6 September 1983.
13. Bernie Stein, interview with Lowell Tarling 29 March 2002.
14. Tiny Tim, interview with Lowell Tarling, 6 September 1983
15. Tiny Tim, interview with Lowell Tarling, 24 August 1982.
16. Tiny Tim, *Keeping My Troubles To Myself* extended play 45 rpm, a Noive & Voive production for Street of Dreams. Acoustic guitar: Tommy Emmanuel. Electric guitar: Phil Emmanuel. Harmonica: Jim Conway. Piano: Alistair Jones. Bass: Chris Haig. Drums: Steve Hopes and Buzz Bidstrup.
17. Martin Sharp, interview with Lowell Tarling, 1 February 1983.
18. Tiny Tim, interview with John Singleton, Radio 2KY, 18 August 1983. Also, Kate Fitzpatrick, *Sydney Morning Herald,* 3 September 1983.
19. *Newcastle Herald,* dated 11 July 1983.

12

Australian Tour
August-September 1983

I was working about the same time doing collages and Tiny was doing it with songs – transposing styles. He was doing with songs what I was doing with images. That's why I clicked with him.
Martin Sharp, artist

Featuring Dave Newland's contemplative Tiny portrait on the cover and at least 2800 words from me, my *Southern Flyer* article was generally well received.

I didn't care what others thought, I simply wanted Martin and Tiny to like it and I got pretty excited when they did. I was so enthused that I wrote a few more pieces about them for a couple of other publications.

Early in 1983, Martin invited me to stay with him at his home in Bellevue Hill, next time I came to Sydney. My wife Robbie and I, and two children Amber and Joel, lived five hours south in Bermagui, a little fishing village on the NSW south coast. I frequently needed to drive to a Sydney publishing house for work. So yes Martin, I'd love to!

Wirian 1983

I came up within the fortnight. Martin gave me a room, showed me around the kitchen and said I could join him in his studio any time and maybe 'assist' him. I wasn't sure what that meant as, at the time, he was cutting up pieces of red and green cardboard and gluing together shapes and letters for a poster for a Jeannie Lewis show called *So You Want Blood*.

Later, Martin explained that he was looking into circumstances surrounding the Luna Park fire and he'd like me to read through news clippings and type up a chronology of events. Synchronicity was an important theme. So that's what I did for a time, against a background of wall-to-wall Tiny Tim music, which I really enjoyed. Every day was a new discovery! A new song (new to me) like *The Luna Park Song* on 45 rpm! Or, Tiny's single from America (new to me) - *Do You Think I'm Sexy?*

Martin owns a grand house called Wirian, mortgaged to the hilt to finance the film. The heart of the house was once a grand dining room. This became Martin's studio, where he entertains guests, plays tapes, reads, write and cuts up pieces of coloured cardboard and paints. Friends called it the 'Inner Sanctum'.

The right wing of Wirian was once a ballroom. It is now filled with about 5000 figurines of characters like Mickey Mouse, Popeye, Boofhead, Asterisk, Darth Vader, *Le Petit Prince,* Ginger Meggs, and so on…it's known as the Dream Museum. Between the Inner Sanctum and the Dream Museum is the old smoking room, now film editing room, full of Tiny Tim memorabilia and film editing equipment.

I was given an upstairs room in the old servant's quarters, alongside several other people who lived there at the time. Some only stayed overnight, others stayed a few days, but when I first came to Wirian, the following five people lived there with Martin:

- Musician, Alistair (Al) Jones, who played piano on the *Chameleon* and *Keeping My Troubles to Myself* records, backed Tiny at the Opera House Concert and would be working with Tiny on his next visit. Al was pretty irreverent, calling us *Wirianettes*, etc, though keen to assist Martin where he could.

- Some people described Marilyn Karet as the only sane one amongst us. I don't know what they meant by that, but she had the room next to mine and kept mostly to herself. During the day, she helped Martin with the film. In the evenings she kept away from his studio, which had stream of visitors, some pretty crazy. She'd seen it all before, too often, I guess.

- William Yang had a bedroom and photographic studio under the house. He quietly went about his business, photographing Martin, his paintings and posters, as well as photographs of the house itself. Sometimes he even took shots of us. One night he called the household together and held a slideshow shown against the theme music of the new television program, *Brideshead Revisited.*

- Fergus Lindsay was the handyman. He did odd jobs and had contacts in the print sector, which he occasionally used as required by Martin. Martin designed a business card for one of Fergus' mates – *Acme Printing.* Fergus also organised Martin's framing work.

- Most people thought her the nuttiest, but I thought Les Bean was the sanest amongst us. Whenever things got spilled or someone made a mess, it was she who usually sorted it. She painted all her clothes in acrylic paints and didn't necessarily wear anything as designed to be worn. For example, she wore 50s-style old women's knickers as a hat. (Painted, of course.) She was a genuine Tiny Tim fan.

When Tiny came to Australia later in the year, all these people were constantly around him - at Wirian, at gigs, maybe placing a bet on his behalf or helping in some other way. There were others too, who didn't live at Wirian. Peter Royles was constantly dropping in, often drunkenly strumming his Takemine guitar and breaking into roughhewn early Dylan songs.

There was also Martin's friend, Yensoon – shy, polite and flat-chested - who had a white painted face, wore traditional Chinese clothes and talked a lot about the Tao. Sometimes I thought of her more as a spirit than an actual person. Or Martin's friend from OZ magazine, Richard Neville. Whenever he dropped in there was always raucous laughter pouring from the Inner Sanctum. While I was there, Richard and his wife Julie moved in briefly, when they were between homes.

Yellow House artists, like Tim Lewis, or some art school student no one had ever seen before, might be helping Martin one day and gone the next. The people traffic was pretty constant. I once spotted artist Brett Whiteley vanishing out the front door, 'Was Brett here?' I asked.

Listening to Tiny

I really couldn't believe this was happening to me – staying in this big house, reading Harry Stein's biography that I'd never heard about, being gifted several of Martin's posters, listening to Tiny talking to Martin on tape and here I was, about to be a bit-player in a tour by an international star!

Martin would tell me what Tiny was doing in America or he'd show me clippings from the latest magazines. Like, in 1983 Tiny contacted NASA as one of the first volunteers to take up the offer to take non-astronauts for a ride in the Space Shuttle. Those who had known Tiny for a long time were not surprised. They recalled 1951 when he'd unsuccessfully applied to join the Space Program.

Martin and I often stayed up late, listening to Tiny's recordings or conversation tapes. One morning Martin played a cassette of the 1968 Albert Hall Concert, which Richard Perry had sent. Again, I couldn't believe my circumstances - listening to this extraordinary concert, as if I'd been there!

Tiny often called Martin late at night (our time) to discuss obtuse subjects like, 'If I were Pope…'. Sometimes I'd leave the room and let them talk. Other times I'd keep doing whatever I was doing and overhear Martin chuckle, as Tiny would tell Martin about his latest crush.

I did try to piece together news of what Tiny was up to. Martin said Tiny was playing the clubs. And his Mum had moved in with him. And Bill Hollander had handed over his management to his son Neil. Martin taped all this and, soon after I arrived, I started taping everything too. Training perhaps, for Tiny's return.

After all that, I'd come home to Bermagui and tell my family and friends what I'd seen and heard. I played conversation tapes and music. Some loved it, others openly mocked. But at least Tiny got played often. On a good night, we'd have friends skipping around the lounge room to the strains of the *Mickey Mouse Club March*.

Some people called Tiny a no-talent has-been. I'd let them laugh, then I'd put *Keeping My Troubles to Myself* on the turntable, which stunned even the most hardened cases. '*That's* not Tiny Tim!' they'd exclaim. *Keeping My Troubles to Myself* was on the latest 4-song EP that Martin had pressed ready to present to Tiny on his arrival. I could hardly wait!

Even though I'd met and interviewed Tiny precisely one year prior, somehow this felt like the first time.

Tiny Arrives

On Sunday 21 August 1983, Tiny arrived at Sydney's International Airport at 8.00 in the morning accompanied by manager, Neil Hollander. Seven of us were there to welcome him, including Martin, who presented him with the new disc. Looking exhausted, Tiny greeted each of us personally, then Martin arranged for Tiny to come to Wirian in the evening. After that, I imagine Tiny went to his room at the Cosmopolitan Hotel (the Cosmo) and grabbed some rest.

Martin invited about 35 people and by 5.00pm, along with Al, Marilyn, William, Fergus and Les, I was hanging out in Martin's studio, awaiting Tiny's arrival in a room full of celebrities, socialites, musicians and artists, some of whom were involved in the tour. Among them was a guy called Tony the Tailor, who was creating a suit for Tiny, patterned on one of Martin's Tiny Tim posters. Then, just five minutes before 5.00 the doorbell rang…

…and it was Peter Royles, drunk. 'Where's Tiny?'

Tiny wasn't here yet. However, Peter had barely stepped inside when a car pulled up with Tiny in it, along with the new Mr Hollander and his Australian tour manager.

'Good', said Peter, 'C'm here Tiny, I wanna show you something'. And before anyone could say anything, Peter gripped Tiny's arm, whisked him away from the guests, into the Dream Museum – and closed the door.

Meanwhile, guests wanted to know where Tiny had gone? Martin wasn't sure. Les couldn't find him. Hollander said 'he's in the end room with a little guy'. Ten minutes passed, guests were getting impatient. Fifteen minutes…then a terrific crash, followed by a howl of pain.

Tiny emerged from the room, uncertain what had happened and horrified by the sight of blood. Then out bounced Peter holding his shin and complaining that he'd dropped a Fender Twin amplifier on his leg. 'How did it happen?' I asked. Peter replied, 'I was showin' Tiny this amp and I fucken dropped it of course!'

Next morning I checked my cassette recorder, to make sure the Peter Royles incident had come out clear, then I drove home while Tiny flew to Hamilton Island Queensland, to perform a few shows. After a couple of days, I returned, bringing Robbie, Amber and Joel with me. (1)

The Kinselas performances were quite gracious shows. Old time tunes, songs from Chameleon and Wonderful World of Romance that we, the audience, now associated more with Tiny than the original singers - Al Jolson, Rudy Vallee, Russ Colombo and Perry Como.

Kinselas Nights

Martin had worked something out with the Australian promoter where, after fulfilling the promoter's crap venues, he would organise some special shows. He hired musicians who had worked with Tiny on previous recordings and created a new poster for every occasion. On this tour, the centrepiece was four consecutive late-night shows at the Kinselas nightclub in the hip part of town.

These were quite gracious shows, introduced by Adrian Rawlins, and backed by a trio of bass, keyboard and drums. Old time tunes, songs from *Chameleon* and *Wonderful World of Romance* that we, the audience, now associated more with Tiny than with the original singers - Al Jolson, Rudy Vallee, Russ Colombo and Perry Como.

By now, we'd got used to Tiny rapidly switching songs – say, from *Babyface* to *I'm Looking Over a 4-Leafed Clover* to *I'm Gonna Sit Right Down and Write Myself a Letter* then *Please Don't Talk About Me When I'm Gone.* We'd got used to the band occasionally playing catch-up. That was all part of the show. Tiny would announce the song ('Great song, written by that great singer Mr Henry Burr in the 20s...') turn to the band, say, 'Maestro, the key of C...' and away he'd go for sometimes up to 20-minutes without a pause. Somewhere near the peak the audience would start singing along with something like *It's a Long Way to Tipperary!* I couldn't believe how hard he worked!

The Kinselas performances started at 11.00pm. Before this, Tiny'd already played some shithole club that didn't appreciate him. But the Kinselas crowd certainly did. There was always a core group present – Martin – and probably 20-30 Martin-supporters who were there for Tiny. Nicola, Sue, Stefan, Richard, Julie, William, Robbie, Peter, Tim, Fergus, Marilyn, Les, all their friends, as well as well-known people, who came because Martin told them to.

Meanwhile lots of people dropped in to see Martin, hoping to catch a glimpse of Tiny. William warned me this would happen. All these people telling Martin they absolutely *love* Tiny Tim! He'd play them something off the *Chameleon* record and they'd be starstruck. So he'd give them the record free. I have no idea what his bookkeeper said, but Martin also gave away posters and heaps of tickets to Tiny's concerts.

Neither Robbie nor I really talked to Tiny in that initial period after he'd arrived. We'd just be 'around' while Al showed him film rushes, or when Martin organised a press conference at Kinselas with Tiny and singer Pee Wee Wilson of the Delltones. Back in Wirian, it was like Sigmund Freud's consulting room. Tiny would vanish into a room with some journalist. Then off again into the Dream Museum with Yensoon, and when they came out after an hour, it was like they'd had a consultation session. Tiny occasionally talked to Al about various song arrangements. And he talked to Martin a lot.

At last, it was my turn.

Second Interview, 30 August

For our second interview, Martin told me to take Tiny upstairs into his spacious bedroom in which there were a couple of lounge chairs and a side table for the recorder. We talked two hours on tape, everything was about sex and religion, and that's where we got to know each other a bit.

Basically, I lost control of the interview and couldn't control the questions. It was okay, because Tiny needed to get all this off his chest. He discussed his sympathy for the Devil and something about oral sex, then in the middle of some dogmatic pronouncement on where the s-e-e-d should fall, he turned to me and said, 'But Tiny Tim could be wrong, I'm only a human being. I am saying what I believe to be Jesus Christ's law. What you have to do, however, is search on your own. I could be wrong. God will understand if I'm saying things and think them up. What you must do however is rely on God in your own life. You must seek out different religions and pray in your room alone. I'm putting myself in your shoes...'

From this, he actually told me how I should pray.

O blessed Lord Jesus
I don't know why I'm on my knees.
I talked to Tiny Tim yesterday
He told me certain things and I seem to be puzzled
I don't know what you're about
I don't know if he's telling me the right truth or what?
But something there seems to be ringing a bell within me.
I may be in the position of fornication... (...or whatever?)
But you know my position before I came to talk to you
And you know now I'm finding something new out, right now
I'm willing to change my life and be born again.
All I'm asking O Lord Jesus (always mention the name 'Jesus)
Is to come into my heart and show me the way. (2)

Knock knock. It was Robbie with a tray of drinks. Black coffee for me and tomato juice for Tiny – straight from the bottle – because Tiny never drank from anything touched by human lips. Like, a glass.

'Ooh, Miss Robbie...' he exclaimed. But she didn't want to interrupt the tape and quickly left. Later though, they did converse.

*

Our children, Amber (10) and Joel (8) met Tiny at a shopping centre event, in Chatswood. Mum was there too, but she refused to approach him because Les was pirouetting through the Men's Shirt's Section where Tiny was again enthroned in a Grace Bros chair.

Elle est fou! Mum exclaimed (she usually spoke in French). She'd never before seen anyone wearing clothes that looked like a Jackson Pollock painting. But Amber and Joel weren't bothered. They knew Les, joined the queue, and said hello to Tiny.

She Left Me With The Herpes

Lots of things happened over the next few days. Tiny went to the studio and recorded, *She Left Me With The Herpes, I'd Rather Die Die Die For My Country (than live live live with my wife)*. He appeared on the Channel 9 Breakfast Show, held several more press conferences and played a few more clubs. Later, Tiny was interviewed by actor Kate Fitzpatrick, a star in her own right. He told her, 'I believe in miracles, last week I believed I could marry Miss Koo Stark, this week she's gone. Something will turn up'. (3)

Tiny also held several discussions Pee Wee Wilson who later in the week, along with his Delltones, would back him at Kinselas on a cover of the Presley song, *Are You Lonesome Tonight*. Les followed Tiny around a bit, cavorting wildly to his music in shopping plazas, clubs and through the Wirian kitchen. Tony the Tailor turned up with the b/w Martin Sharp poster suit. Peter Royles got drunk and tried to climb on the stage at Kinselas when Tiny was in full flight, until some audience member head-locked him, tried to strangle him and knocked over our table. Some memories are quite startling. Like, when Robbie and I came back to Wirian one afternoon and there was Tiny in the hall singing *Love You Funny Thing* with Marvin Lewis playing the piano. I can't believe we simply walked past, as if this was an ordinary event. Another time I drove Tiny to his hotel and we had to walk past a classy restaurant to get to the lifts. The entire restaurant went silent when we appeared. First - Tiny. Followed by a woman with a white painted face dressed traditional Chinese vestments. Followed by a woman with painted clothes and an old lady's underpants on her head. Then me.

Les Bean

Wentworthville Leagues Club is located in a Sydney suburb better known for its panel beating shops than anything else. Neither Martin nor Robbie wanted to go. They would attend the 11.00pm Kinselas show later.

Les and I said we'd go. I spent my afternoon with her berating a sober Peter Royles who was very sorry about the other night. After that Les and I got into my car and headed for Wentworthville. On the way she told me her story and I taped everything, including her background, how badly she fared in school, that she'd been a Devo fan and sadly, that some of her family thought her certifiably insane. Then I parked the car.

We could hear Tiny singing as we walked in. He'd already started his set, which was similar to the Revesby RSL Club – *Stayin Alive, It's a Good Day, Goody Goody*...

Les and I signed ourselves in, strode past the poker machines, said 'Hi, Mr Hollander' and before anyone could speak, Les proudly strode through the tables and hit the barren dance floor. Tiny acknowledged her with a nod. Half-ballet, half-punk she gyrated and within seconds two women leapt out of the crowd and joined her. For a moment, it looked as if the place might explode into fun!

Then someone called security. They grabbed Les and ejected her. Then Hollander – absolutely furious - turned on me and ordered me to leave.

'What for?'

'Because you brought her here!' he exploded. 'And I promise you that if she don't leave Tiny alone, he won't be playing Kinsela's tonight! YOU TELL MARTIN SHARP THAT!' Which is why the tape I brought back to Martin that night wasn't of Tiny singing, but people shouting at me.

According to Hollander, Les was not to come within a 100 metres of Tiny. I returned to Wirian, reported this to Martin. He was pretty calm about it. I collected Robbie and off we went to Kinselas. Martin, Yensoon, Robbie and I, took our seats. Tiny took the stage. Then a weird thing happened. I heard a noise behind me, turned my head, blinked and there were three Les Beans sitting four rows behind us. Three of them, with painted clothes and old people's underpants on their head sat side-by-side. I swear I couldn't pick the real Les Bean, nor even if she was there.

A couple of days later, Tiny performed the Newcastle Funny Festival, an hour-and-a-half north of Sydney, which Les and I also decided to attend. It was quite an event. For the occasion, they published a special edition Tiny Tim poster by artist Michael Bell. (I bought two – one for Martin.) The Funny Festival had made an effort to promote Tiny who revealingly told the Newcastle press, 'I consider myself a singer of serious songs, but if people want to laugh that's okay'. (4)

The Festival organisers provided a spectacular showband to back him - Newcastle's own Castanet Club, a 9-piece conglomerate of performance and comic musicians who were prepared to rip into songs like *Rock Around the Clock* for Tiny. The stage was ablaze with colour, and I'd invited half a dozen friends. *Goody Goody, Hound Dog*...one of those upbeat songs saw Les stride through the audience and hit the dance floor. Again, she was instantly joined by a couple of women. This time Les wasn't thrown out, she was lauded. Soon six gay women were rotating, swirling and jiving directly in front of Tiny's microphone stand. My friends and I got up and danced too. Tiny met them afterwards and signed autographs.

Tiny slowed the pace for his newest composition, the *Koo Stark Song,* which I'd never heard him sing in public before. Then he moved on to the medley. By now everyone was on the dance floor. I taped all this excitement and played it to Martin when we got back.

'Did you listen to it?' he said.

'What?'

'The song *Down Under...!*'

'Huh?'

'He sang, *Can you hear can you hear the thunder – you better run, you better take cover!*'

Third Interview

Our third interview was held in Tiny's room at the Cosmo. Neil Hollander ushered me in. The place smelt of limburger cheese. Before Tiny could welcome me, Hollander started berating him about his eating habits and of course the smell. Tiny didn't say much, knowing Hollander would be gone in about minute. But he didn't like it.

When Hollander had gone, Tiny's main concern was that he had received a bouquet from someone called 'J Hover' and he didn't know how to respond. The 'Jehovah' connection was spooking him a bit. So he made a phone call, which didn't settle anything, though he relaxed enough to talk to me on tape for another couple of hours. We'd already done sex and religion at length, Tiny really couldn't go through it all again, so I asked what it was like being a star and getting the best of everything?

Thoughtfully and eloquently, he leaned back in his chair and told his story, which I have quoted extensively in Chapter 6. 'When you make it, after 20 years…etc'. He talked a lot about food, the money he never saw, and the late-60s period where he lived in five-star hotels with 24-hour service and plates of food costing $170 each. 'I ain't lying!' he emphasised.

Looking to the future, he was emphatic that he really wanted to 'make it twice'. He hoped a dramatic film role might come his way.

Then we talked about Steve Paul's Scene NY and the period leading to the *Tiptoe* hit. He also reminisced about staying at the Big Pink, recording with Bob Dylan and the Band, and playing Phillip Granger in Dylan's film. Looking around, I could see Tiny travelled light. Apart from an array of costumes and make-up, he only seemed to have his ukulele and Bible. I asked him about loneliness, he replied 'Maybe sometimes, but I always have Jesus Christ to talk to…'.

Then I got personal and asked if he put Henna in his hair? Boy, he didn't like that. 'Are you kidding,' he thundered, 'Loving Care!' as if there was a world of difference between the products.

I asked about his eating disorder, which he explained stemmed from his early teen years, where he couldn't eat with his father watching. He explained it as quoted in Chapter 1. Then I asked whether he'd ever smoked a joint or taken a recreational drug? 'Never touched it,' he replied, 'I don't believe in that, I don't need a high. Thank Jesus Christ for that!'

And then we discussed circumstances concerning his 3-day abstinence from sex 'for the glory of God' during his honeymoon with Miss Vicki. I also asked about the spiritual marriage to Miss Dixie. Tiny seemed to enjoy talking about s-e-x. Some people do, that's not unusual. What was really unusual was that I was recording all this really personal stuff, with him occasionally making sure that the tape recorder was on.

Recording Studio

Towards the end of the tour, Tiny went into a recording studio and Martin decided to go too. He asked Fergus and me if we wanted to tag along and we said yes. Martin drove us to Sun Studios near Sydney's Central Station, and – after retrieving his keys that he accidentally dropped down a drain - Martin, Fergus and I showed up inside.

There were lengthy breaks between takes, enabling the three of us to enter the recording booth, meet the band and chat, while Tiny – who was unapproachable – talked intensely to musical producer, Nathan Waks. The song was *Highway to Hell* and I found myself chatting mostly to bass guitarist Denny Burgess, who later became a friend.

Then, after 10 minutes or so of talk, Nathan and Tiny would agree on something, snap into gear, and Martin, Fergus and I would move back behind the panel and off they went, playing their robust 6-minute version of AC/DC's *Highway to Hell,* which was an entirely new direction for Tiny. I didn't know what to make of it.

Fame

As part of Martin's team, sometimes I had to accompany Tiny or drive him somewhere. Most of the others involved were inured to fame in a way I wasn't.

Martin had lived with Eric Clapton and was quite famous himself. William had photographed Mel Gibson, Les had got pretty close to Devo, Al was in the Slim Dusty Band, but I had never experienced anything like this level of fame before. And you don't really feel it until you're in a public place with Tiny. Not a recording studio, not Wirian's kitchen, not even in the audience with him onstage. Out in the street amongst people gave me a real taste of what fame must be like. Pretty frustrating, I thought.

Martin, Tiny and I went to see Adrian Rawlins (Mr Poetry) recite at Grace Brothers Bondi. The three of us comprised Adrian's entire audience. It was a non-event, but it was okay. Then Martin asked me to drive Tiny back to the Cosmo. To get to my car, Tiny and I had to walk through the Bondi Mall. I didn't give it a second thought until people started milling around and blocking our progress. *That's Tiny Tim!* some spotter exclaimed. Next thing the people were swarming. The rush of people was like being thrown into a beehive. Voices here, there and everywhere. A stranger telling Tiny that her mother owned his first LP. Another said her boyfriend saw him at Luna Park. Someone else said something or other about his appearance on last week's TV breakfast show. He signed someone's arm. Signed someone's pocketbook. He just signed stuff.

Suddenly, he turned away from the throng and walked into a chemist shop. The crowd didn't enter the shop, but three counter staff immediately came over to him, dropping cold whomever they were serving. Tiny picked up an Elizabeth Arden sample and explained to me and a small group of customers that he owed his youthful skin tone to this particular skin cream. He got me to pinch the back of my hand and note how the skin retracted slowly, then he rubbed the sample on his, pinched it and pointed out the difference.

'If I buy one for my mother-in-law, will you autograph it to her?' I asked.

'Mr Tarlin, of course!' he beamed, while all three counter staff competed to hand the fragrance to Tiny.

'What's her name?' he asked.

'W-I-L-M-A', I replied.

I snapped this on a Polaroid camera, in a room above the Kinsela's nightclub. It's Tiny in a press conference with Peewee Wilson of the Delltones, Tiny is telling the assembled journalists that he and Peewee love Mr Presley's music and are going to join forces on Are You Lonesome Tonight , as a feature of their upcoming show.

Lowell Tarling

Tiny in the Lion's Den

Before leaving for Bermagui, and feeling that I'd seen every unusual thing there was to see, I drove Yensoon, Martin and Tiny to Circus Royale in a southern Sydney suburb, where they actually put Tiny into a Lion's Den.

Tiny is scared of corgis! Yet he actually got into a cage with a lion (and lion-tamer) and they filmed it for morning TV. How does having a hit record, *Tiptoe Through the Tulips* logically lead to getting into a cage with a mangy lion years later?

Then Robbie, Amber, Joel and I went home. Later, we received the extraordinary news that Tiny in the lion's den in Revesby was picked up by the US press. (5)

Footnotes:

1. Much of this chapter is taken from by 1983 Diary.
2. Tiny Tim, interview with Lowell Tarling, 30 August 1983.
3. Tiny talks about the Tiny Tim Tiptoe Trail to Kate Fitzpatrick, *Sydney Morning Herald,* 3 September 1983.
4. Tiny Tim, *Newcastle Morning Herald,* 5 September 1983, speaking before his stage appearance at the Castanet Club.
5. Tiny Tim at the Circus Royale, taped by Lowell Tarling, 7 September 1983. Also, Michael O'Regan, *Sunday Telegraph*, 24 August 1986.

Martin found this picture of Tiny crowned as a King, in Arthur Rackman's book, Cinderella (published in 1919). In my edition it appears on page 82 and is worth checking out. It inspired a print and a CD concept titled 'King for a Day', which Martin and Dave Rowe have been/are working on. Martin also referenced this Rackman image on Wonderful World of Romance, recorded in 1979 with a limited LP release 'for fans only', and released to CD in 2006.

13

Tiger By the Tail

I knew his one song 'Tiptoe Through The Tulips'
only because it had my name in it.
Miss Tulip

Tiny started composing songs almost as soon as he started performing in the late-40s. They were usually 3-chord ditties about his latest 'Miss'. Miss Elizabeth Taylor, Miss Stephanie, Miss Snooky, Miss Tuesday Weld, and so on. Tiny occasionally – not often - included his newest composition in his live acts, like *Forever Miss Dixie* at the Sydney Opera House concert, and *The Koo Stark Song* in Newcastle Australia.

When he returned to the States, apart from performing his heart out, he created, collected or worked on many of his own compositions. This selection included *Santa Claus Has Got The Aids This Year, She Left Me With The Herpes, Cheryl Tiegs Don't Leave Your Husband* and *Dietetic Baby* some of which he sent to Martin, who played them constantly.

From his childhood, Tiny worked best in solitude. He wrote these songs when he was alone, probably in his bed or sitting on it, in his respective bedroom/hotel rooms. He didn't have much else to do in hotel rooms, which had become his way of life. I recalled his room at the Cosmo, with a phone, a shower, a TV set, a Bible, his uke, cosmetics and not much else.

Recluse

What did he do in those hotel rooms in the mid-80s when cris-crossing America?

When not in his room, he would spend time playing the pokies (ie. slot machines) in hotel lounges. He told me this was the only time the attention of fans really bothered him. When playing the machines, he preferred being left alone to 'concentrate'. In 1983 he was keen enough about it to take up reading *How To Win On Slot Machines,* 'It doesn't work, of course', he told interviewer Kate Fitzpatrick. (1)

*

Alone, he would usually pray, read his Bible, telephone people and talk for hours, or learn new songs. That's how he got to know thousands of songs. He'd made a study of them all his life, so he always had something fresh. For example, he even learned Michael Jackson songs like *Billy Jean* and *Bad.* The only reason he never performed them in public was because he never had the appropriate backing band.

In his room he would also eat and watch the Dodgers Baseball team or the Toronto Maple Leaf ice hockey games on TV – again, always alone without distractions. He also liked to watch certain films in private, especially where the girl was exceptionally beautiful. Tiny didn't like to share his screen crushes.

Australian journalist, Caroline Jones certainly got it right when she interviewed him in 1978 and started with, 'Many people have seen you as an extrovert. I have always thought of you as a gentle, sensitive and shy person'.

Tiny liked that and replied, 'I tell you Miss Jones, you hit it right on the nose. The thing is you can't blame them for what they think, because they only see the show for five minutes or half an hour. And if I were in their position I might think the same way. But the thing is, I am a recluse and some of my brightest moments happen when I'm alone'. (2)

Repository Of Old Tunes

Tiny's repertoire varied with his band. He needed the Burgess Brothers for *Highway to Hell*. And Nathan Waks, for the *Chameleon* repertoire. But back home, with a small trio (organ, sax and drums), around this time his US show comprised something like this selection: *The Very Thought Of You, The September Song, That's You That's You, Jingle Jangle Jingle, Sioux City Sue, Someday You'll Want Me To Want You, You Are My Sunshine, Don't Fence Me In, If You Knew Suzie Like I Know Suzie, Margie, Avalon, St Louis Blues, She'll Be Comin' Round The Mountain, The Old Gray Mare, I've Been Working On The Railroad, Hail Hail The Gang's All Here, Always, Dancing With Tears In My Eyes, How Much Do I Love You, Goodnight Sweetheart* and of course he would peak with his hit, *Tiptoe Through The Tulips*.

Furthermore, Tiny was never shy about including straight hymns on his song list, hymns like *Amazing Grace, Throw Out the Lifeline* and *He's Got The World In His Hands*. And while Elvis, Little Richard and lots of others have made one-off Gospel LPs, there are not too many stars who mixed hymns with their secular songs in their live acts in clubs and bars, yet Tiny did it so naturally.

Cousin Hal and Miss Tulip

During this period Cousin Hal took his wife Sherry to a Tiny Tim performance in a club in Pennsylvania, where they lived. Hal described the performance this way, 'He was like a repository of old tunes. Tiny was wearing one of those unusual costumes. He was on the stage for a full hour and a half without stopping, going from song into song into song. I don't know if he'd memorised them but it was like natural. He would go into an old vaudeville song then pick up another tune, then do an impersonation of Elvis Presley and keep going. He kept going without regards to anything. He wouldn't even take a drink.' (3)

Meanwhile, Miss Tulip had started writing letters to her father. At age 13 she left her mother and moved into the Olcott Hotel with Tiny and her grandmother Tillie. That's how Miss Tulip spent the summer of 1983. Though she knew he was famous, Miss Tulip knew little else about Tiny. 'I knew his one song *Tiptoe Through The Tulips* only because it had my name in it.' And she got to hear *On The Good Ship Lollipop* because Tillie had the record.

Prior to this, Tiny's only real contact with his daughter had been through occasional phone calls of which she says, 'He would call every once in a while. I didn't really have any impression of him because I just talked on the phone. He seemed like a nice person'.

Her stay at the Olcott didn't really add much to this impression. 'He worked most of the time, so I didn't really see him.' (4)

Miss Jan

Around this time, Tiny met aspiring singer Miss Jan Alweiss at the Williams Club, a private alumni club located between Grand Central Station and Times Square New York.

Tiny was attracted to her glamour and they became romantically linked. Tiny's third wife, Miss Sue, explains the relationship, 'Miss Jan was a very New York person. She's intelligent, wily and worldly. And Tiny, by then had been around the block too, so they kind of understood each other. She was very interested in show business and publicity, and he was looking for a woman that he could take around to these social events.

'He took her to the *Laugh-In* reunion. She made a big splash there and he was very pleased with that. Miss Jan was really sophisticated and very much of a glamour girl, a very good dresser who knew how to handle herself in some ways, although not always. Sometimes she could embarrass Tiny at these events because she was the kind of person who could say *anything*. She wasn't afraid to speak up and she was not under his control any more than Miss Vicki had been.

'I think Tiny in some ways was drawn to these tempestuous relationships. Because he grew up in a family that was that way, it had a familiar feel to him, a feeling of excitement and passion, whereas a more sensible relationship seemed a little dull to him – actually. He wanted someone very glamorous.' (5)

In 1984 Tiny married 23-year old Miss Jan Alweiss in Las Vegas and then a second time, one year later in a synagogue, for her parents' sake. (6)

They never lived together and the question of divorce was always hanging in the air, yet they remained married 10 years, though they were both dating other people while also regularly seeing each other. Miss Sue explained, 'I think, to both of them, he was just one of the guys she was seeing, and she was just another one of the many women he was seeing'. (7)

With Tiny on the road constantly touring, Miss Jan had no intention of living with Tiny's Yiddish mother (who died in July 1986, age 93). Even though the marriage seemed doomed from the start, Miss Jan was Tiny's longest married relationship.

'I'm married to a very beautiful wife – Miss Jan,' said Tiny in 1991, 'It pains me to be so tired of her and she's tired of me. We'll have to sit the marriage out, if that's what the Good Lord wants. I haven't had an affair with her since 1989 - I mean, I haven't seen her body. All she does now is come over and touch me because I tell her I need something every day. I mean, she's given me so much love she doesn't have to.'

Tiny said, 'Miss Jan lives just two blocks away. We don't live together because she has her own apartment, but she comes here every weekend. I have to be alone, she has to be alone. She's a great artist, a commercial artist. We had five million fights before and after the marriage. It's a miracle we're still together. Praise the Lord, unbelievable!' (8)

Over the years a lot of people have criticised Miss Jan. Like a lot of the criticisms of Tiny's wives, much of this stemmed from his management. But Tiny wanted her, Miss Vicki, Miss Sue – and all his Misses - treated with respect. Prior to meet Miss Sue, Tiny summed up his first two marriages in a sentence, 'Miss Vicki and Miss Jan had the looks I want'.

Great American Circus

Tiny spent from March to November 1985 touring with Allen C Hill's Great American Circus, which he joined in Miami. He performed a 10-minute medley, appearing after Mumbo Jumbo, the star gorilla. The Great American Circus is a circus road-train that travelled all over the American eastern seaboard. Once again, Tiny found himself in a funfair environment.

Tiny explained, 'Ironically the idea started in Australia. While I was there last in 1983 I did a show for the circus and I had to get in the lion's den and of course the papers got the story and the idea came to one of the agencies here for me to try out with the circus.' (9)

He also performed an endless round of bars and clubs, all over the States. One of his most significant performances was in Columbus October 1986, where his backing was the chic 5-piece band, Campervan Beethoven.

Tiny performed 10 songs with this arty, punk, ska, world music band, which gained him a lot of credibility amongst a hip set who were 20 years too young for *Tiptoe* (which he played in the middle of the set). As a nod to the times, Tiny included the Carl Douglas disco hit *Kung Fu Fighting* in his set. (10)

Blood Harvest

Tiny often toyed with the idea of doing movies. At the close of our 1982 interviews he told me he wanted to play the Phantom of the Opera. He said, 'I'd love to do movies, it's a must!' In 1983 he was telling the press he wanted to play either Dracula or a space creature. (11)

In 1985, local filmmaker Bill Rebane was in the audience when Tiny made an appearance at a beer garden in Lincoln County Wisconsin. Rebane had an idea for a horror film, which he put to Tiny, and Tiny agreed to play the lead role and sing the theme song. Although Tiny had made several film appearances, this was his only dramatic role.

The film is called *Blood Harvest* and it was released in 1987. Tiny plays Marvellous Mervo, a social misfit who wears clown makeup and dresses like a circus escapee – (which was kinda true).

Tiny is the best thing about the film, everything else is terrible, right down the camerawork. The lazy script is peppered with a few gems, spoken by Mervo, which only Tiny could have written. In his soliloquy, Tiny uses almost identical words as his monologue in the *Great Pretender* on the *Chameleon* LP.

Another flashback is the theme song, written by songwriter Tom Zane. Tiny sings, 'I just want to make the whole world laugh, even if the laugh's on me…'. which lines up with what Tiny told the press in Newcastle Australia, 'I consider myself a singer of serious songs, but if people want to laugh that's okay'.

The film was shot in a farming community, Gleason Tennessee, a smalltown environment (population less than 2000) in which Tiny was spectacularly out of place.

The antagonist is an all-American lad called Gary. This guy is nuts. He grotesquely hangs naked women upside down in a barn, cuts them, makes a proper mess of them - it's a real tomato sauce blood splashfest. In the end, it's Tiny who saves the day. The message (if anyone ever got that far) is something like: *don't judge by appearances.* (12)

The Wedding Singer

In 1987 Bear Family Records released another Tiny Tim single that failed to gain attention, *Tip-Toe Thru The Tulips/Resurrection*. However, the cover photo, of Tiny tiptoeing through a field of red tulips beside a creek, became quite a famous picture of Tiny in his mid-career years. Never out of work, Tiny was on the road most of the time, playing the full range of venues – from dives to concert halls. Married now to Miss Jan, he was seldom home. They never lived together anyway.

One highlight was 15 February 1987 when Tiny attended Cousin Hal's wedding to Sherry Horowitz. Sherry recalls, 'When Hal & I were married Tiny flew in from somewhere I really cannot remember. It was a Sunday afternoon.

'The marriage was the second time around for us – no large production - 30 people. My friend told Tiny we had no music, so he sang and played his uke when we walked down the aisle. Our friends said was the best wedding they had ever attended!' (13)

Brighton Arts Festival

I was in Melbourne when Martin was organising his contribution to Brighton Arts Festival, held in Brighton England in May 1988. A lot had changed for my family and me in the lead-up to Tiny's second world professional non-stop singing record to be held there. We'd left Bermagui and from 1986-1992 I worked in various publishing houses in Sydney and Melbourne.

The Brighton Festival is England's biggest Arts Festival. It features dance, theatre, classical and contemporary music, books, street art and film. It also features world premieres and UK premieres. Before Tiny would agree to perform, he wanted *Street of Dreams* screened at the Festival. This meant Martin and his team had to get the film into a rough format for public viewing. The 'Brighton Cut' was achieved in a fluster, but in time.

Miss Jan accompanied Tiny to Brighton, where he was a headline act. The presence of Miss Jan kept Tiny somewhat apart from his Australian supporters and friends – like Martin, Nathan Waks, Marvin Lewis, Alistair Jones, Martin's cousin Roz Sharp and others who had flown in for the big event.

Starting at 7.00pm on Friday 27 May, before a respectable, not sold out, crowd, Tiny came onstage at the Zap Tent, outside the Brighton Dome. He wore a white shirt, dark tie and a new suit, printed from Martin' black and white Tiny Tim 'Eternal Troubadour' posters. Tiny carried his uke on stage and opened up with *Mr Phonograph* – the tribute to Thomas Alva Edison who invented recorded music – followed by mostly old time songs peppered with some surprising inclusions. For example, *Ace In The Hole,* Fats Domino's *I'm Walking* and B B King's, *The Thrill Has Gone.* There were no original compositions and only few songs taken from his albums, which is remarkable considering the enormous body of work he was presenting. From *God Bless Tiny Tim* Tiny sang *Tiptoe Through The Tulips* precisely at the point when he broke his own record. He also sang *Million Dollar Baby* and *Love You Funny Thing* from *Wonderful World of Romance.* And from *Chameleon* he sang *It's A Long Way To Tipperary.*

Certain parts of the marathon-medley did recall previous English performances. He sang You Call It Madness (But I Call It Love), My Time Is Your Time and The Maine Stein Song, all sung in 1968 at the Royal Albert Hall. He also featured There'll Be Bluebirds Over The White Cliffs Of Dover and There'll Always Be An England, which had worked so well 18 years before at the Isle Of Wight Festival. There'll Always Be An England was positioned near the climax, which peaked with When The Saints Go Marching In, We'll Meet Again, Hello Young Lovers and finally, Heartbreak Hotel. One hundred and forty-eight songs in a total of three hours, 11 minutes and 30 seconds - Tiny well and truly broke his previous Non-Stop Professional Singing Record. For an encore, he brought Miss Jan on stage and sang a duet with her.

The Brighton marathon was released by Street Of Dreams in a limited edition 3-cassette pack. Tiny's liner notes suggest that it was very much on his mind to present 'the great melodic songs that were written by the finest songwriters of their day and sung by the greatest singers of their day. Singers like Billy Murray, Henry Burr, Max Miller, Byron G Harlan, Rudy Vallee, Charles Coburn'. This intention is well reflected in the song list and goes a long way to explaining his selection. Not only was it a marathon-medley, but also a presentation of the history of popular song, which was a theme ever close to Tiny's heart. (14)

'Amazing…' drawled the patron of the Festival, Sir Richard Attenborough in Martin's ear, as they watched Tiny steaming through song after song without a pause. 'World Beater!' screamed the British press after his powerful performance, 'Tiny Tim Really Is Tops'. (15)

On his return, Martin wrote me the following, 'I had a great trip. I can't say it was a triumph, though TT's marathon of 3 hours 12 certainly was. IS. More relaxed than Luna Park, he got into some more relaxed songs, Time On My Hands, White Christmas, Bluebirds Over the White Cliffs of Dover'. The cutting room floor is being prepared for the next cut of the film, got the wedding footage from London at last. They hadn't forgotten me over there'. (16)

Later in life Miss Sue commented on the Brighton Marathon. She said, 'Tiny was a person that had three times a normal person's energy. Even when he was old he had tremendous stamina. He could stay up for several nights in a row without affecting his performance too much; he was able to sleep sitting up in almost any kind of conveyance – whether it was a car or a plane, or anything. If you ever stopped talking for even a minute he almost fell asleep almost out of habit, as though being on the road for so much you're happy to catch sleep when you can. He could go without sleep, he could go without food, he could do without sleep for 2-3 nights and he could go without food a day-and-a-half easily. And he had a lot of physical strength. He didn't have a lot of muscle strength, but he was a big person and in some ways he could just go on and on like the Energiser Bunny.

'I suppose there was probably a lot of determination there, to just keep going. He was just winging it, making it up as he went along. I don't think he had that much of a plan. He was good at that kind of thing – thinking on his feet, figuring out how to get the audience interested and involved, keeping them involved.' (17) Tiny told the British press, 'I think it is the most important concert I ever did'. (18)

THE ETERNAL TROUBADOUR

Tiny Tim

& THE TIME MACHINE 2

THE WORLD
PROFESSIONAL
NON-STOP
SINGING
RECORD

A CENTURY OF SONG
IN ONE SMASH HIT!

At 7.00pm Friday 27 May Tiny broke his World Non-Stop Singing Record at the Brighton Arts Festival UK. He sang for three hours and 12 minutes and invited Miss Jan to join him on stage for an encore. This is the cover of the 3-cassette pack released by Martin and Street of Dreams Productions.

The Eternal Princess

In 1988, James Big Bucks Burnett – musician, entrepreneur and owner of the world's only 8-Track Museum (until New York got one) - brought Tiny to Dallas Texas to headline his third Mr Ed Music Festival held at *Club Dada*. Bucks had asked Tiny to record two songs, the Led Zeppelin classic *Stairway To Heaven* and one written by himself, titled *Fourteen*. Tiny acceded to both requests and so, backed by a band called Brave Combo Tiny cut the tracks and promptly developed a fierce crush on Bucks' former girlfriend Miss Stephanie Bohn who showed up backstage at a concert with a ukulele for Tiny to autograph.

Miss Stephanie was encouraged to play up to Tiny's affections through a series of love-letters. It was a heartbreaking time for Tiny who lived in hope, and whose on-again/off-again relationship with Bucks fluctuated in the turbulence of each deception. Despite mixed feelings for Bucks, Tiny never really shook off his crush on Miss Stephanie. (19)

Despite Tiny and Bucks' rollercoaster relationship, the recordings were sounding great! In 1990 Tiny returned for more sessions with Brave Combo after which he suddenly broke contact. Bucks explained on the CD's liner notes, 'Tiny returned to Denver in 1990 to record more songs with the Brave Combo. Everything went well, and a month after the session something odd happened: Tiny abruptly ceased all communication with me, and as months turned into years it seemed the album might never be finished'. (20) Tiny had a sharper explanation. He said Bucks was playing him for a sucker and Miss Stephanie was the bait. Bucks strongly denies Tiny's interpretation of these events. Much later they patched up their differences and they completed the *Girl* CD, released in 1996 on the Rounder label. Around this time, Big Bucks Burnett announced himself as president of the Tiny Tim Fan Club (with 200 members). He issued the *Tiny Tim Times*, a small newsletter. He also claimed to house the Tiny Tim Museum in Dallas Texas. But when I asked Tiny, he didn't seem to know anything about it.

'A Tiny Tim museum?' he said, 'Mr Sharp's house - I don't know anywhere else'. (21)

Leave Me Satisfied

In 1989 Tiny recorded the single, *Leave Me Satisfied,* for Gordon Stinson's NLT Records. Australian fans did not pay much attention to Tiny's newest US recordings like, *Mr Ed, Tiptoe/Resurrection, I'll Never Get Married Again* and *The Chicken Dance* - but the first-rate production of the Country-flavoured *Leave Me Satisfied* caught everyone's attention. Martin was sent a promotional copy. As far back as 1968, Tiny's potential as a Country singer had been noted by Richard Perry. (22) Stinson had caught the same vision. He produced an album of Country songs titled *Leave Me Satisfied*. (23)

Two years later, I visited his studio in Burns Tennessee, a small town (population 1500) outside of Nashville. The studio is a third-class construction with first-class equipment. For the album, Stinson hired the best session players, best photographers, best of everything. Tiny spent three months living in Burns, a place similar to Gleason Tennessee, the location for *Blood Harvest*.

One of the tracks was the Buck Owens song *Tiger By The Tail*. Owens agreed to perform the song alongside Tiny on television. Stinson organised the video shoot, which included Tiny singing *I Wanna Get Crazy With You*. Further promotions included Tiny being awarded the keys to the City of Kentucky, and being made an Honorary Colonel by Colonel Sanders of KFC fame.

The single *Leave Me Satisfied/I Wanna Get Crazy With You* entered the charts at No 88 with a bullet, which was the first time Tiny had charted in America since the glory days.

Footnotes:

1. Kate Fitzpatrick, *Sydney Morning Herald,* 3 September 1983.
2. Tiny Tim, interviewed by Caroline Jones, *ABC Radio*, 25 October 1978.
3. Harold Stein, interview with Lowell Tarling, 1 April 2002.
4. Tulip Stewart, interview with Lowell Tarling, 2 April 2002.
5. Sue Khaury, interview with Lowell Tarling and Michael Wilkinson, 1 April 2002. Sue said, 'He always said in many ways he was a great admirer of beauty and glamour. I'm not the glamour type, the other two (ie. Miss Vicki and Miss Jan) were'.
6. Tiny Tim, interview with Lowell Tarling, 4 October 1991.
7. Sue Khaury, interview with Lowell Tarling and Michael Wilkinson, 1 April 2002
8. Tiny Tim, interview with Lowell Tarling, 4 April 1992. Also, Michael O'Regan, *Sunday Telegraph*, 24 August 1986,
9. Tiny Tim at the Circus Royale, taped by Lowell Tarling, 7 September 1983. Also, Michael O'Regan, *Sunday Telegraph*, 24 August 1986,
10. The Tiny Tim/Campervan Beethoven session was recorded (26 October 1986). A bootleg recording is available, with some degree of difficulty.
11. Tiny Tim, interview with Lowell Tarling, 24 August 1982, and Michael O'Regan, *Sunday Telegraph*, 24 August 1986.
12. *Blood Harvest* had a limited release in 1987, again in 1992. After Tiny's passing, and with the development of online purchases, the 2002 release reached a bigger audience. It is available on DVD.
13. Sherry Horowitz Stein, email 18 March 2013.
14. Tiny Tim & The Time Machine 2, *The World Professional Non-Stop Singing Record,* 3-cassette deluxe edition, 1988. Also, Tiny Tim, interview with Lowell Tarling, 4 October 1991.
15. *Evening Argus,* 28 May 1988.
16. Martin Sharp, Letter to Lowell Tarling, dated 8 October 1988.
17. Sue Khaury, interview with Lowell Tarling and Michael Wilkinson, 1 April 2002
18. *Evening Argus,* 28 May 1988.
19. Ernie Clark, interview with Lowell Tarling, 30 March 2002.
20. James Big Bucks Burnett, liner notes, *Girl* CD, 1996.
21. Tiny Tim, interview with Lowell Tarling, 4 October 1991.
22. Richard Perry, interview with Lowell Tarling, 1 April 2002.
23. Tiny Tim, *Leave Me Satisfied,* NGT Records. The tracks are: *Leave Me Satisfied, Any Time You Need Some Lovin', Tiger By the Tail, Everytime I Get to Dreamin', Business of her Own, I Wanna Get Crazy with You, That Old Country Waltz, Put Me on Your List of Easy Lovers, Atlanta, When You Leave (Don't Slam the Door).*

14

In Search of Tiny Tim

Before Jim Morrison became a star he offered me a song that he wrote. It was called, People Are Strange. And the next week Light My Fire was a big hit.
Tiny Tim

In September-October 1991 I take a trip to America, in search of Tiny Tim places. And because the *Leave Me Satisfied* album has stalled, Martin asks me to suss the situation.

So I check into the Opryland Hotel in northeast Nashville. I hire a Pontiac car, get a driver called T-Bone (a story in itself) and after a couple of days sightseeing, T-Bone and I head for Burns, a straggly little place, with horses, paddocks and barns, an hour and a half out of Nashville.

Gordon Stinson is the man I want to meet, the executive producer and owner of the *Leave Me Satisfied* package. The house is the recording studio. He lives in a trailer, which has Southern décor, like red velveteen upholstery and as much gold-coloured trim as possible. Maybe he's got a wife, maybe he hasn't, I can't tell. Stinson wears rhinestones and the biggest belt buckle I've ever seen on a small man.

It's a goodwill mission. I aim to find out why the album is no longer available and if there's anything that Martin can do to help? However, Stinson and I are at cross-purposes. To me, it's an exploratory visit, to him – it's a sell-job. Stinson wants sell 50% of the *Leave Me Satisfied* project (ie. video, single, album, tapes and marketing) to Martin for $75,000 for a 50 per cent share, despite no cooperation from Tiny.

Stinson shows T-Bone and me precisely where Tiny recorded. He explains Union Master Scale and shows all his receipts. I mention there are three names listed as producers on the album, B Bishop, JS Brown and GD Stinson? He shrugs it off, replying that he is the sole owner of NLT Records, 'but would need 15 days to check with his people' before we can conclude the sale. What sale?

Next, he screens some promotional videos, underscoring that he's got Buck Owens – the legend himself – accompanying Tiny on guitar, performing *Tiger By The Tail* on national TV. That's quite a coup, giving a lot of legitimacy to the song that was a smash hit for Buck Owens and his Buckaroos in 1965. It reached No 1 on the Billboard Country Charts and No 43 on the Pop Album charts. *Leave Me Satisfied* was the last vinyl record Tiny ever cut. After this, it was all CDs.

'Ah'm telling you this Loll (*ie. Lowell*) so you can see we did everything right - right down to his Tony Lama boots. But,' says Stinson - unaware that I tape everything to do with Tiny and am running tape right now - 'How often does a Tiny Tim single chart? It charted, and ah pulled it.'

'Why the hell would you do that?'

'Ah did it because ah felt Tiny was being most unreasonable in not promoting the LP.'

'Doesn't sound like the Tiny I know.'

'How well do you know Tiny?'

'I'll be seeing him this week in New York.'

'Well, you tell him from me ah'm ready when he is. Ah love the man!'

'I'll talk to him, as well as to Martin, but there's nothing to talk about if there's no relationship between you and Tiny.'

'Yes siree, ah love the man, but ah'll never work with him again.'

'Sure you would,' says T-Bone who has been silent the whole time.

'Okay, maybe I would.'

'Can we patch up the past?' I ask.

'You can try,' Stinson replies.

'What's the problem?'

'Oh Lord, he says ah owe him money.'

'How much?'

'$1500.'

'Is that it?' Apparently so. 'When I talk to Tiny, what do I say about the $1500?'

'Ah love the man, tell him ah'll do the right thing.'

'No worries then, I've got your drift.'

'Good boy! And tell Mart'n that if there's anyburdy that's got kernfidence, Loll, you know by now ah must have – because you have seen it from the inside-out. In fact you and T-Bone know more about the working of what ah have in preparation than does Tiny himself! That's fact er the matter. But ah believe Loll, we can stir up one heck of a kermmotion. Ah jess want to make sure that ah am dealing with honesty. An ah feel that if you and Mart'n would assist in guiding me, Mart'n would not allow an unscrupulous decision being made on my part in Orstralia. He too wants to see the best for Tiny…'

'That's all mighty interesting, Gordon. You get together the $1500 and I'll talk to Tiny. We'll do what we can from Australia and we're back in business, right?'

'Raaht own!'

We shake, then T-Bone and I are outta there.

'Whoo-hoo!' I yell speeding down the highway. 'I've just about patched everything up between Tiny and Stinson!'

'Ah doan think so,' says T-Bone.

'You heard him – he's gonna pay Tiny – then we're all back on track.'

'Is Martin gonna to buy a half share?'

'Pro'bly not.'

T-Bone shakes his head and says, 'You jess doan understand Good Ole Boys…'

In the afternoon, I phone Tiny who is pleased that Stinson has promised to cough up the money by the end of the week.

But Tiny adds, 'We'll see it when I get it. But there will be no cooperation between us until I receive the money. It's a question of honour Mr Tarlin. I know he loves me. But let me tell you about Mr Stinson.

'He did send me a cheque for $1500 – and it bounced. Unfortunately I cannot go to the Garden Checking Cash Company again even though I did nothing wrong. I have a mental block because that cheque bounced and I had to pay from my mother's account back in 1988. I talked to him about it and he promised to send the money but he never did. I tell ya, as soon as he returns the money, I'll buy him a pitcher!

'I'll take this to the courts of Heaven!' Tiny continues, 'Because when he returns the $1500 out of principle, we got no more problems. I'll get on that album quicker than he can breathe!'

We agree to catch up in New York this coming Friday afternoon.

One Wonderful Moment's Time

A few days later I fly to New York and check in at the Wellington Hotel on 7th Street just up from Carnegie Hall. The television doesn't work. The cooler doesn't work. I have a single bed and not much else. The cleaner says 'shu' for 'you'. Like 'Shu want a towel?'

I catch a cab to Greenwich Village and find *Café Wha?* 115 MacDougal Street where Tiny and Bob Dylan hung out a bit in 1962. I talk my way inside and stare at the stage where Tiny, Dylan and Hendrix have performed, until a bouncer asks me what the hell I am doing there? And escorts me out. Then, at 1.00 in the afternoon, I head to Hotel Olcott to meet Tiny, the only person I know in New York.

When I visited him in New York, Tiny couldn't understand why I wasn't eager to photograph him. 'My tool of trade is the tape recorder Tiny,' I said, 'I leave the camera work to real photographers - like William Yang, Jon Lewis, Greg Weight and Dave Newland...' (all of whom took classic shots of Tiny in Australia). Yet, he insisted. So I bought a disposable camera across the road from the Olcott Hotel, came back - and snapped this.

*

He comes down the lift and looks great in a red-zip top jacket, grey – near white – elastic topped trousers and awful footwear, as usual. Yes, he is carrying the trademark calico bag. Yes, probably with an alarm clock in it. He takes me to the Olcott Eatery, orders a pitcher of beer for himself and food for me. He also orders cornbread – plus 10 corncobs and coleslaw to be sent to his room. While we talk, he nibbles the corn bread, which is the first time I have seen him eat anything.

'Mr Tarlin, I can't complain. You know, it's *One Wonderful Moment's Time,* words that are so true – especially here. *I'd trade all of my years for one wonderful moment's time.* That was written by Shelley Cohen – may he rest in peace – who died in a drowning accident. Miss Bronwyn was one wonderful moment's time. I forget the name of the club in Sydney. Was it Kinselas? It was right in the heart of Sydney?

'It's been re-named, *Mars.'*

'Well she took *me* to Mars. She came in from nowhere. It was the second show. It was as if the Good Lord said, *This is what you want. I'm giving her to you for one moment.* One wonderful moment's time – but be careful. She was like a diamond. She was everything I dreamed of. That was one wonderful moment's time.

'The early times just in Australia alone were Miss Cameron in 1976 in Martin Sharp's house – one wonderful moment's time! Going back to the 40s – be it from Audrey Dash in 1942, to one of the greatest of the 60s, Catherine James. And Marilyn Rosenberg – they were all one wonderful moment's time. And I've had these moments with only one stipulation: Look but don't touch unless you're going to marry.'

Tiny's in good form. He pays for my meal, which he really should not have done. Then he takes me up to his dingy little flat. Along the way, he tips big – like $5 or more for whoever presses the lift button. Every time he even talks to a porter, he hands over a bloody note! Shouldn't that be the other way around?

His quarters comprise kitchenette, small lounge sitting area – where his mother slept when she was alive – and his bedroom. In his bedroom, a large bed, dressing table packed with cosmetics, a phone near his bed and not much else. No memorabilia. He pulls out a 1976 *Oui* magazine from the top drawer of his bedside table and opens to Miss Vicki's nude centrefold. When I visit them, most people don't show me nude shots of their ex-wives. At least, not for openers.

We discuss how we should spend our afternoon and agree that if I hire a limousine for two hours, he'll show me his childhood places. Then he calls reception and places the call for the limo in a camp voice. *Hello, this is Tiny Tim here…*

The limo arrives. Arvie is our driver's name and he follows Tiny's directions.

'Ah Broadway,' Tiny sighs, 'This is where the late *George Gershwin* used to live in 1919. *Ted Lewis* – one of the kings of jazz in 1919-1929 also lived up there. Also *Frankie Lyman* of the *Teenagers* lived up there. And the late great *Freddy Prinze,* who used to be a star in the 70s. *George Raft* used to dance at the *Autobahn Ballroom* in 1922. So we're passing a neighbourhood where a lot of celebrities from 1918 lived.'

'This is Upper Manhattan?' I ask.

'This is Mid-Lower Manhattan. Upper Manhattan is where we are going. Over here is the *Beacon Theatre* where they still have Rock acts but back in 1940 it was a movie house. In fact everything here was movies back in the late 30s and the 40s when movies were the biggest thing in the world.

'In 1935, this was one of the greatest neighbourhoods in this country. Back in 1937 the greatest comic strip in the world was *Dick Tracy*. Ooh, there was nothing but Dick Tracy! I was one of the few that did not like him. My favourite comic in 1937 was *Mutt and Jeff. Nancy* by Ernie Bushmiller. I don't know if you remember Nancy? And also I liked *Loony Tunes* with *Porky Pig* and *Bugs Bunny*.

'Anyway, this whole area here in 1935 was strictly movies and the chicken-type markets. Now we're heading into Harlem. These project homes were starting to be built in 1957. The blacks started to settle here from 1904, but by 1920 a good portion of blacks were already situated in Harlem. *The Cotton Club* was near here, I don't know exactly where. By 1920 this was really starting to move. My mother used to work around here in 1955.'

We drive a little further.

'I used to go to school right over here in 1937. I went there for about six months in 1936-37. I used to live on Amsterdam Avenue at 147th Street. This is 141st Street, right? We're talking 1935-36, mostly everything was white up here. Over there where it says *Beverages* was the *RKO Hamilton*. That's where I saw *Snow White* in 1937. It was a great theatre at the time, it's all gone now.' And then he points to shady characters on the pavement and adds, 'You're also passing the biggest coke area in this country. This is the biggest uptown coke area in the world.'

'What about Greenwich Village?'

'Not Greenwich Village! You might find transients down there, but over here is the biggest coke-drug area in the whole world.'

'So if I walked here I'd get beaten up?'

'If you walk around here you have a wing and a prayer and good shoes to run, ha ha ha!' he laughs at me and points out the window.

'You know, this store used to be here for years under another name. This was here for over 50 years. Unbelievable but it's true. That Candy Store that says *Toys and Cards* – the original owner was here since 1935. And it's still here! This is the *American Indian Museum* on the left here. Over there, down there is *Sugar Lane* – used to be a beautiful territory. The very wealthy used to live down that area.

'This is West Broadway. *The Olympia Florist* was here for more than 60 years. When Rudi Vallee was a star in 1931, this place was here. The Olympia Florist is a landmark of this area. Now as you go beyond 162nd Street, here's where I lived in 1942. In 1941-42 this is where I bought early issues of *Marvel Comics, Planet Comics, Jungle Comics, The Ranger, Captain America* and *Prize Comics*. In 1940 comics were the biggest thing in this country – now Mr Arvie, if you don't mind we'll turn left here.

'This is where I lived. This is the block I lived on. I lived in this white house here with my parents – may they rest in peace. I lived here from '42. My parents lived here at 601 West on 163rd Street. This is the place. Two houses here on the right hand side was where George Gershwin lived for a while in 1919. This is 601 West, 163rd. That's exactly where I lived from 1942 to 1967. My parents lived here til 1981. Right here.'

'That door?'

'You can take a picture if you want, Mr Tarlin.'

'You've got a good memory,' sparks Arvie, joining in at last.

'Thank you, you can't forget certain things. Things that are close to you, you can't forget', Tiny replies.

'You born in New York?' Arvie asks.

'Yes.'

'Cos you know better it than me.'

'Where are you from?' Tiny asks.

'Israel.'

'Listen, if I went *there* I wouldn't know anything!' Tiny laughs.

'Charleston Court?' I read, above the pale blue lintel.

'Yes. At one time it used to have elevator men. It used to have everything. And I used to live in Apartment 1B and then we moved up. In fact, I think this is the original gate, which was put in here in 1950. This whole area was very wealthy, of course it's all changed. Down here is where I played Curb Ball. I used to hit it off the stoop, a little curb – four on a team. I'll never forget it.'

'I'll never forget it either, Tiny!' I exclaim, amazed to be taking a snap of one of the places I'd read so much about.

'Turn right here and we're going up to Broadway again where I will show you some very historical mementos. I had friends in this block too, they used to call me *Herbie* ha ha ha. Wow, they used to call me Herbie! They left me out of the games, but so what? Who cares?'

'You were here from 1942-1967?'

'Yes.'

'You travelled from here to Greenwich Village to play gigs?'

'That's right.'

'How?'

'With a subway. But this has all changed now, boy has it changed! On the right you see the famous *Autobahn Ballroom*. This is where Malcolm X got shot in 1965. It used to be the most famous movie house in the Heights.'

I see a great big building with white pillars, boarded up. There is a Cuban flag, a Rasta flag and some other red, white and blue flag that I don't recognize. Messy graffiti tags the building.

'Did you see that sign - Malcolm X Lives?' I point.

'I missed it', says Tiny, 'but that's where George Raft danced. On the left side this used to be the *Yankees Stadium* back in 1902.'

'They're the Bad Guys, right?'

'Well, to me they are. Back in 1945 this was the most prestigious building of its kind. It's all changed as you can see. It all used to be Jewish here. Jewish and Italian. We're in Upper Heights. I can show you where Dr Ruth still lives. Dr Ruth is the famous sex doctor. She's about 85 and talks of sex.'

He shows me a church in Edgecombe Avenue where he met a beautiful girl in 1935. He shows me where Reverend Ike preaches, where he saw Errol Flynn in 1940, where the RKO Coliseum was, the site of the old *Heights Theatre,* the location of the Stamp Store and the George Washington High School from which he was expelled for calling the headmaster an 'old man'.

Then he's not so sure. There's a long pause. Eventually Tiny indicates to Arnie, 'We're going to my wife's house, then to 42nd, and then up to where I was discovered on 46th'.

'Have you and Miss Jan ever lived together?' I ask.

'Well here and there, but never really,' he shrugs.

'You met her here in New York?'

'Sure did – 1983 at the Williams Club.'

As the streets of New York flash by, I decide to resurrect the subject of the aborted *Leave Me Satisfied* project, 'Stinson asked me to call him after seeing you, if that's okay with you?'

'Call him any time you want, it don't bother me.'

'I'll explain the problem about the money…'

'And he'll give you a million excuses. If you really want to make a call, you call Bernie Bishop. He's listed in the book in Dixon Tennessee. You want the real story, you call Bernie Bishop.'

'Stinson told me that he has poured $150,000 into that project.'

'Call up Bernie Bishop and see who put the money up.'

'T-Bone was there when he said it, Stinson told me to tell Martin that he totally bought out Bernie Bishop's rights to the record?'

'Maybe he did, maybe he didn't,' Tiny shrugs. 'But Bernie Bishop was the main money-man. Who's T-Bone?'

'Well, I reckon I should give Stinson a call, if that's okay with you.'

'Please. He's a fantastic talker. Be careful yourself. He sounds good when he talks. But it's *deeds* that count and there's no $1500 here. It's a matter of principle. When he puts it down, we start to talk.'

'He should do exactly that and then release *Tiger By The Tail*,' I enthuse.

'That's one of the best ones on the album. He's a brilliant man. Another genius,' Tiny sighs. Then he addresses Mr Arvie, 'We'll turn on the right side of 42nd Street and we'll go up to Miss Jan's block, then I'll show you where I was discovered on 46th…'.

As we approach Miss Jan's building, Tiny looks increasingly nervous. 'Right here – 257! Where this white building is…' (There's a guy having a smoke on the sidewalk.) 'Oh-oh, this guy may be waiting for her…who knows who she's with? But that's where she lives,' he smiles uneasily. 'We can now turn right and go straight to 42nd about 7th Street towards 8th and I'll show you where I played Hubert's Museum. Sometimes called Hubert's Flea Circus, this legendary freak show is where Tiny featured as the Human Canary, which was his first paying gig – more than 30 years ago. 'Is Hubert's anything now?' I question.

'*Anything* is right! That museum was there since the 1920s. I got that job in 1957. That's when I sang with the high voice. Boy time flies.

'What happened to the other people who were there with you?'

'You mean the Elephant Lady? And the man who played *Anchors Away* on 10 glasses? And also Professor Hubert's trained Flea Circus – 25 fleas dancing to music – among other acts? They were freaks of nature.'

'What happened to them all?'

'I was there only a week, my friend…' he says, voice deepening. Then to Arvie, 'We'll now turn into 42nd. They play chess here on the streets. Now where it says *Private Booths, Peepland, Multi-video booths*…'

Tiny points to a dark-coloured building with gaudy lights and a big yellow and red eye as a logo - a type of sex joint, I think. There's nothing memorable about it, it's neither run down nor run up.

'That's where Hubert's Museum was,' he says as we pull over so that I can take a picture.

A young black guy spots Tiny Tim in the limo, 'Tiny Tim! Want some weed?'

'Oh, I never smoke that,' he replies with a brush of the hand. 'Thank you, ha ha ha.' And the dude goes away. We drive off too.

'Over here is the Port of Authority Bus Terminal. You want to keep away from that place. This is where the homeless have their homes, unfortunately in cardboard boxes. We're now going to Steve Paul's Scene, where I was discovered. This is 9th Avenue… no no, keep going … past that parking lot.

'And the Scene was …boy, where the heck was it? Keep going, keep going. This is where the Scene was, right here.' And he points to a black door next to a gift shop.

It looks like the side door of an Aussie pub where they roll in the beer barrels. It's couple of steps down from the sidewalk. There is plenty of dirt and graffiti on the walls. Pigeon shit everywhere. I can't imagine this place ever being trendy, then again – I never saw it from inside, in 1966.

'Yep,' Tiny sighs. 'Jim Morrison played here before he became a star. The Young Rascals too…this was the in-place'.

'How did you get along with Morrison?'

'Before he became a star he offered me a song that he wrote. It was called, *People Are Strange*. And the next week *Light My Fire* was a big hit. When he was here, you couldn't get in – even before he charted. The women would go crazy over him.'

'He was a very good looking man,' I admit.

'One of the best looking men I've ever seen. Unfortunately, he passed away. The Lord gives, the Lord taketh away, praise be the name of the Lord. I tell you … whatever the gift is, you have it for a season. Once it goes…?'

We remain together for a while, but the Dodgers, are playing tonight at 8.30 and he wants to watch the game alone.

Haw Haw Haw, Son

Back at the Wellington Hotel, I phone Stinson.

'Good evening Loll, how are you living son?'

'Like a monk - but let's not talk about my sex life.'

'Ah ha ha ha! Well you've got things timed right on the money, oh Lawd. Within the next couple of days I'm going to execute. Now Loll – if you can – make an attempt to speak with Mart'n.

'Here's what I would like to do once I get Tiny straightened out this week. I think it would be wise to work toward getting a reliable honest record label in Australia to pick up on it because I can furnish everything. I think we can all do well with this – Mart'n, you, me, Tiny – everybody – if it's handled totally above board and with an honest effort.'

'You're way ahead of me mate, what about the $1500 you're sending Tiny?'

'Just give me a couple maw days to see where my situation is. Legal work does not go rapidly,' says Stinson. 'Haw haw haw son, the other thing I am very aware of – y'know how Tiny is when you tell him something? Y'need to be reasonably accurate when you execute because he gets tripping on things. So you just sit tight until the close of the week and I shall call you when you get home to Orstralia. Meantime put your efforts into seeking an approved label in Orstralia. When you get home send me a kangaroo and a few koalas. Have you ever heard of a Darwin Stubbie?'

'I sure have.'

'I need about 10 of them now! Haw haw haw! I'll catch ya later.'

Footnotes

This chapter is taken from my September- October Diary written at the time. Also a 3-hour tape with Tiny dated 4 October 1991. And a taped conversation with Gordon Stinson, dated 21 October 1991.

15

1992 Australian Tour

Tiny is a survivor.
There wouldn't be too many that could put one over Tiny!
Dave Rowe, Australian tour manager

Stinson made the crazy assumption that Martin's financial resources were bottomless. The truth was, the film, concerts, recording sessions, hiring assistants, purchase of song copyrights for *Street of Dreams,* fabulous suits for Tiny, had all cost Martin around $2 million dollars. His house was on the line.

Financially speaking, Tiny's 1992 Australian tour came at a most inopportune time. Desperate for a royalty cheque from his Cream song, *Tales of Brave Ulysses,* Martin was under a lot of pressure, trying to hold the show together.

Martin's Scene, Wirian

While the promoters were responsible for Tiny's main bookings - when Tiny toured Australia, Martin always released a new album, got Tony to tailor a new suit, booked studios and session musicians for further recordings, organised film crew as needed, created a new Tiny Tim poster and booked a good venue (plus band) for a special concert, which was always a spectacle.

By this time, the people around Wirian were different from 1983. Les was married, living in Queensland and had stopped painting her clothes. Peter Royles quit drinking and moved to Goulburn NSW. William Yang moved out, Willy de la Vega moved in. Terry Stanton also moved in, a musician who understands carpentry. Yensoon was still around. People like light-artist Roger Foley (aka Ellis D Fogg) and comic Sandy Guttman (aka Austen Tayshus) dropped around, as well as Yellow House friends like Tim Lewis and others, like barrister Toto Renshaw. Me? I had a 9-5 job, financial pressure and a 5-year old daughter called Zoë, who wasn't quite sure who Tiny Tim was?

Tiny's 1992 Australian musos was essentially the same band used in the frantic 1983 *Highway To Hell* session. Then known as *His Majesty,* they changed to The Burgess Brothers Band - Denny Burgess (bass), Col Burgess (drums), John Bottica (guitar), Claude Woodward and Mac Lancaster (keyboards), with old faithfuls in the studio like Nathan Waks (studio production) and Al Jones (studio engineer). Tiny's other band was the cowboy band, the Prickles, whose meeting came about by chance. Five days before Tiny's arrival and with no connection to the tour, bassist Chris Löfvén, phoned Paddington RSL Club to enquire about Tiny's concert that he'd heard about. The booking person gave Chris, Australian tour manager, Dave Rowe's number. So Chris called Dave, told him the kind of music the Prickles played. Dave replied, 'We need that!' and invited the Prickles to meet Tiny and Martin at Wirian, nine days later. (1)

From out of nowhere, the Prickles were in. They were used for studio recordings as well as Tiny's backing band for the Country segment of his Paddington show, before handing the stage to the Burgess Brothers who handled the Rock. Around Wirian, Marilyn was still there, quietly working on the film. Martin's two main assistants were Miss Blazey who helped with publicity and Dave. Willy de la Vega sat up with Martin and talked things through, long into the night. And no one was crazy any more.

New York, New York

Back in America, though that excellent album, *Leave Me Satisfied* was dead in the water, Tiny was doing fine. He was still at the Olcott. Jim 'Mayor' Connolly was his current manager, and from 1991

Tiny starred in the *Ron Kurtz & Donnie Brooks' 30 Years of Rock N Roll* show. Remember Donnie Brooks - a star in 1960-61 with hits like *Mission Bell, Memphis* and *Doll's House?*

The rock n roll show guaranteed regular work. Tiny toured with former hit-makers Micky Dolenz (Monkees), The Tokens, Jewel Atkins, Al Wilson, Bobby 'Boris' Pickett (the *Monster Mash* guy) and of course Donnie Brooks himself. Commenting on the show, Tiny said, 'Micky Dolenz was on tour with me this year. There must have been three or four 19-year old women screaming after him. Every place we went they were screaming for him – 19, 18, 17, 20 were in the line waiting for him – wow, I tell ya. It became so wild that I went to Colony Music after the tour was over and bought a book of Monkees songs – maybe *I'll* have some luck!

'So right now I'm learning *Take The Last Train To Clarksville*. The last time I sang that song I got somebody about 80-years old! So Mickey Dolenz ain't crying. One girl came to see him from Florida, from Ford Lauderdale, she came all the way from Illinois and she went away again. I said, 'Boy if that girl came to my room I'd need a lot of prayer'. ((2)

Tiny also played spot bookings, like Hollywood High School, in April 1991, (a bootleg recording exists). Tiny sang all-American songs, a very different song list to Australian ears – *California Here I Come, Yankee Doodle Dandy, She'll Be Comin' Round the Mountain, America the Beautiful, God Bless America, I'm Coming Back to California...*

Tiny also did at least three good-paying ads. The Kenwood ad was self-deprecating, with the headline, 'True, Kenwood can make anything sound good...' then a photo of Tiny, 'But come on, we even have our limits'. Ha ha har. I never liked Tiny being presented that way, neither did Martin, Dave, or anyone else on the team, but it wasn't worth complaining. I'd learned that with Tiny - all publicity is good publicity. The Pepsi ad was better. Dave told me they paid Tiny $10,000 for that one. Plus he made another $5000 for the test run of an ad for Budweiser Beer. So Tiny was doing fine.

People Are Strange

In March 1992 Tiny comes to Australia for the eighth time - according to my calculations = 1971, 1974, 1976, 1978, 1979, 1982, 1983 and 1992. It was called the *People Are Strange* tour, after the song Jim Morrison had offered Tiny all those years ago at Steve Paul's Scene.

Tiny Tim arrives in the country! And I'm at work, not at the airport. I'm launching a new magazine called *Dynamic Small Business* (now, *Dynamic Business*). I can only get to see Martin and Tiny weekends or afterhours.

On the day of Tiny's arrival Dave urgently phones. Dave is in a panic because Tiny can't be driven in a small car to Radio 2UE. A small car doesn't look right and we own a Mercedes Benz that looks a bit like a limo. In the course of my writing career I haven't been asked to do many radio interviews, but tonight happens to be one of those nights. It's a telephone interview with Brian Wiltshire on Radio 2GB about the 'exciting new magazine' I am editing.

So I sit alone in my study, sipping wine, awaiting Wiltshire's call and constantly flicking from 2GB to 2UE to hear what Tiny has to say. Then comes the call and I tell Wiltshire's audience stuff like 'every big business was once a small business...etc', get him off the line and phone 2UE to congratulate them on playing Tiny. Somehow I go straight to air (twice on the one night!). I tell 2UE's listeners that Tiny is great – yay! - so the deejay gives me two free tickets to the Paddington RSL show, which Robbie and I are attending anyway. After that Dave accompanies Tiny to Melbourne. They return on the Saturday that I show up at Wirian with my 16-year old son Joel. We sit around the kitchen table with Terry Stanton Tim Lewis, his wife artist Bernadette and Miss Blazey. They are all sitting around as if waiting for something to happen. 'What's going on?' I ask.

'Well', someone explains, 'Martin is flat out at Australian Galleries, where his show *Sharp On Paper* is opening in nine days. Tiny is being interviewed in the film editing room by *Drum Media* and

Dave is managing the situation. Tiny's already done TV today – he was on the Ray Martin Show with Chad Morgan.'

Chad Morgan! There's a name!

Wearing the Mickey Mouse suit, Tiny finally comes out and Dave sees *Drum Media* out the front door. I say hi and Tiny warmly responds. Offering me his left hand he says, 'Mr Tarlin! Nice things always happen when you show up. Like, Miss Vicki phoned right after you left me at the Olcott in NY!'

'And this is my son, Joel…'

'What happened to your leg?'

Joel explains a skateboarding accident, so Tiny gives him medical advice. Dave briskly enters the kitchen and says they have to go. Having charmed everyone in the room, Tiny waves and says he'll be back in 10 minutes.

I chase after Dave, 'what's going on?' Tiny is on Clive Robertson's *The World Tonight* radio show. 'Ten minutes?' he laughs, 'fat chance!'

Interviewing Tiny

Before the week is out Joel and I return to Wirian to catch Tiny, who is running late.

While we wait, Martin, Joel and I talk to Tony the Tailor. His name is Tony Bechini, a Pitt Street tailor who employs 10 people. He makes clothes for showbiz people like the Delltones, singer Demi Heinz, everyone on ABC-TV, stage shows like *Nicholas Nickleby,* and *Les Miserables,* plus opera costumes. He loves opera. I find myself asking all these small business questions – now, after 30+ years in the business he doesn't need to advertise. Not only do people seek him out, he actually reprimands customers if they're not correctly wearing his suits! While we wait for Tiny, Martin gets measured for a new suit.

Tiny then arrives, flustered and embarrassed because he's late. Tony promptly whips out his tape measure and efficiently measures Tiny. 'There's a history there in the suits…' I express, suddenly realising that I should have kept track of how many? What years? And which of Martin's posters were printed on fabric and worn onstage?

Joel and I tinker around until all is done. Tony leaves, then Martin says he has to go back to Australian Galleries, and could Joel and I assist Tiny with 200 posters to be signed?

'Sure', Tiny replies, sounding exhausted at only 2.00 in the afternoon.

So we set up a production line in the hall, Joel picking up each poster and placing it in front of him, Tiny in the middle signing, and me on the right removing each signed poster and placing it on the stack. Signing 200 posters takes ages. It's difficult to run a good conversation under such circumstances. It's pick up, sign and place. Pick up, sign and place, 200 times. Poor Tiny, he starts to fall asleep. A young woman, who possibly lives here, brings Tiny a drink of tomato juice 'straight from the bottle', which lifts him a bit. Pick up, sign and place. Pick up, sign and place.

To keep Tiny awake, I play some songs on Terry's guitar, because he starts falling asleep while signing. Tiny wants me to keep playing, to keep him going. I hammer out *Da Doo Ron Ron* with enthusiasm that would wake the dead.

'Oooh yes!' Tiny laughs, waving his hand before signing poster 154.

King Bee gets us to 172. *La Mer* takes us to 189 – and seeing as that's the same chords progression as *Tiptoe* (C-Am–F–G7, as I play it), *Tiptoe* is the song I strum when we hit 200. (Orchestrated synchronicity doesn't count.) Then we're all done.

Having completed our task, I call for another round of drinks – tomato juice for Tiny, coffee for me, soft drink for Joel. Then the three of us move into the Dream Museum to talk on tape. As usual, he launches into his views on Jesus Christ, cancers, hysterectomies, S-E-X, etc. This time, I want his childhood – schools, cousins, parents, comics, first job, first kiss and what the heck started him playing ukulele? (Much of this conversation is incorporated into the first two chapters of this book.) Building on our drive through New York, I try to put flesh on the bones, and feel I mostly succeeded. I also try to get him to talk about Cousin Hal – who seemed to be his best childhood friend. And Cousin Bernie, who I didn't know anything about, even though they spent a lot of time together as kids. Auntie Leah, Tillie and Boutros of course. And then Pop culture - Superman comics, Miss Elizabeth Taylor, Mr Lenny Bruce, Captain America, Dick Tracey, Jack Benny, Mr Sinatra and a dangerous moment with Miss Betty Wallace.

'Mr Tarlin, you don't mind me saying this in front of your son?' he asks, moving to the topic of premature ejaculation. Joel appears agitated.

The Dream Museum setting is perfect for our taped conversation. All of Tiny's references seem to be around us - Popeye, theatre posters, Rudy Vallee's biography, Luna Park Marathon imagery, old comic books in glass cabinets. After two hours the tape runs out, though before leaving, Tiny and I play a few songs together with me on guitar, which we've never done before. Tiny produces his uke from his shopping bag and sings '*You are my sunshine…*'. He then asks for the guitar, and finishes the afternoon singing and playing that. I've never seen him play guitar.

Joel and I drive Tiny to the Savoy Hotel and go home.

Photo of Tiny in front of Michael Bell's 'Castanet Club/Tiny Tim' poster, at Wirian. I took a few snaps too, but Tiny seemed to sparkle more when my daughter got behind the camera.

Photo credit: Amber Tarling 1992

Sharp On Paper

It's another day at the office. Robbie picks me up at 5.00 and - along with 18-year old Amber, we battle Sydney traffic and arrive on time at Martin's exhibition, at Australian Galleries.

For us, this one is rather special, because Martin has painted Amber's portrait which is hung alongside big collages of Elvis newspaper billboards and Boofhead album cover designs for Regular Records.

Even without Tiny Tim's presence, Martin's always has a packed house on opening nights and this is no exception. The throng spills into Roylston Street. There are way too many people crammed into the gallery to stand back far enough away, to enjoy the pictures. We plan to come back another time to do that. Martin arrives with Tiny. Then, omigod, doyens of Australian art, Margaret Olley and Charles Blackman enter! There's a temporary hush, then a swell again

Inching his way through the pack, shaking hands along the way, Tiny makes his way to the microphone. After speeches, gallery director Stuart Purves introduces Tiny, who sings four songs, including one I'd never heard before, about an artist painting a portrait of a mother. *Paint her just as you find her, leave every wrinkle there...but my friend be careful, when you're painting that mother of mine!*

Then we all battle the crush of bodies and the heat of the room. Excellently dressed people are melting. Their make-up glistening with perspiration. Hello Garry and Judit, hi Jonny, nice to see you Tim, g'day John, Russell – I knew you'd be here, nice to meet you Andrew, hi Al, Victoria – how nice, nice to see you Clare, sure Dave - I'll drive Tiny to the Remo shop, Martin Fabiyni – pleased to meet you – I'm Lowell and this is my wife and daughter, and so on.

The *Mental as Anything* band are scattered around. And, Denny from the *Highway to Hell* session is there, with his shock of white/blonde hair and red leather jacket. It's all pretty frantic, after which we go home whereas Tiny returns to the studio with the Burgess Brothers Band and records the Billy Idol song *Rebel Yell* and a 25-minute version of Barry McGuire's song, *Eve of Destruction*. What a night!

Remo, Eternity & Tiny

Another day at the office, I drive to Wirian. Dave asked me to chauffeur Tiny to Remo's store in Oxford Street (a fashionable retail strip, in inner-Sydney) for an in-store appearance.

I pick Tiny up at Wirian, drive one suburb away to Paddington and pull up right outside Remo's store. I open Tiny's door, as any chauffeur would, Remo Giuffré is there to welcome him. Tiny gets out of the car and causes a minor traffic jam, which he doesn't appear to notice.

The store itself stocks according to Remo's tastes. Oddball things like Westclox fob watches, Tiger Balm, classy cutlery, 'statement' t-shirts and t-shirts featuring Martin's images, like Vincent van Gogh and Eternity. There's a huge Eternity picture hanging in Remo's shop window.

A couple of people from work come to see Tiny, who socialises a bit, signs autographs and good-naturedly agrees to being photographed wearing a sleeping mask for the Remo direct mail catalogue.

I drive Tiny back to Wirian, where I hang around with Tiny, Martin and Dave until way after midnight.

Tiny Turns 60

Tiny's age was always a bit of a mystery, even from those closest to him. After the Paddington RSL Concert, there was no longer any doubt. When the clock shifted to midnight and the calendar switches to 12 April 1992 – Tiny celebrated his 60th with a cake-cutting ceremony and a hall of 800 Aussie fans.

*

Nathan Waks introduces the Prickles who start us off with a hoe-down Country music set. There's a break, then Martin takes the mike and introduces Tiny. Dressed in a Mambo 'insect' suit, blue-patterned shirt and tie, Tiny walks onstage, blowing kisses. He performs another mini-marathon, a history of popular song, beginning with *Mr Phonograph*.

Oldies are enchanted by hits from their childhood, while the Emo-Generation seems fascinated by this white-faced troubadour who wears more make-up than they do. Robbie and I dance a bit then talk to a couple from work, who surprise me by attending. I go to the bar, order a couple more drinks, Tiny still hasn't taken a pause. This goes on for an hour.

Sensing that Tiny is peaking – and *When the Saints Go Marching In* is usually a clue - I move right down the front, where people are watching, gently dancing or waving their arms.

Roll Out the Barrel…Tiny rolls from song to song. *I've got a Loverly Bunch of Coconuts,* and there it is – *Tiptoe, Happy Trails,* back to *Tiptoe.* Then he stops. There is rousing applause, Tiny does a brief encore, then thanks Nathan, Martin, Dave, Mr Ellis D Fogg (who provided the light show) and the band.

Right then, a woman who calls herself Miss Josephine asks me to help her get onstage to kiss him. 'I guess it's okay,' I equivocate, 'singers seem to enjoy being mobbed'.

'I love his uke!' she remarks. Next thing, she pushes through the front row by herself, scrambles onto the stage, kisses him – he kisses her too – and she's gone. What was that all about?

There's another break then Tiny + the Burgess Brothers Band play a set of goodtime hard rocking music. Tiny is unrelenting, working and working, with white-haired Denny on bass, striding the stage and grinning, knowing everybody is having a good time.

At midnight a cake comes out and Tiny's celebrates his 60th birthday with Martin, a cast of musicians, assorted celebrities, friends and fans.

While this is going on inside, out in the street Martin's car is broken into and Tiny's ukulele (a 'Martin' uke) gets stolen. Also Martin's professional Walkman, its microphone and song lyric sheets. When we talk about it later, Martin questions me about Miss Josephine.

'Did she actually mention the uke?' he enquires.

Next day, Martin organises the purchase of a new Martin uke, because Tiny cannot be without one. Terry writes a press release about the whole saga. And Martin plays us the recording of *Rebel Yell* that Tiny laid down with the Burgess Brothers Band last night. Also, a 24-minute beldam-esque *Eve of Destruction.*

A couple of days later, I rush across to Wirian where I chat to Roger, Dave, Terry, and a New Yorker called Chris who has been flown out by the *National Enquirer* (USA), to write about Tiny's Australian escapades. After that, Dave and I go eat somewhere and he talks to me about travelling to Melbourne with Tiny. With Tiny, he says, one constant theme is that he definitely wants to 'make it twice'.

Dave tells me of rather jovial moments together, a side not often seen by others. One evening, the two of them were sipping beers and Dave turned to Tiny and said, 'You don't have to spell out s-e-x, you could just say the word…'

'Haw haw haw, I couldn't Mr Rowe.'

'Just say it – sex. And *breast,* it's just a word.'

'Oh no, Mr Rowe…' Tiny flutters.

'Or cunt!' Dave suggests.

'Oh! Oh! Oh! Mr Rowe! Never!'

Later, Dave and I attend the Tiny Tim recording session at Festival Studios. Next day, a change of pace from Rock to Country, Tiny records a 12-hour session with the Prickles, at Powerhouse Studio Alexandria.

Bassist Chris Löfvén says, 'We had a discussion with Martin about the recording studio, because Regular Records had dropped the idea of paying for it. On the 16th we go to the studio. The session started at 4.00pm. Doug Henderson was the studio manager. Nathan Waks was the producer. We laid down seven tracks with Tiny: *In the Middle of the Night, In My Backyard, I'll Never Get Married Again, I Know God Still Loves Me, Banjo Picker's Wife, Courage My Friend* and *Bobby McGee*. The session ended at 4.00am.' (3)

And then Easter. On Easter Sunday I do chauffeur-duty again and drive Martin, Miss Blasey, Peter C and Tiny to the Norths V Easts NRL football game in North Sydney. As far as I can tell, none of us know enough about the game to explain it to Tiny.

We arrive. I get privileged parking. We walk through Norths' changeroom. On seeing us, footballers in underpants stop getting dressed and greet Tiny. Then someone leads Tiny one way, and someone else ushers us to our seats. After a few preliminaries, one of the football executives makes an announcement before Tiny walks onto the stage, in the middle of the North Sydney Football Oval, and sings about American Football.

Tiny gets his ukulele back today, found in the rubbish at the back of Kinsela's. Everything else remains lost. Two days later, Tiny flies home. He returns, only to find the bookings have - after all this time - dried up, which makes it increasingly difficult for him to pay his rent at the Olcott Hotel.

I call on Martin who is exhausted. He expresses some disappointments about the tour, but great enthusiasm for the song *Courage My Friend,* recorded with the Prickles. Dave tells me that although Martin's finances have been dented, there's a royalty cheque on the way.

'Don't go worrying too much, Lowell', Dave adds, 'Martin always comes out on top'.

Miss Tulip

In October 1992 Tiny spent time with Miss Tulip and the meeting went well. The *National Enquirer* dramatised the reunion under the headline, 'Tiny's Desperate Plea To Daughter…Please Forgive Me'. (4)

Miss Tulip was doing fine. After a spell as a rebellious teenager - giving birth to Charisse (Tiny's first grandchild) at the age of 16 - she adopted the Jehovah's Witness faith and so in a sense inherited her father's religious nature. Her musical interests though didn't follow her father's. She runs more towards Rhythm & Blues than Swooner-Crooners. (5)

Footnotes:

1. Chris Löfvén, interview with Lowell Tarling, 25 June 2005.
2. Tiny Tim, interview with Lowell Tarling, 4 October 1991.
3. Chris Löfvén, interview with Lowell Tarling, 25 June 2005.
4. *National Enquirer,* 22 June 1993.
5. Tulip Stewart, interview with Lowell Tarling, 2 April 2002.

This is a photo of Tiny recording the Rock album. It was meant to be fluorescent in its original design. That didn't work out. I didn't have the fluorescent inks and I couldn't get that effect.

Martin Sharp, 22 October 2003

16

Eve of Destruction

It's braver if I go and better for the business if I go, because even though I may have to be the sheep
for the night, when it passes they can say, that man was nasty
but he kept his composure and he kept the image.
Tiny Tim

Although he didn't have many bookings when he returned to New York, Tiny had several recording opportunities, unfortunately the kind that don't yield significant royalties. The vinyl era was over, it was all CDs now.

Big Bucks Burnett had come back into the picture, successfully resurrecting the *Girl* project. Martin's *Rock* album was about to be released. There was another idea on the table, a good one - tribute album of Russ Colombo songs. Tiny had been talking about it to his friend, Jim Foley, who was getting plans underway to make it happen. (Three years later, Foley would be the recipient of Tiny's last phone call.)

And while listening to the Danny Bonaduce Show, someone called Pink Bob got enthused about Tiny. Pink Bob started playing through Tiny's back catalog and wanted to record him for his label, Ponk!

And then - Des Moines.

Des Moines

Stephen Plym ran an event management company from Des Moines Iowa. He booked celebrity hosts for baseball events, people like Clayton Moore (the Lone Ranger) and boxer Joe Frazier. Plym admits he regarded Tiny as a 'national joke' in the early 70s when he was a star. Nevertheless, Tiny was a 'wild and zany, a guest host who would positively shock people' so Plym called him up to host an event.

Tiny misunderstood the nature of the gig, he thought Plym was asking him to *play as a team member*. Wild with excitement, he agreed. Somehow Tiny wound up on the baseball pitch as a player. He was so funny, dropping catches, pitching easy balls and scurrying from base-to-base. The audience went wild!

And that is how Tiny – dressed in a Mickey Mouse suit and tie – made regular appearances at baseball stadiums in Des Moines, pitching, catching and batting. Ticket sales went through the roof. The players and the crowd laughed themselves silly, as Tiny missed easy strikes and ran the bases in little stutter steps. (1)

Meanwhile, back in New York, something wasn't right. Going back to Tiny's original contract with Frank Sinatra's Reprise label, back to the days of Caesar's Palace, there had always been whispers that Tiny was being managed by the Mafia.

Alarmed that he was being controlled by New York mobsters and in debt (presumably to them) in early-1993 Tiny fled his room in the Olcott Hotel in the middle of the night, leaving behind most of his possessions. He went to the mid-west city of Des Moines where Stephen Plym became his new manager during the darkest period of his career. Tiny appeared at Fireman's Fundraisers or alongside retired sporting heroes to sing for their cause at various baseball games. Sometimes he'd simply sing the national anthem. (2)

Notwithstanding a queue of four good albums somewhere in the pipeline: Martin's *Rock,* Big Bucks' *Girl,* Jim Foley's *Prisoner of Love* and Pink Bob's *I Love Me* – when he took on Tiny, Plym was the kind of manager who gave up before he started. About Tiny, he wrote, 'There was no question about it, he would never, ever, ever have another hit record'. (3)

In Australia, Tiny's *Highway to Hell* was released as a 'cassingle'. People have probably forgotten, but in the late-80s/early-90s the cassette was challenging vinyl, hence the cassette-single. A frantic film clip of the song was screened on MTV (worth a look on youtube). And Martin was working on *Courage My Friend,* to present to Tiny at their next meeting.

Also negotiations were taking place for a 1993 Australian tour. Tour promoter John Kannis planned to bring Tiny out, with Martin making a significant financial contribution. Even so, that was not enough to clinch the tour. They needed a third party to make it happen. That would be Australian rock band, the Hoodoo Gurus.

Big Bucks Burnett

Halfway through the year, Tiny picked up the phone and called Big Bucks Burnett, they patched up their differences, and Tiny went back to the studio and completed the *Girl* album, recorded again with Big Combo.

Big Bucks' side of the story runs like this, 'In mid-1993 Tiny unexpectedly called to explain his silence. His unrequited love for Miss Stephanie was too great to allow him to work with me, as my introduction of the two in 1988 had irrevocably forged she and I together in his mind like Siamese twins. If he could not have *her,* he could not bear to work with *me.* It all made perfect sense. Miraculously this situation reached a happy conclusion.

'After much negotiation, Tiny returned to Denton in August 1993. A special meeting with Tiny, Stephanie and myself produced an unlikely reconciliation and work on the album resumed. Tiny and Brave Combo worked their magic on a wide variety of songs, bringing new life to both the classic and the obscure. Stephanie even sang on *I Want To Stay Here.* (4)

Tiny had a sharper explanation, but it doesn't matter. (5) The point is, they patched up their differences and finished the *Girl* CD (released in 1996 on the Rounder label). On this album *That Old Feeling* is beautifully sung by Tiny and his backing vocalists, against his gentle ukulele strum. Martin played me that track around this time, and Tiny sure didn't sound washed up to me. It's one of my favourite Tiny Tim songs - right up there with the *Chameleon* LP. I don't know what Plym was thinking when he said Tiny was all washed up!

1993 Australian Tour

At the end of October, Tiny came to Australia for the 9th time. The tour was anchored by an 8-gig tour of five cities - Adelaide, Melbourne, Canberra, Newcastle and Sydney - in which Tiny would support the Hoodoo Gurus band. He also had a solo gig in Brisbane, and two in Sydney organised by Street of Dreams, which was essentially Martin and Dave now. Add to this, eight scheduled media events and the inevitable recording sessions with Martin.

The Hoodoo Gurus are a pop-rock band with punk sass. Their manager, John Kannis, got Tiny to be the Special Guest at all their venues. Martin and Dave reckoned it was singer Dave Fawlkner's idea. They said Tiny's take on *Highway to Hell* was the band's favourite song at that time. (6)

A group of us met Tiny at the airport, though he took so long coming through customs that we didn't get to greet him properly until after he'd settled into his room at the Savoy Hotel, Double Bay (near the Cosmo). We met up at Café 21, close to the Savoy, and agreed to another interview.

This time he travelled alone, without a manager. There was no accompanying Mr Plym (as there had been Messrs Hollander). Instead, Dave Rowe travelled around the country with Tiny, as a kind of personal manager. Two days after arrival, Tiny met the Hoodoo Gurus and their management and he expressed grave apprehensions that he would be heckled in the rock venues. They assured Tiny this could never happen, because the band would gradually join him and ultimately take over. Dave wasn't so …sure!

Meanwhile, Martin was considering his recording options. One idea was to create a *Twentieth Century Suite* from everything they'd recorded together - which I'd estimate being in excess of 300 songs, if you include the two marathons. Martin suggested, 'We'll just deal with the whole Twentieth Century through him, mixing all those songs in together. A collage sort-of effect, as a vehicle to put all those different styles.' Then he quickly added, 'This is just an idea'.

'He's very happy with this record', Martin continued, pointing to *Rock*. 'He's interested in the Rock stuff. I'm disappointed the cover wasn't printed in fluorescent colours, which it was meant to be and promised. But the quality of the sound is fine.'

Commenting on Des Moines, Martin said, 'Tiny's getting some support but he needs better management than he's getting. He's just keeping a roof over his head, playing a few gigs here and there. He hasn't missed New York. He's not complaining about it. It seems he's done quite a few recordings in America.

'The Olympic Games are coming up. Tiny would like to sing his marathon at the Olympics!'

A Week Later

Tiny played a difficult crowd at Selina's on the Friday night followed by Saturday night's roughneck crowd of 2000 Hoodoo Guru fans, which was impossible. Singer Dave Faulkner had originally agreed to introduce and personally endorse Tiny. In fact, Fawlkner might have cranked up the band and backed Tiny like they did in Canberra. He didn't do it, leaving Tiny to the surging mob with only his 'little ukulele in his hand' (to quote George Formby). His thin ukulele backing didn't impress the young yobbo crowd who only wanted kickarse rock.

A friend from my work was there in the mosh-pit - young James Tetley. He said the hostile crowd started hooting and chucking beer cans at the stage as soon as Tiny appeared. Poor Tiny struggled impossibly through his half hour set. 'Scary is exactly what it is,' said Tiny later, 'It's like going into the desert with only a slingshot. My ukulele sounds like four rubber bands'. (6)

Next day, Martin phoned me to borrow a video recorder, which I didn't own. But friends – the Levitch's – did, but didn't have the time to do the filming. But another friend, Pete Jensen knew how to work it and had no commitments. So Pete surprised himself by winding up in the studio at night, filming Tiny recording Jim Morrison's *People Are Strange,* the Rolling Stones' *Satisfaction,* and Neil Diamond's *I Am I Said.*

Next night, *Rainbow on the River, Satisfaction* (again), *St Louis Blues,* and another shot at *I Am I Said.* Pete stayed in the studio until 3.00am, shooting film.

Before returning to the States Tiny also recorded more Rock songs, this time with *Nitocris,* an all-female punk band. He also recorded tracks for a new idea - *Tiny Tim's Christmas Album,* as well as a 1993 Christmas message for his fans.

Album Launch

On Thursday night, 18th November I go to a ritzy 30-room mansion called *Iona,* around the back of Kings Cross, with Amber and her boyfriend, for the launch of Tiny's *Rock* album.

This is the Regular Records crowd, the Martin Fabinyi set. There are people associated with the Mambo Graphics surf and street clothing brand, the band Mental As Anything and their supporters, Japanese photographer Satoshi (with a connection to Japanese record label, Zero Communications). Also, photographer Robert Rosen, Mambo entrepreneur Dare Jennings, Rock people, film people, artists, bohemians. Martin, of course, is there.

It's another of those socialite-type occasions, with Tiny being introduced around the room and people keen to meet him. Amber and I hang out a bit with Dave. Talking to Martin is impossible in this throng, everybody wants to say hello Martin, hello Tiny.

The formalities are okay. Fabinyi launches the *Rock* CD, it pounds through the speaker system. Tiny plays a few songs and so do other musos. The weirdest moment of the night is when the almost-cartoonish backdrop (painted in vivid colours by Mentals/Dog Trumpet guitarist Reg Mombassa) peels off the wall and drops on drummer John Bliss, right in the middle of a song. Otherwise everything else goes according to Regular Records MD, Martin Fabinyi's plans.

Three Weeds

Let the tour organisers handle clubs, the Hoodoo Gurus and the Grace Brothers gigs. Martin always organised something special for Tiny. It was for Martin's own crowd, who by now had seen the Luna Park Marathon, Opera House Concert, Kinsela's concerts, Tiny's 60th and now this at an inner-city pub, the Three Weeds. Not a rough pub, one known for its folk/roots music and art connections.

One of Tiny's support bands is *Dog Trumpet*. I first heard they'd formed at Iona, where they performed Cream's song *Strange Brew* in their set. Over a drink, I found myself chatting to bass player, Peter O'Doherty, a real nice guy. Peter told me that he broke three tendons last night taking a piss in the bushes. It must have happened between sets because he supported Tiny last night too. Peter said that last night Tiny's ukulele got somehow broken, just before him going on. He explained that's why Tiny's uke is patched up with gaffer tape.

His Majesty's (Burgess Brothers Band) took the stage with energy. Denny strode the planks, clearly enjoying himself and smiling to brother Col on drums. *See See Rider* was a highpoint. Oh yeah.

When Tiny took the stage, the crowd (about 150) went berserk. Yay for Tiny! These were TV and radio people, like Monty the Channel 9 Weatherman and a deejay called Maynard. Reg Mombassa (ie. *Dog Trumpet)* was present too, along with many from the Mambo and Regular Records crowd. Martin's friends were there, Wirian people and friends from the Yellow House and other projects. Robbie was present, as well as seven people from my work. It was a packed house, all crazy for Tiny, Dog Trumpet and the Burgess Brothers Band.

But what should have been a triumph didn't turn out that way. I blamed the keyboard player - but what would I know? Robbie blamed the sound. Maybe the problem lay with Tiny himself, maybe something happened last night when his ukulele got hurt, maybe the Selinas gigs were fresh in his memory, maybe the mood was wrong, maybe he had Miss-Someone-or-Other on his mind, maybe he was worried about Des Moines, maybe he'd given and given and given, and maybe he was exhausted now.

We could see he was unhappy by the way he slumped off stage. It wasn't an exit I was used to. I raced backstage to see if there was a problem?

Martin and Dave were there, along with someone from Regular Records and a staffer from the venue. The crowd was yelling for an encore. Dave suggested he do it. He wouldn't. Why not?

'Because it's a *forced* encore', snapped Tiny. 'And you can leave', he said to the venue-person. He then turned to me, 'As for that interview tomorrow…' he said, 'I refuse'.

*

My mind flashed back. I saw myself in Bermagui back in 1982, having been instructed by the *Southern Flyer* editor to line up an interview with Tiny. After the brief, I got on the phone to Martin requesting Mr Hollander's phone number. I recalled squeezing in a question before Martin hung up.

'Has he got a sub-personality?' I asked.

'He has,' Martin replied, 'but I'll let you find it'.

I'd been searching ever since. I also recalled Tiny talking to me about never losing his cool in front of an audience, 'because they've knocked the star out of it...' he explained. And here, the star had momentarily been dislodged.

In that moment, Tiny gave me more than an interview. He gave me a sense of completion. I actually saw Tiny properly pissed-off. I saw the other face of Janus. Sure, I was a bit embarrassed, this happening in front of Bobby Dee from work, who'd accompanied Robbie and me backstage. But I felt good too, I felt like phoning Steve Elias and telling him that at last, the job was done. I'd gotten his *Southern Flyer* story more than a decade later.

And how did Tiny handle anger?

He dismissed everybody and isolated himself. When he'd composed himself, he came out.

Then off he went to Wirian with Martin and Dave - probably also Willy de la Vega, Jameson, Terry and whoever else wanted to join them. They sat around Martin's big kitchen table, Tiny strummed his bandaged uke, sang and laughed with them til 3.00am. All of which Martin taped, of course.

*

Martin summed up the tour like this, 'I think we got some great work done. As far as I knew he was the Hoodoo Gurus' special guest but they threw him on - just before them - with just his ukulele. He found it very tough. They're meant to be big fans, but they left him just with his basic instrument and the audience was getting a bit restless.

'I'm just hoping to do the *Christmas Album*. I don't know if there'll be anybody interested in putting it out. *Silent Night* is probably the best track', said Martin a few days after the tour. (7)

1993 Albums

The two albums released in 1993 were *Rock* (Regular Records) and *I Love Me* on Ponk.

Back in the States there was an illusion that Tiny had become a real has-been, whereas in reality there was a bank of records, five/six albums deep, that the world had actually never heard.

1. *Leave Me Satisfied*.
2. *Girl*.
3. *Prisoner of Love* (the Russ Columbo tribute album).
4. *I Love Me*.
5. *Rock*

Plus the *Christmas Album* somewhere in the can.

Ah, what more do ya want!

Footnotes:

1. Vivien Kooper and Stephen Plym, Tiny Tim and Mr Plym, p. 70, Edee Rose Publishing, California, 2004.
2. Sue Khaury, *Memories Of My Husband Tiny Tim*, 1998, unpublished.
3. Vivien Kooper and Stephen Plym, Tiny Tim and Mr Plym, p. 27, 59, Edee Rose Publishing, California, 2004.
4. James Big Bucks Burnett, liner notes, *Girl* CD, 1996. Ably backed by the Grammy-nominated Brave Combo, *Girl* is a collection of popular songs taken from all eras. They are: *Girl, Bye Bye Blackbird, That Old Feeling, Sly Cigarette, I Want To Stay Here, New York New York, Stairway To Heaven, All That I Want Is You, Stardust, I Believe In Tomorrow, Hey Jude, Over The Rainbow, Springtime In The Rockies* and *Fourteen*. The best track is *That Old Feeling*, and *Sly Cigarette* probably the most popular.
5. Ernie Clark, interview with Lowell Tarling, 30 March 2002. He said Bucks was playing him for a sucker and Miss Stephanie was the bait.
6. Martin Sharp, interview with Lowell Tarling, 2 November 1993.
7. Martin Sharp, interview with Lowell Tarling, 2 November 1993.

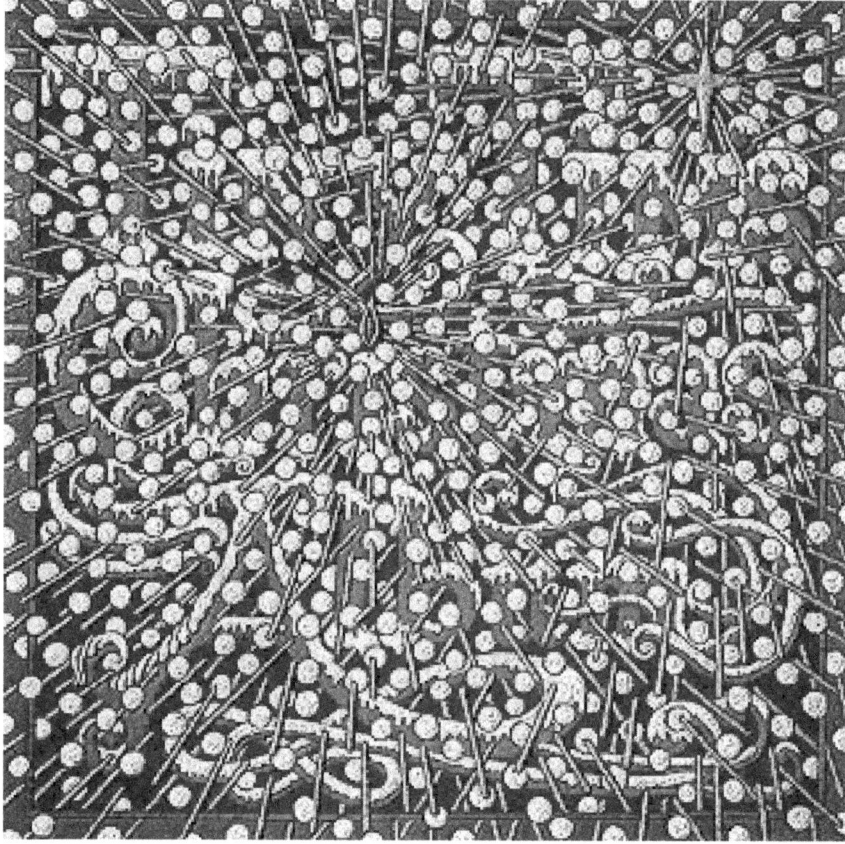

I'm tidying up Tiny's stuff, keeping it alive, hoping to release the Christmas Album. I don't know if anybody will be interested in putting it out. Silent Night is probably the best track. How Tiny brings Amazing Grace into a Christmas medley is also very interesting.

Martin Sharp 18 January 1994

Miss Sue

Two different people brought me news clippings saying Tiny was living in Des Moines Iowa in an old run down hotel. It had a very unflattering picture of him looking quite overweight and quite elderly, but I was still totally intrigued with the idea of meeting Tiny Tim.

Miss Sue

Des Moines is nothing like New York and Tiny's new manager Mr Plym didn't seem like a real manager. Friend? A promoter? A guy with an eye for gimmickry? Probably, bits of all three. Plym put together a conglomerate of Iowa business people who offered Tiny lodging and a guaranteed him a weekly salary of $1000 against future earnings. The deal quickly fell apart. Apart from the occasional celebrity appearances at baseball venues, Tiny was now very much alone.

From his lonely room at the Fort Des Moines Hotel, Tiny watched Robert Schuller's TV show *Hour of Power* – his favourite. For his public, Tiny played a sprinkling of celebrity bookings and did innumerable telephone radio interviews with shock-jocks like Howard Stern, who encouraged Tiny to be more and more outrageous on air. When Tiny's phone bill ran to $3000 in a 3-month period, his Iowa backers had his line cut off.

In Sydney Australia, Martin was pressing on with his *Street of Dreams* film and *Tiny Tim's Christmas Album*. In London, a young musician, David Tibet heard Tiny's *God Bless* album for the first time, and wanted more. In Dallas Texas, Big Bucks Burnett was holding together a 200-strong fan club and struggling to keep Tiny going. Big Bucks was looking for ideas, using his *Tiny Tim Times* newsletter to publicise Tiny's upcoming shows. But the career was definitely bottoming out. Martin wrote Bucks, 'Somehow we have all got to pull together to give Tiny our best support. I don't know how we can do this; perhaps we should hold a convention or develop an effective network'. (1)

Tiny was also quite out of touch with his family. Miss Tulip married Eric Stewart, but Tiny could not attend the wedding. Cousin Hal was living in Pennsylvania. Miss Vicki accepted his calls, according to her moods. Likewise, Miss Jan was sometimes too preoccupied to talk, and in April 1994 raised the prospect of divorce, which Tiny strongly opposed. 'Look,' he said, 'I am not getting a divorce. I did not give one to Miss Vicki and I am certainly not going to give you one'. But the divorce went ahead anyway. (2)

'You're in a room and nobody wants you…', Tiny told the *Washington Post*, '…you're afraid of getting put out in the streets because you can already hear the taunts, "Oh, there's a former star, look at him now folks. He was strange to begin with, but he finally got what he deserved".' (3)

Turning to the press for help, Tiny gave the *National Enquirer* the story they were after. Headlined, 'Down & Out In Des Moines' it upset Tiny's managers, because it made them look callous and unprofessional. How could the press do this to Tiny? Who leaked the story? Eventually the penny dropped. They figured out it was coming from Tiny himself. 'Who's gonna want to book you now?' they anguished.

The *National Enquirer* attracted a lot of attention to Tiny at this period. If it was a cry for help, it certainly worked, attracting two new people who would become important to his closing scenes, Miss Sue and Ernie Clark.

Ernie Clark, a fan from Tiny's *Laugh-In* days and a deejay from Battle Creek Michigan, read that *National Enquirer* article and speculated with a friend about seeing Tiny in concert, 'I wonder how we could get hold of him?'

Running with that thought Clark phoned the publication and was given a number for a Fred Farmer from Des Moines, which he called. A receptionist put him through and Fred Farmer answered. 'I was kinda hoping to talk to Tiny Tim…' said a disappointed Clark, into the phone.

'It's me!' Tiny exclaimed.

'I just passed out,' Clark laughed. 'At the time I didn't realise Fred Farmer was one of his aliases. I was a bit surprised'.

Clark and Tiny talked on the phone for almost three hours. Since then, Clark has gradually built up a library of Tiny Tim video, sound and picture archives, which in time became a second repository (like Wirian) for Tiny Tim material. Clark currently manages the Official Tiny Tim Memorial website (www.tinytim.org) which is well worth visiting. (4)

Miss Sue

Enter Miss Sue. She was wonderful. She turned the whole plot around. Instead of Tiny spending his final years in that lonely hotel, Miss Sue provided Tiny's story with a comfortable conclusion and – ultimately - a cathedral burial.

Miss Sue Gardner was an heiress. Her father, George Gardner, had built a tidy fortune from the production of pneumatic stapling, nailing guns and shrink-wrap. Tiny was her first crush. As a young teenager Miss Sue fantasised about marrying 'Paul McCartney, Paul Simon or Tiny Tim'. She had 55 pictures of Tiny on her bedroom wall. *God Bless Tiny Tim* was the first LP record she ever bought.

After leaving college, she made a big effort to find Tiny, but did not succeed. 'It's hard to maintain fever pitch when you don't have sight of someone, and he did disappear completely,' said Miss Sue, who finally tracked him down in 1995. (5)

Knowing her continuing interest in Tiny's career, friends drew Miss Sue's attention to the *National Enquirer* article, 'Down & Out In Des Moines'. She was living in Minneapolis at the time, and decided it was time they met. Miss Sue called his hotel, left a message and was astounded that he returned the call. He did so in a deep gravelly voice, with the words, 'This is Tiny Tim'.

Miss Sue effused how much she'd loved him as a teenager and, after a while, she asked if they could meet, to which he said, 'What do you look like? Are you slim?' She said yes. And although Tiny wasn't keen about her bringing her fiancé, Dennis Dungan, they set up a meeting. Along the drive, Dennis and Miss Sue joked about the chances of having Tiny sing at their wedding.

Strawberry Tea

Miss Sue, Dennis and Tiny met for dinner at Tiny's hotel. She initially felt Tiny looked old, but 'after five minutes' she stopped seeing that and became attracted to him again. And then, Miss Sue and Dennis found out the hard way that you can't go anywhere with Tiny without causing a sensation.

Sue described this occasion, 'Tiny did all the talking at the table. The people around us sat staring at their empty plates, eavesdropping. Then Tiny began to tell some ribald stories and they all got up and left. Dennis and I played with our food. We tried not to laugh, but Tiny talked on, oblivious to all. He was charming and polite, but he went into embarrassingly intimate details.' The ribald stories were about groupies. She asked him lots of questions.

Strawberry Tea was the song Miss Sue loved best on the *God Bless* album, and was disappointed to find out that her favourite song was a throwaway and Tiny was disinterested in it. He told her, 'They *made* me sing that one'.

After this the three of them retired upstairs to a room ('Not his room,' said Miss Sue, 'He didn't want us to see his, it was very squalid') and Tiny talked for six hours straight – about aliens, President Nixon, this and that. At one stage Miss Sue said she was tired, to which Tiny replied, 'If you're tired, you may lie on the couch, but I must go on!'

As they left, Tiny seemed totally keyed up about something and in an attempt to console him Miss Sue patted his left hand and said, 'It's okay'.

As they walked away from Tiny, Dennis said to Sue, 'So that's your dream boy, huh?'

She replied, 'Yes, he is'.

Dennis and Miss Sue saw Tiny again, at a Fireman's Benefit. While Dennis was gone Tiny started singing romantic songs and Miss Sue said that she got the feeling that she was been serenaded, to which she thought, 'This can't be?' As they drove off Dennis told Miss Sue, 'I think you're going to marry him and *I'll* sing at *your* wedding! From here began a courtship, with Dennis stepping aside for Tiny.

Having been granted a divorce from Miss Jan in the same year, Tiny and Sue were free to follow their own path. One day after kissing and petting, Tiny wanted to sing some hymns. Miss Sue said, 'I don't feel comfortable singing hymns when we've been messing around a little bit, I don't feel right about it'.

'There's only one thing we should do,' Tiny replied, 'we should get married!'

And so Tiny and Miss Sue announced their forthcoming marriage, which sparked a round of media interest, including appearances on Jay Leno's *Tonight Show*. (6)

Mr Clark

After a two-year telephone friendship, in August 1995 Ernie Clark met Tiny in person when he performed in Clark's hometown of Battle Creek Michigan. Clark described the show as three opening songs – one of which was, *Are You Lonesome Tonight* - before an extended medley.

In his shows, Tiny usually wore one of the several suits that Martin had designed for him over the years – perhaps the Mickey Mouse suit, the red-and-white stripe suit, the Sydney Opera House suit – and he would use the house band to enhance his ukulele backing. On this occasion it was a 3-piece band called *The Sinatras*.

The Sinatras were Clark's friends. He phoned the bandleader and said, 'How would you like to back Tiny Tim?' This floored them and they didn't at first believe him. Clark spoke to the bandleader and said, 'He thought I was joking. When he realised it was true he was thrilled to death!' (7)

Tiny's Favourite Tiny Album

Meanwhile two new Tiny Tim CDs were released on two different labels, and before the year was out there would be two more.

The first, *Tiny Tim Live In Chicago* released by Pravda/ Bughouse, was a live performance put to disc. There were a lot of CDs like this around now, if you knew where to look. Tiny was being taped in America and England, just as Martin had been doing for years.

Martin, or one of his assistants (sometimes me), had taped Tiny incessantly when he was in the country. The film editing room alternated as a studio where Dave transferred Tiny's live performances from cassette to CD. Not for bootleg release, but for archive purposes. We had Tiny live at Revesby RSL Club, live at Kinsela's, live with the Castanet Club in Newcastle, just lots of them. *Live in Chicago* is a bit like that.

For Tiny Tim aficionados, the songs are a retrospective of his albums: *Tiptoe Thru The Tulips, Great Balls Of Fire, On The Good Ship Lollipop, Highway To Hell, Rock Around The Clock, Are You Lonesome Tonight* and *When The Saints Go Marching In*.

Then, from the Vinyl Retentive label came, *Prisoner Of Love – A Tribute To Russ Colombo*. It was recorded 22-25 September 1994 in Tampa Florida and arranged, conducted and produced by composer of contemporary classical music and experimental rock musician, Paul Reller.

Associate Professor of Music at the University of South Florida, Reller got his BM from the University of Minnesota, and his Masters and PhD at the Eastman School of Music. He has also received many awards. Reller's understanding of 20th Century music made him ideal for Tiny, who had always wanted to record a library of albums, each dedicated to individual singers of the past. *Prisoner Of Love* is the Russ Colombo volume. Redolent of *Wonderful World of Romance,* Tiny is at ease with every song. Of the 10 tracks only three were regulars in Tiny's repertoire: *All Of Me, Prisoner Of Love* and *Auf Wiedersehen My Dear,* all of which usually featured in Tiny's marathon-medleys.

It's not Miss Sue's favourite Tiny Tim album. She said, 'I like *Chameleon* and *Wonderful World of Romance*, I think they're both of equal quality with the Warner Brothers material. But Tiny's favourite was his tribute album to Russ Colombo'. (8)

Important Troubadour

Meanwhile, Tiny's *Songs from an Impotent Troubadour* was released to CD. Documenting in song Tiny's enormous crush on Miss Stephanie was not music to Miss Sue's ears. The background to the release runs like this. After hearing his friend, Lloyd Wright, constantly describing Tiny as a 'genius', 24-year old hallucinatory Gnostic English musician David Tibet, purchased the *God Bless* album and he loved it. Not a person to enjoy his passions passively, Tibet wanted to do something about it.

Sensing his friend's enthusiasm, Wright passed on Big Bucks's contact details. Tibet joined the fan club, subscribed to the *Tiny Tim Times* and purchased everything he could. After a time, Big Bucks suggested, 'Why don't you try to speak to Tiny Tim?' So Tibet telephoned Tiny and they spoke at length. 'I think I got on well with him,' said Tibet.

Tibet wanted to deepen his involvement. He explained, 'This always happens when I become obsessed with an artist, then I want to release something by them and Bucks said, "Funnily enough I've got this thing that we did in a recording studio" which was this *Impotent Troubadour* album'. Burnett then gave Tibet Martin's contact details, which subsequently led to the UK release of *Tiny Tim's Christmas Album.* Tiny later came to London and performed at the Union Club.

Songs From An Impotent Troubadour was recorded in 1994 and released in 1995 by David Tibet in collaboration with Big Bucks Burnett. As a historical document it's a must. It's a walk through Tiny's original compositions - from the 1947 *Poem for Elizabeth Taylor* to his 1994 *Ice Skater's Song* for Jessica Hahn. *Songs From An Impotent Troubadour* is the only Tiny Tim album on which he wrote all songs. There are three about Miss Elizabeth Taylor, one for Miss Tuesday Weld. Miss Snooky is in there, so is Café Bizarre and the Page Three. *Forever Miss Dixie* is an anthem from the days of his spiritual marriage. Jessica Hahn gets three songs and two are for 'the Eternal Princess' Miss Stephanie Bohn. (The first *Stephanie* track dates back to 1958 and is about another Stephanie.) As far as the story of Tiny's crush-life goes, he wraps it up with *I Used To Love Jessica Hahn But Now I Love Stephanie Bohn.*

The most startling track is the closing one, *Just What Do You Mean By 'Antichrist'?* - Tibet's creative contribution to the set. It's something Marilyn Manson might have thought of and unlike anything else in Tiny's entire repertoire. Of the Anti-Christ Tiny says, 'In my opinion, he will come from out of space'. Tiny felt contact with outer space was closer than most people thought, in 1989 he said, 'I believe in 1995 – earlier or later – we are going to experience the first visit from outer space. It will be the beginning of a new dawn. In 159 years from now the question parents will be asking is, "Why are you marrying that hideous Martian?" We're going to want to know what the No 1 hit in Venus is, and what's the best nightclub on Saturn'. (9)

He should have called it *Important Troubadour* not 'impotent'.

Miss Sue said, 'I don't know why he called it that…?'

Martin was equally miffed, 'isn't a premature ejaculator *more* potent, or *too* potent, not less?' (10)

Musical History Tour

On 11-12 November 1994 Tiny performed for home video a five-hour *Musical History Tour,* covering the history of popular song.

In some ways, this film is the notepad for the project of his life, something he had always aspired to do, starting with 'The Great Crooners' article he wrote for *Playboy* through the mini-marathons and marathons, to many interviews where he talked about about Popular Song. It's the beer-soaked version of Martin's *Twentieth Century Suite.*

You have to let your imagination run to enjoy this one. It's a home video, filmed in a lounge room, for persistent fans only. But if you imagine these songs, this patter and an entirely different production, set on a magnificent stage, with Richard Perry's Orchestra, Martin Sharp imagery, Miss Vicki the dancer, Marvin Lewis on piano. Then Tiny appears, dressed in a Tony Bechini suit and Tony Lama boots…you'll find *God Bless, Chameleon, Wonderful World of Romance, Prisoner of Love* and more, all in there.

His friend Johnny Pineapple assisted the spontaneous project, filmed to video in the presence of his young son and then circulated to interested Tiny Tim aficionados.

Miss Sue, Just You

Outer space has certainly always interested Tiny. He suggested to Miss Sue that they should wed in a space capsule at Cape Canaveral. The *Spooky World* show encouraged these plans. She preferred a church.

Next, *Spooky World* called Jay Leno who wanted to televise the event. With that, Tiny launched out in a completely different direction, he decided to renew his vows to his second wife Miss Jan on TV(!?). Miss Sue watched it at a neighbour's house who asked her what it felt like watching your fiancé renewing the vows of his second marriage. 'I smiled wryly,' she wrote, 'The next day divorce papers were filed and Tiny announced his plans to remarry'. (11) Before marrying Miss Sue, Tiny insisted on a pre-nuptual agreement that made clear that he was not entitled to a cent of her fortune.

Tiny and Miss Sue were married by Rev Dale Korogi on 18 August 1995, and Tiny made an album of unreleased music in honour of the wedding, (which again adds to the year's CD total).

It was a huge Catholic wedding. Tiny's new manager, Gil Morris, was Best Man and friend Johnny Pineapple was a groomsman. Johnny relates that they were one groomsman short and asked a random guest, who didn't even know Tiny, to get into a suit and join them at the altar! Over 750 people attended, as well as five camera crews – one was *E!* from New York. Tiny sang at the reception, 'including a matchless version of *Always'* says Miss Sue. *I'll be loving you, always…*

After the wedding, Tiny moved partly into Miss Sue's Minneapolis suburban home. Conscious as ever, of not taking advantage of his partner's financial situation, Tiny continued to maintain his hotel room in Des Moines at a cost of $750 per month. He insisted on generating his own income. But Tiny was in poor health, diabetic, had troubles with varicose veins and within two months of the marriage, after a small drama in his room in Des Moines he was diagnosed with congestive heart failure. He refused to be admitted to hospital and never missed a performance.

There really was no longer any logical reason to retain his Des Moines apartment nor to continue exhausting himself with live performances. Miss Sue told him he didn't have to work, but Tiny had no intention of retiring. In his last interview eight days before his death he told *People* magazine, 'I have to work. Even carrying luggage through airports is exhausting, but I need the money'. (12)

After a time, Tiny did give up his room at Hotel Fort Des Moines, but he was away from Miss Sue a great deal. They were married 14 months, during which time Tiny spent 300 days on the road. No doubt Tiny was encouraged by a surge of interest in his career. There were plenty of bookings now that public interest had been reactivated thanks, in part, to the publicity generated by his marriage. He was back to $1000 a night gigs, a slot on a television commercial that paid $10,000, and US shock-jock Howard Stern was a committed fan, frequently interviewing Tiny on radio and television.

Other TV appearances in 1995-96 included *Roseanne, Maury Povich, Joan Rivers, Real TV, Prime Time Country, Jay Leno Tonight, A Current Affair, Get Down With It, Mike and Maty, Danny Bonaduce, Rolanda*. He made cameo appearances in two movies and was featured in the *Ukulele Hall of Fame* documentary video. (13)

Radio Interviews

Describing Tiny as she knew him Miss Sue says, 'I was amazed by how many radio interviews he'd do, sometimes 2-3 hours. He was such a good person to have on the radio that everybody wanted him and there were a lot of repeats, because anybody who'd had him before knew what a good interview he was and also he would take them at any hour, so they'd sometimes call at 4 or 5 in the morning – 6 or 7 – for the morning commute show. It could be someone calling from Kansas City. And he loved that because he felt that God had really placed him in that position.

'He felt that he had accumulated wisdom in his life about various things and he wanted to give that back – so many older people do want to give other people the benefit of their experience. Some of it was very ordinary, avoiding haemorrhoids was extremely important. Taking care of your skin was extremely important. All the things you talked about to him were terribly relevant, and all sort of equally, although he always said God was No 1, and if he had the opportunity to talk about God then that would take precedence over everything. But once you get out of that category you get into things like why Nixon should never have resigned, or something about Elvis Presley, or something about face paint, it was all kind of the same.

'He felt that people needed to get themselves right with God and repent of their sin, and it was a very Biblical message. Sometimes people would laugh because they'd think he was an inappropriate person to be saying it, but I don't really know why. He lead a pretty clean life. He drank – most Christian denominations do, so that's nothing so radical and he was a virgin when he was married which is very unusual. He was faithful within his marriages. He wasn't a church-goer but then that's impossible because of his lifestyle. He was really upbeat with people, very accepting, cheerful and optimistic, an uplifting person to be around.

She said, 'I remember early in our relationship he said to me, 'Would you like to watch me put on my make-up?' I said, 'Sure.' And he put on layer after layer of creams, then he'd say, 'Tissue off, tissue off, tissue off...' and using this one, 'Tissue off, tissue off...' The tissues were flying as he'd discard them and they were flying from the table to the ground, and he's carrying on a running commentary on what he was doing. Then he'd put on the base, and it was all smeared like finger paint all over his neck. What a mess. And I'd say, 'Let me smooth this a little bit' and of course it was all over his shirt and his tie, and all his hands, and in his hair, and it was just awful. And then he had this pink powder puff and the last thing was that he'd puff this powder over everything which of course just caked into his eyebrows and all over his clothing. He'd get all done, and he'd look at me just like a little child that was so happy with this mud pie that he'd made, 'Isn't it wonderful?' 'Oh yes, it's lovely dear' – what can you say?

'Sometimes – if he was going to be here for a day or two, he wouldn't never get out of his pajamas all day. He'd wear a little tie with his pajamas and I always thought that was funny. He said, "A gentleman should always wear a tie". I remember one time he had on his pajamas with a tie, and then he was going to put on a suit to go down to the front desk of the hotel, so he had on two shirts and two ties and a coat, and the pajamas and the other tie was showing at the neck. He'd applied make-up every day of his life since 1953 or something. He said, "It seals the skin..." – I don't know. He did look great and you can't argue with success.' (14)

I Love Me

Towards the close of the year Ponk Records released *I Love Me,* which takes its name from a song Tiny performed at the Royal Albert Hall. This is a collection of hard-to-obtain remixed singles like *I Saw Mr Presley Tiptoeing Through The Tulips, The Laughing Policeman, She Left Me With The Herpes.* There was a strong disco influence on the new recordings, for example *Sweet Sue (Just You)* switches from its Old Time musical hall origins to disco rap - then back again. Given the timing of the release, and lines like, 'Her body may be thin and small but when she romances she's 10 feet tall' he can only be singing for Miss Sue.

At first, Tiny's father-in-law – a man only four years older than Tiny - thought he was 'weird', an impression no doubt fuelled by Tiny. Said Miss Sue, 'Dad stared at Tiny with a confused look and he never lost that look'. (15)

Sue added, 'I felt that my Dad had accepted our marriage just from the fact that he knew I was set on it, and I had been alone for a long time, so my Dad was glad that I was happy'. (16) In time Tiny and his father-in-law developed a convivial relationship, with Tiny joining in get-togethers and singing *Happy Birthday* at family gatherings.

Miss Sue's stepmother, Jacqui Gardner, was a socialite who loved taking Tiny to parties. Tiny loved attending parties.

Footnotes:

1. *Tiny Tim Times*, January 1994.
2. *Tiny Tim Times,* April 1994.
3. Tiny Tim, *The Washington Post*, 19 February 1995.
4. Ernie Clark, interview with Lowell Tarling, 30 March 2002.
5. Sue Khaury, article by Jim Walsh, 'The Strange Afterlife of Tiny Tim', *Night & Day,* 5 January 1997.
6. Sue Khaury, interview with Lowell Tarling and Michael Wilkinson, 30 March 2002 and 1 April 2002.
7. Ernie Clark, interview with Lowell Tarling, 30 March 2002.
8. Tiny Tim, *Prisoner Of Love* CD, 1994. Sue Khaury, interview with Lowell Tarling and Michael Wilkinson, 30 March 2002.
9. Tiny Tim, interview by John Toohey for *Ram*, 14 June 1989.
10. Tiny Tim, *Songs Of An Impotent Troubadour,* CD 1995. Recorded and produced by David Tibet. David Tibet, interview with Lowell Tarling, 7 April 2002.
11. Sue Khaury, *Memories Of My Husband Tiny Tim,* 1998, unpublished.
12. *People* magazine, 16 December 1996.
13. Sue Khaury, *Memories Of My Husband Tiny Tim,* 1998, unpublished.
14. Sue Khaury, interview with Lowell Tarling and Michael Wilkinson, 1 April 2002.
15. Sue Khaury, telephone conversation with Lowell Tarling, 2002.
16. Sue Khaury, interview with Lowell Tarling and Michael Wilkinson, 30 March 2002 and 1 April 2002.

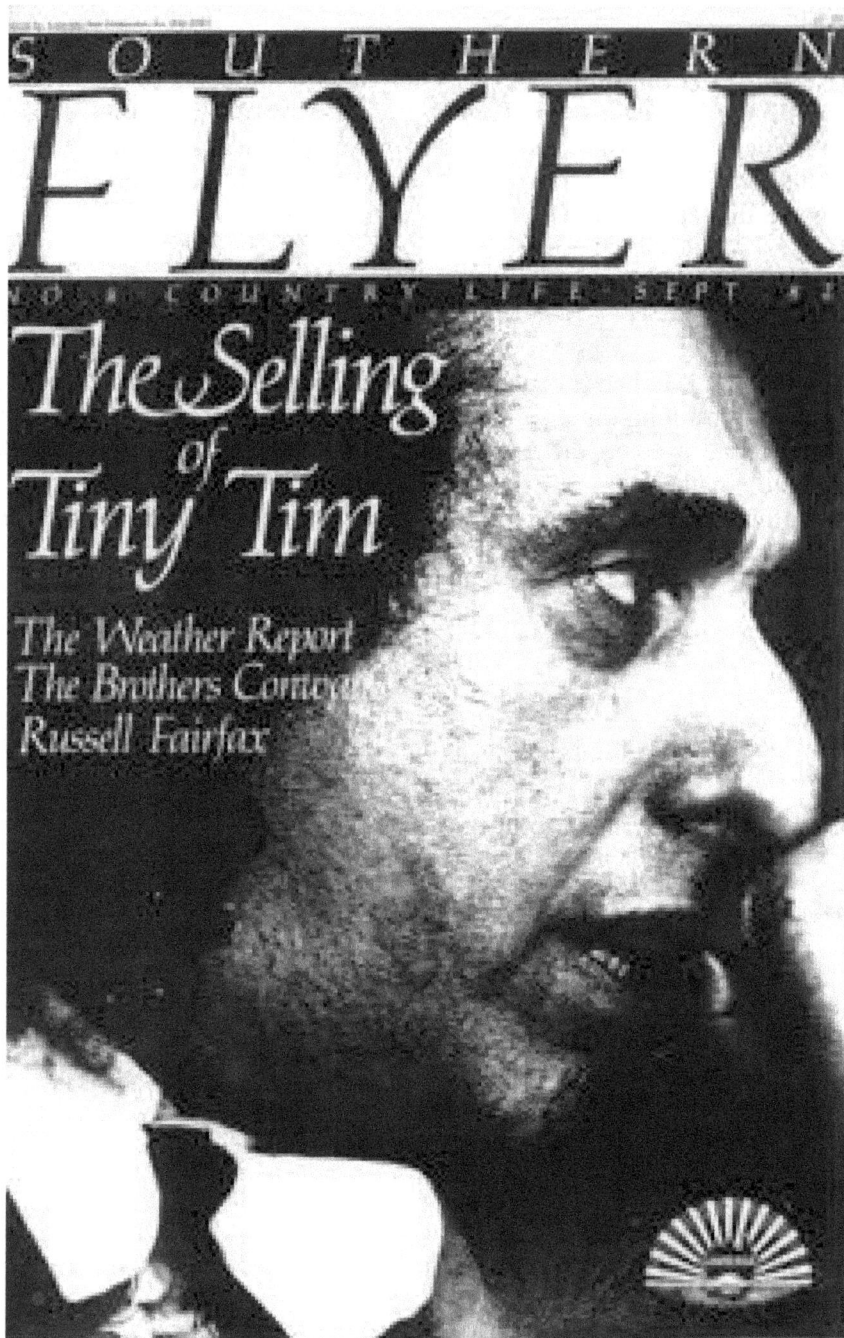

Excellent cover photo for the Southern Flyer, thanks to Dave Newland and the Art Department.

18

The Show Must Go On

I don't feel great. I've got this pain in my side
Tiny Tim to friend, Mark Mitchell

Tiny no longer resembled the beanpole-slim falsetto-warbling Human Canary of the 50s and 60s. Although he always loved his skin cleansers, Tiny's cosmetic habits were now less extreme than in his youth. (1)

Some other changes too. In the mid-90s Tiny usually sang baritone – saving his falsetto for *Tiptoe Through the Tulips,* which he usually sang towards the close of his performance. Although his personal habits were often still a topic on which he'd dwell, he mostly dropped his sexual fantasies from media interviews.

Tiny's manager, Gil Morris usually accompanied Tiny to performances. Says Miss Sue, 'At the end Tiny was having a lot of trouble getting around, he was having trouble walking, he was having trouble carrying things, he just didn't want to do it any more alone. He wanted somebody with him and Gil would pick him up at the airport and had a little apartment. Gil would be with him for all his meals and drive him there and stay there.

'But Gil was selling autographed pictures for $10 apiece and he'd sell hundreds of dollars worth of them every night and every now and then he'd give Tiny $10. It wasn't right, but Gil made much more out of the pictures than he did off the percentage, so that's why he was there. But even though Tiny knew it was not out of the kindness of his heart, he still appreciated it.'

Still Mobbed

Sue continued, 'Once we were married I picked him up at the airport a lot. Sometimes it would take hours to get out of the airport because he would be mobbed repeatedly as we walked down the car course. I learned how to manage the crowd a little bit, because sometimes I could just see he wasn't up to it. I noticed that if we kept walking that people wouldn't stop us so much, so if I did see he was weak in his knees, I'd take him by the arm - he'd want to stop and talk - and I'd say, 'C'mon honey, keep moving'.

'There are three things that cause people to come up to you – one of them is if you're standing still, one of them is if you make any kind of eye contact with them, and the other thing is if you're not talking to each other. So I'd try to avoid all of those things, I'd keep him talking, keep him moving, keep him looking at me and not let his gaze fall on anyone else. As long as we kept moving and talking and looking at each other and no one else, I could see out of the corner of my eye all this pandemonium taking place from people seeing him and wanting to come up – but they wouldn't approach. So that way I could get him through the airport in a relatively short time.

'Sometimes he wasn't happy with that, we'd get all the way to baggage and I thought, "We're almost home – free" but of course the baggage area was a danger place because you had to stand still. I remember one time, we went all the way down to baggage and nobody had talked to us the whole time. He said, "Nobody cares for Tiny Tim no more" and I looked around and there was 75 people standing there wanting to approach, that I had managed to fend off by keeping him involved in conversation. It was very easy to call them over, all you'd have to do is just look up at them and smile a little bit. He'd stand there until every last person had gotten their autograph, said what they had to say and ask what they wanted to ask. That's why we tried to avoid it, because he'd be so exhausted.

'He used to have conflicts with his manager – Gil Morris – because Gil would not book him in a sensible way. I would think really he should go out to the east coast, do several things in a row and then come home. Maybe there was nothing he could do about it but it seemed the jobs would come up here and there, constantly jumping every place. And then Gil didn't have a lot of money, and he was paying the transportation, so often times you'd get these flights that would stop and stop and stop. Sometimes only a difference of $20 would have saved hours. By the time Tiny could get back or arrive at some place, often times he was completely out of it.

'When he was home, he was so tired. He travelled 300 days over the 14 months we were married, and he was flat on his back on his bed the last two months - so he didn't really have a lot of time to do things in. But I did go with him out to Wisconsin, which is a little vacation area where there is a river with some odd rock formations, kinda made a tourist trip out of the town. There's a lot of things to do there, you can take these little boats rides and that sort of thing. The rock is a wonderful attraction for strange old antiques of many kinds of music-making machines - all kinds of curios. We went there and he often got tired. I wished I hadn't brought him because he was so tired.

'Really – after we were married – I started to feel the frustration of being married to someone who was so ill and unable to do things, unable really to go out. I went with him to Nevada. I wanted to walk along the river, stroll up and down, but he couldn't do that. He'd walk out and he'd be mobbed immediately – and then walking was so hard for him. I just came to accept that Tiny spent most of his time in bed unless he was performing, then he'd get up and perform – which took all his energy. There was very little left and it was becoming almost impossible for him, but he kept it up right to the end, it's really all he wanted to do.'

Miss Sue did not accompany Tiny on tour, 'He was not terribly interested in staying home with me. He loved the excitement of performing and being on the road. I saw him perform several times around Minneapolis and other places I went with him. I didn't travel a great deal. Because my diet is very restricted it's almost impossible for me to travel. But I saw him perform on many occasions and I know there was a high to that that he was completely addicted to. That's what his life was all about.' (2)

Having been at the beck-and-call of his work all year, Tiny spent the month of December in Minneapolis with his wife, as promised.

Tiny Tim's Christmas

Happy Christmas. Tiny's in-laws gave him an electric blue dressing gown covered with gold stars, 'which he put on immediately', said Miss Sue. Her brother gave him a clock that looked like a wolf playing the saxophone. When the alarm went off it said, 'Hey, hey, it's time to get up so you can get down – whoo-hoo'. Tiny pressed that button over and over, said Miss Sue, 'like a little kid'.

And so, Tiny in his new dressing gown, with a new alarm clock proceeded to reminisce to the Gardner family gathering about his television appearance with Mr Crosby all those years ago. The stories went long into the night. Everyone wanted to have their picture taken with Tiny,' says Miss Sue. 'It was a joyous time.'

Sue said, 'I think my Dad would rather have been a musician and not just a businessman. So Tiny kinda lived the life that my father would have liked to have had the nerve to live, but my Dad grew up poor and he could never stand that. He wanted to have money. He didn't want to be at anyone's mercy the way his father was at the mercy of the bosses at the factory. So my Dad was very into that and Tiny had chosen to be poor most of his life - in fact all his life. Even when he made his money, he never saw any of it'. (3)

That Girl Again

The March 1996 release of Big Bucks Burnett's *Girl* album revived the memories of Miss Stephanie and hurt Miss Sue. Although she'd heard all Tiny's fantasies, copping it again - with Miss Stephanie's photograph right there on the cover - Miss Sue broke down and wept. Finally she turned to Tiny and said, 'You aren't going to get rid of me that easily, I'm here to stay'.

He replied, 'You are some kind of woman!' (4)

The release of the CD seemed to restore Tiny's sexual confidence. Instead of telling the press that he was a sexual dud, he fought off the old stereotypes with unusual confidence. He said, 'People think I'm an asexual freak, a romantic dud. But you are talking to the sexiest and most romantic person in the world!' (5)

There was a revival of interest in the ukulele instrument in the mid-1990s. People were actually interested in Arthur Godfrey. George Formby and Roy Smeck CDs were re-released. Whereas in the 70s *Tiptoe* had appeared on demeaning compilation albums like *Dopey Ditties,* the song was now treated with more dignity, appearing on *Legends of Ukulele,* alongside Cliff (Ukulele Ike) Edwards, Eddie Kamae, Ian Whitcomb and the Ukulele Orchestra of Great Britain. And while they might have cost $5.95 in the 50s, by the mid-90s a plastic Maccaferri uke cost 20 times that price, if you could find one for sale.

Ukulele festivals starting springing up in America, England, Australia – just everywhere. And, being a genuine troubadour, Tiny was a big favourite. On a trip to an English uke-fest, somehow Tiny's beloved Martin never made it onto the plane. Tiny without his ukulele is a problem requiring an immediate solution. The organisers quickly got him a borrowed instrument - a metal resonator uke. (It is rumoured that ukulele-enthusiast George Harrison funded this festival and that Harrison loaned the metal uke.) (6)

On 12 April 1996, to celebrate his 64th birthday, Miss Sue gave Tiny a metal Dobro-style resonator ukulele (with electric pick-up). It became his favourite instrument, 'because it was loud'. She ordered it from England. Tiny was impressed by the British model.

Tiny Tim Unplugged

Tiny Tim Unplugged was released on Tomanna Records in 1996. While touring a couple of years previously, enthusiast Tom Anderson had recorded Tiny live in concert – in Anderson's music store in Birmingham Alabama, before a handpicked audience.

This is an intimate live recording of a relaxed Tiny before a most appreciative audience. It sounds like an extended version of Tiny entertaining friends around Martin's kitchen table.

Tiny sings songs in 'groups', starting with 'Mother' songs – *Baby Shoes, All the World and it's Gold.* Then 'patriotic' songs, like *You're A Grand Old Flag,* etc. Then songs for girls who leave home and get into trouble in big cities. After that, Tiny launches into standards that have become associated with his live act over the years. Songs like, *Goody Goody, Don't Sit Under the Apple Tree, Just a Gigolo,* half a dozen more, before *Tiptoe.*

The crowd, of course, demand an encore, which is a great version of *Do You Think I'm Sexy* followed by the irrepressible *I Got You Babe.* (7)

Praise My Soul The King Of Heaven!

Playwright Max 'Bunny' Sparber recently made a short documentary - a tour of the Minneapolis locations where Tiny spent this period of his life. Sparber's footage is worth a look on youtube. It shows the smart two-storey house where he lived with Miss Sue, along with actual Tiny Tim places in this period of his life. This doco reminds that Tiny - this hardcore New Yorker - spent his closing years in a suburban environment.

Generally, Tiny seemed content when at home. Every morning he would sing hymns before singing anything else because he wanted to give the Lord the 'first-fruits' of his talent. Sue recalls, 'Never would he sing his romantic songs unless he'd sung one hymn. *Praise My Soul The King Of Heaven* was his favourite and sometimes he'd say, "I want to sing for you but I can't yet because I haven't sung to the Lord" and he'd sing *Praise My Soul The King Of Heaven* one way through, and then he'd sing the other song'.

He set up many religious icons and Miss Sue was impressed by the fervour with which he recited the Rosary, Hail Marys and the Lord's Prayer. Religion was something they could share. They prayed and sang hymns together. However, Miss Sue was surprised that Tiny had no actual sleep cycle, he might not sleep for two days, or he could sleep any time. His only regular habit, as far as time was concerned was to always try to say his prayers at midnight.

'He was very religious,' said Miss Sue, 'Even if it was the 10th time through a Hail Mary or Our Father, he'd do it with as much gusto as if he was performing. He thought that his way of serving God was to mention Jesus to people as part of interviews, on stage and that kind of thing, and that he was reaching a group of people who would otherwise not hear anything about God and weren't really seeking him out – because you don't come to clubs to hear a sermon and he didn't give a sermon, but he would make mention of God'. Miss Sue's favourite Tiny Tim song is his little-known rendition of *The Rosary*. (8)

They sang together many songs, alone, on tape and in the presence of friends. And Tiny had many friends like, Johnny Pontes, Joe and Lindy Roth, Martin Sharp, Miss Jan Gianopolous, Mark Mitchell, Jim Foley and Ernie Clark. He stayed in touch with all these people, usually through lengthy telephone calls. Johnny Pineapple was a good friend who lived across the road, he played a lot of Hawaiian music, and as fellow musos, they shared experiences and swapped songs. (9)

Miss Sue recalls that although he did not visit Miss Tulip, Tiny maintained a telephone relationship with his daughter. A visit had been scheduled, prohibited by what comes next. (10)

Miss Sue said, 'We were together almost two and a half years, counting the year of courtship. I met a lot of extremely unusual people with Tiny, showbusiness people, some of the fans – very different. It was amazing to go from being "an old maid and an invalid" to suddenly being a celebrity wife, being in the tabloids, and meeting all these unusual people. And it had hardly begun and it was all over.' (11)

Ukulele Expo 96

On 28 September 1996 Tiny was booked as a performer at the *Ukulele Expo 96* in Massachusetts. Miss Sue stayed home. Tiny's next gig was to have been his old nemesis, Las Vegas. But Tiny had not felt well all day and, apart from his manager Gil Morris and Pink Bob, there was nobody present at the expo who Tiny knew. He was anxiously awaiting the arrival of friends Mark Mitchell and Jim Foley.

Meanwhile, Tiny spent time with Pink Bob talking and singing on tape for a Ponk project called *Videosyncracies*. It was his last serious interview in good health and he really doesn't look like a man about to have a heart attack. It can be seen on youtube under the title, *The Last Interview, 28 Sept 1996, Uke Expo 1996 at the Bookmill, Montague, Massachusetts*.

When Mitchell located him, in the back seat of Gil Morris' car, he thought Tiny looked tired. On seeing Mitchell, Tiny said, 'Let's take a walk,' which they did, and when they were by themselves Tiny told Mitchell, 'You know, I don't feel great. I've got this pain in my side'. He pointed and said, 'What do you think it is?' Mitchell said, 'Jeez, Tiny, I don't know – that's where your kidneys are'.

After a brief discussion about health matters, they joined the others at the dining table where Tiny didn't eat. Finally, the stagelights went on, cameras started flashing and it was time for Tiny to go on stage. The place was packed. Every performance was being videotaped by the organizers, everybody was anxious to hear Tiny sing the old songs. He was one of the few genuine troubadours at the show, most of the other players were younger and newer to the instrument.

Tiny made his way through the packed house, walked on stage, introduced the band, hit the first note and went straight down, like a felled tree. Nobody knows what that song was to be, there was one note and that was all. *Pearly Shells* was a possibility, as Tiny had spent some time earlier in the day practicing it with the band.

The audience surged as soon as Tiny fainted. He'd fallen from the stage - lucky it was less than a metre high. Being several rows back, Mitchell had to scramble through the crowd. Foley – a 'bodyguard-type of guy' – also forced his way through and held the crowd at bay. Paramedics too pushed their way in, and when Tiny started coming to, the first thing he saw was an intravenous needle about to be whacked into his arm and he panicked. Tiny didn't like needles, so Mitchell had to talk him through that. 'It's just for a second Tiny, then you won't feel anything'.

Tiny's next concern was for his jacket, which the paramedics had cut, in order to reach his arm without moving him. The place was total chaos, people coming too close, yelling, and all the while the cameraman kept his camcorder rolling. This footage was screened on national news.

Mitchell accompanied Tiny in the ambulance. Tiny went straight to Emergency Ward and Mitchell left him in good spirits at 3.00am. Externally, Tiny had only one scratch on his face, and there were no broken bones. TV news bulletins showed him in a wheelchair, smiling for the cameras.

Tiny was diagnosed as being in need of by-pass heart surgery, to which he would not agree. He feared the surgeon's knife more than he feared death and said, 'When my time is up, it is'. He did not want to be cut open. (12)

Three Grandchildren

Tiny's hospital stay got lots of media attention. Contact with Miss Tulip was re-affirmed and Tiny was excited about his three grandchildren, Charisse, Jade and Trey. Said Miss Sue, 'Tiny was so excited, he couldn't wait to hold his new grandson - but he never got the chance. We invited the entire family to come out to Minnesota for the holidays and stay with us. I was even redecorating a spare bedroom for them, but time ran out'. (13) The media also reported that Tiny had made his peace with Miss Vicki.

After 11 days, Tiny was flown home by Air Ambulance to Minneapolis where he was again hospitalised. Says Miss Sue, 'We were told that he had one or two years to live at the most. He was advised not to perform anymore, at least until after the 1st of the year', (ie. 1997).

'He came home and seemed to be doing remarkably well,' said Miss Sue. 'After a month he was walking around the house singing at the top of his lungs. One night we got a call from a place where he had been booked to perform. The gig had been cancelled but they just wanted us to come for dinner and to say hello. He got up and sang a song or two. It turned into a 20-minute set and he was fine. A week later he did a benefit but seemed shaky. He was spending much more time in bed now and seemed to be more uncomfortable.'

Adios

Miss Sue said Tiny wasn't really taking care of himself. He certainly wasn't eating well. She said, 'He'd always give me his receipts for everything while he was on tour because of tax reasons, and he wasn't eating anything. They were providing him with food but he had to go to the cafeteria to get it but he wouldn't go down there because the people were staring at him, and so he was eating candy and peanuts and it was terrible.

'Then I insisted to the management that I could go down to the cafeteria and bring the food up and failing that, I sometimes ordered room service and paid for it myself because he wasn't eating properly. He never did take care of himself. I was talking to Vicki about it one time because I thought he could have lived another 10 years at least if he had taken care of himself and she said, "No, if he had to do it over again he'd do exactly the same". She was right'.

Cousin Hal also knew the score, 'He didn't like to go to the hospital or see a doctor or anything like that. That was unfortunate, if he did he'd still be alive today. Miss Sue took great care of him. He was lucky he lasted as long as he did. The only reason that he died is that he refused to take his medication any more.'

One week before Tiny died, the Martin-produced *Tiny Tim's Christmas Album* gained an international release in collaboration with David Tibet. Also one week before he died, Johnny Pineapple had a vivid dream about Heaven, which he and Tiny analysed at length. Two days before he died, Martin and Tiny had their last phone conversation.

The night before he died Tiny was discouraged because he was in pain. He said to Miss Sue, 'This pain is never going to go away'. (14) That night he phoned David Tibet in England and told him about the Minneapolis Ladies Club gig that he was about to undertake, 'I really don't feel too good. I'm just going to go down and do it because I won't be there long'. (15)

His last phone message was to Jim Foley. Tiny said, 'Hello congratulations. Good afternoon Mr Foley/Mrs Foley, this is Tiny Tim. I just got your call. It's about 2.32 central standard time and 3.32 eastern standard time on Saturday November 30th 1996. Your call came earlier but I was asleep, I had the phone shut but I just got the message right now: congratulations on the birth of your wonderful baby girl. May the Good Lord bless it real well, thank you Jesus Christ. And I just pray that you both have the best. And I thank you for keeping me in touch and we will keep in touch. But thanks again for letting me know and congratulations Mr & Mrs Foley once more. This is Tiny Tim signing off.'

'Signing off?' Foley remarked. 'Tiny always says *Adios*'. (16)

Footnotes:

1. Sue Khaury, interview with Lowell Tarling and Michael Wilkinson, 1 April 2002.
2. Sue Khaury, interview with Lowell Tarling and Michael Wilkinson, 30 March 2002 and 1 April 2002.
3. Sue Khaury, interview with Lowell Tarling and Michael Wilkinson, 1 April 2002. Also, *Memories Of My Husband Tiny Tim,* 1998, unpublished.
4. Sue Khaury, interview with Lowell Tarling and Michael Wilkinson, 30 March 2002.
5. Tiny Tim, *Daily Telegraph,* 31 March 1996.
6. Sue Khaury, interview with Lowell Tarling and Michael Wilkinson, 30 March 2002.
7. Ernie Clark, interview with Lowell Tarling, 30 March 2002.
8. Sue Khaury, interview with Lowell Tarling and Michael Wilkinson, 30 March 2002. Tiny recorded *The Rosary* in unreleased sessions in the early 80s.
9. Sue Khaury, interview with Lowell Tarling and Michael Wilkinson, 1 April 2002. Sue Khaury wrote out the following names of people who she believed were important to Tiny either personally or professionally when she knew him: James Big Bucks Burnett (record producer), Kent Fadness (video photographer), Sharon Fox (60s Fan Club president), Janet Gianopolous (friend), Joe Karpik (photographer), Rita McConnachie (TV contact), Gil Morse (manager), Johnny Pineapple (friend and fellow muso), Bob Pontes (friend), Roslyn Rabin (cousin), Joe and Lindy Roth (friends), Martin Sharp (friend, film-maker, artist and record producer), Tulip and Eric Stewart (daughter and son-in-law), David Tibet (UK record producer), Artie Wachter (childhood friend).
10. Tiny usually spoke of Miss Tulip with much affection. Tiny Tim, interview with Lowell Tarling, 24 August 1982 he said, 'Sure I'm fond of her, there's no doubt about it. Ernie Clark, interview with Lowell Tarling, 30 March 2002, Clark said, 'Tiny was always aware what was going on with Miss Tulip's life. He was elusive about the whole thing. I think he felt bad because he wasn't around for her when she was growing up. There were a handful of visits but I think it was mostly contacts by phone.' Sue Khaury, interview with Lowell Tarling and Michael Wilkinson, 30 March 2002, Sue said, 'There's a quiet dignity about her, she has humour, she's bright and she likes to write. Some of her kids have an interest in art, so there is creativity there.'
11. Sue Khaury, interview with Lowell Tarling and Michael Wilkinson, 1 April 2002.
12. Mark Mitchell, interview with Lowell Tarling, 30 March 2002.
13. Tulip Stewart, interview with Lowell Tarling, 2 April 2002. Also, magazine article, 'Tiny's Last Swan Song', December 1996.
14. Sue Khaury, interview with Lowell Tarling and Michael Wilkinson, 30 March 2002 and 1 April 2002. Harold Stein, interview with Lowell Tarling, 1 April 2002. Martin Sharp, interview Lowell Tarling, 1 February 1983.
15. David Tibet, interview with Lowell Tarling, 7 April 2002. Also, Tibet writes about his experience recording Tiny in London on the liner notes of *The Eternal Troubadour.*
16. Ernie Clark, interview with Lowell Tarling, 30 March 2002. This telephone message is a bonus track on the CD *Tiny Tim Live At The Fat Black Pussycat.*

19

Minneapolis Women's Club, 30 November 1996

Death is never polite, even when we expect it
Tiny Tim

'Death is never polite, even when we expect it,' said Tiny. 'The only thing I pray for is the strength to go out without complaining. (1)

Against the doctor's advice, and as a favour to his mother-in-law Jacqui Gardner, Tiny insists on fulfilling an unpaid fundraiser on 30 November at the Minneapolis Women's Club, a club for wealthy ladies. For the occasion, Tiny dresses in a Tweed jacket, blue shirt, blue trousers and a dark-coloured tartan tie. He elects to play the wooden Martin ukulele tonight, not the resonator uke.

Miss Sue is uneasy about his condition all day. She asks him if he has taken his medication and he says no. 'Why not?' Sue questions, 'It's so important!'

'What's the use?' replies Tiny. 'They're just going to give me more and more and it'll work less and less. I'm going to go eventually, so what's the point?'

Miss Sue has tried many times to stop him performing and never succeeded. She has given up trying to persuade him against his will.

Miss Sue wants to cancel the Minneapolis Ladies Club gig. 'This is too much!' she thinks as Tiny stumbles while getting into the limo. She implores her stepmother to call the whole thing off. But they press on.

When they arrive at the venue, they are disappointed. The bandleader snubs Tiny and refuses to back him. Turning to Tiny, Miss Sue shrugs and says, 'I guess they think that you're not supposed to be here'. Although they feel unwelcome, Miss Sue and Tiny sit politely, patiently putting up with a big band whose sound system is much too loud for the room.

Despite having been informed that Tiny has been invited to perform, the band does not invite him to take the microphone. The first set seems never-ending. Miss Sue figures this is going to be a long and exhausting stint. She is quite correct. The band plays for nearly two hours, while Tiny and Miss Sue wait…and wait…

At last the set comes to a close. By now Miss Sue is convinced the band is never going to invite Tiny to take the stage. And if their second set is to be as long as their first, another two-hour wait would be too long. Miss Sue asks her stepmother to find out what the deal is? Meanwhile people are leaving the room in droves.

The message that comes back is that Tiny should take the stage right now – between sets - which he does. He plays his first song to a virtually empty hall, but when the audience realise it is The Man himself, they rush back. The crowd builds to maybe 150 by the time Tiny is into his third song.

His fourth is *When I Grow Too Old To Dream,* during which he fixes his tender gaze on Miss Sue.

And finally he sings an abridged version of *Tiptoe Through The Tulips* and signs off to loud applause. He blows kisses in acknowledgement, the audience claps, but Miss Sue can see that something is terribly wrong. She rushes to his side. Her worry is that he might trip on the many cables on the ground.

She takes his arm and attempts to guide him off-stage – 'Let's go…' But Tiny just stands there, applause ringing in his ears.

'Are you all right?' she asks.

'No,' he replies quizzically, 'I'm not.'

And then he slumps on her with all his body weight bearing down on her tiny frame.

'Help me!' Miss Sue cries out, putting her arms around Tiny to hold him up. But before anyone reaches her, Tiny gracefully sinks to his knees and drops to the floor.

There is a doctor present. He starts working on Tiny immediately. The ambulance arrives within 10 minutes and the ambulance officers work on Tiny all the way to the Hennepin Country Medical Centre. They keep working in the Emergency Ward, bringing the heart back for one or two beats, then they lose it again. This goes on for more than a hour.

At 3.00am Tiny Tim, the time traveller of song, is pronounced dead. (2)

He might have died ingloriously like so many Rock stars, but Tiny had to have an audience. It is uncanny that both his heart attacks were in full character, on stage and with a ukulele in his hand.

Miss Sue tells the press, 'He died singing *Tiptoe Through The Tulips,* the last thing he heard was applause, and the last person he saw was me. It was just like Tiny to die like that. He was a born showman.' (3)

*

I knew him on-and-off from 1982, and in researching this biography, I was amazed at all the references that his closest acquaintances have made to his ill-health, varicose veins and physical pain that I never knew about.

I'd say, 'G'day Tiny, how are you?'

And he'd always reply, 'Mr Tarlin, I can't complain'.

Footnotes:

1. Tiny Tim, *San Francisco Examiner,* 2 December 1996.
2. The material from this chapter is taken from Sue Khaury, interview with Lowell Tarling and Michael Wilkinson, 30 March 2002. Also, Sue Khaury *Memories Of My Husband Tiny Tim,* 1998, unpublished.
3. Sue Khaury *Memories Of My Husband Tiny Tim,* 1998, unpublished.

20

Afterword

On Monday 2 December 1996, Robbie wakes me gently. She says, 'Someone has died and you're not going to like it'. It's Tiny.

Over coffee, I play *When I've Gone the Last Mile of the Way* and then I phone Martin. He says it happened Saturday afternoon, our time. I ask Martin how this will affect things? He replies, 'Nothing has changed, in fact he seems more present than ever'.

This is what Martin told the Australian press under the headline, *Bound for Heaven – My Amazing Friend:* 'It's not often one gets to work with, and for, a truly great artist, and it has been my great privilege to work with the genius of popular song. As an artist myself, my bond with him was on an artistic level....

'I'll miss Tiny's great friendship and advice, but I don't feel sad. If anyone is heaven bound it is Tiny. I have a great treasury of recordings made with him which I am sure one day will be heard by many. I hope to be able to bring a lot more of the work we have done together to fruition, and to listeners who I am confident will be touched by his poetry, his pathos and his humour, but most of all by his courage'.

Martin has continued working on the film *Street of Dreams* ever since. It has been screened as a late night movie on ABC-TV and fairly constantly at Martin's exhibitions, for example his major Retrospective held at Sydney Museum in 2009. The Brighton Cut can also be seen on youtube.

Recordings

Two live albums were released in 1996 – *Tiny Tim Unplugged* (Tomanna) *The Eternal Troubadour, Tiny Tim Live in London* (Durtro) recorded in 1995. Then the Richard Perry recordings came back into the picture. *Tiny Tim Live at the Albert Hall,* (Rhino Handmade, 2000, recorded 1968). Followed by his boxed set, *God Bless Tiny Tim, The Complete Reprise Studio Masters and More.*

Tiny has always had a following in Japan. In fact, when it was impossible to purchase *God Bless* on CD, a Japanese pressing was usually available. In 2006, Japanese company Zero Communications released Martin's *Chameleon* and *Wonderful World of Romance* CDs. They also released a new recording, *Stardust,* which included a previously unreleased version of *Highway to Hell,* as well as songs from the 1992-1993 Sydney sessions like *I Am I Said, Sing Me the Rosary* and *People Are Strange.* These CDs, as well as a range of Martin Sharp posters are available from www.mojofinaeart.com.

There has also been a string of live CDs, some have been legitimate releases, like *Live at the Fat Black Pussycat 2.24.63,* which is available through the Tiny Tim Memorial website. Others, like *Hollywood High School* and *Live with Campervan Beethoven* have seeped onto the Internet and have simply been downloaded.

As I write, Tiny's latest albums are I've Never Seen a Straight Banana – Rare Moments (Collectors Choice Music 2009) and Vol 1 Tiny Tiny: Lost & Found (Rare and Unreleased 1963-1974) (Secret Seven Records 2011).

Stage Show

I quit my editing job in 1993 and went back to freelancing. In 2002, businessman Michael Wilkinson was looking to buy a theatre at the Paris end of Melbourne. He contacted me, I contacted Martin and for a while it was all on.

Michael commissioned me to write the stageplay and Martin was sufficiently enthused to contribute two new drawings, as sets. There was a general agreement that the best person to play Tiny was singer

Mic Conway, who wrote a stageplay concept too. I thought I should ask about Tiny's approach to music. So I called the ukulele player in Mic Conway's National Junk Band, Phil Donnison. Phil backed Tiny in his first tour of Australia in 1971 and explained that Tiny simplified the chords of *Tiptoe*. Phil showed me all the passing chords a house band might play, underneath Tiny's strum.

Mick Reid backed Tiny on guitar at an RSL Club gig in 1993. He explained that Tiny didn't always keep regular time, especially during his marathons. Mick said Tiny could suddenly switch from 4/4 time to a waltz (and back) within seconds, which required the band to stay very alert. Key changes were less of a problem, as Tiny usually called them out, 'Maestro, the key of G…'.

Significantly, the stageshow created the impetus for me to return to America. There Miss Sue kindly showed me where they lived, she showed me Tiny's last bedroom and spoke for three hours on tape. I also interviewed friends Mark Mitchell and Ernie Clark, Richard Perry, Miss Tulip and cousins Bernie and Hal. In London, I interviewed David Tibet. These, added to interviews with Tiny and Martin, are the basis of much of this book.

Hal and I maintained contact. He and his wife Sherry visited Australia and spent an afternoon at Wirian with Martin, sitting in the same places Tiny used to sit, in the same rooms.

Biography

In 2004, Stephen Plym published an account of his time as Tiny's agent. Notwithstanding the claim that he and Tiny were 'like brothers', I have never read a more one-dimensional account of anybody's life.

As for suggesting he knew Tiny better than anybody else? I doubt Cousin Hal, Richard Perry, Mo Ostin, Martin Sharp, the Cappys, the Hollanders, Mark Mitchell, Jim Foley, Johnny Pineapple, Miss Janet, Miss Vicki, Miss Jan, Miss Sue or Ernie Clarke, would concur. The book reads like a missed opportunity to fill in Tiny's Des Moines experience. The author is less interested in dates, places and venues than the fact he bought Tiny a blow-up sex doll as a birthday present.

A better account of Tiny's life was written by Chris Campion and posted on Tiny's Memorial site.

As for my experience, I have been trying to get the attention of publishers ever since I phoned Penguin Books, on the day Tiny was in the lion's den in Revesby in 1982. Penguin had just published my first novel and was looking to my next book. They were appalled when I proposed Tiny Tim as my subject.

So I prepared sample chapters, let it be known that I had around 50,000 words from the man himself, plus interviews with many who knew him, including family members. I contacted the 10 most prominent worldwide publishers of Rock biographies, but I did not fare any better. Although I continued shaping my account, I couldn't even drum up interest from small publishers either.

It was the development of eBooks via amazon.com that has made this biography possible. And Linda Ruth Brooks Publishing, who turned this into an appropriate format.

Cousin Hal kept me motivated, in his quiet way. Again, technology helped - via Facebook contact. When he and Sherry visited Wirian in 2008, Hal's eyes went from one Tiny Tim image to another - the *Opera House* poster, one of Tiny's ukes, a Tiny Tim Head Knockers figurine, the *Chameleon* poster, and Martin's *Song of Songs* painting, 136 x 319 cm long. There was some sadness in Hal's voice when he turned to me and said, 'Who will remember this?'

'I'll give it a shot,' I replied.

Also by Lowell Tarling

Fiction

Taylor's Troubles – first edition 1982
Taylor's Troubles – revised edition 2004
The Secret Gang of Oomlau – 1988
1967, This Is It! – 1990

Anthologies

Hunter Valley Poets 1973-1973
All The Best, A Selection Celebrating 25 Years of Puffins in Australia – 1989
Australia's Best Poetry Volume One – 2001
Visions From The Valley, Poetry of the Hunter Valley 1960-2000 – 2001
The Great Australian Shed - 2012

Non-Fiction

Thank God for the Salvos, The Salvation Army In Australia 1880-1980 – 1980
The Edges of Seventh-day Adventism – 1981
The Australian Handbook of Business Letters – 1989
17 Small Business Success Stories – 1991
Gold Beyond Your Dreams (with Heather Turland) – 1998
No More Cellulite Fast (with Violetta Chevell) – 1999
Beyond Azaria (with Michael Chamberlain) – 1999
Brash Business (with Geoff Brash) – 2000
The Complete Tiny Tim Interviews – 2000
Breadwinner (with Tom O'Toole) – 2000
The Women's Club (with Di Williams) – 2000
My Dad Thinks I Rob Banks (with Joe Sammon) – 2001
Risky Business (with Clare Loewenthal) – 2001
Secrets of the Beechworth Bakery (with Tom O'Toole) – 2001
Guilty to Driza-Bone (with Frank Fisher) – 2002
The Method, A Writer's Handbook-2003
The Business Method, the A-Z of Business Communications – 2004
On The End of a Wire (with Peter Davidson) – 2004
Go For Your Life! (with Chris Grey) – 2005
Busted: 17 Classic Mythbusters – 2007
South Side Story – 2008
Coping with Difficult People – 2010
Coping with Parents – 2010
Coping with Teenagers – 2011
Coping with So!! Difficult People – Three books in one - 2012

www.lowelltarling.com.au
lowell@lowelltarling.com.au

Lowell Tarling

**Lowell in his study, with Martin's 'Chameleon' poster of Tiny in the background.
Photo credit: Konrad Lenz**

Lowell Tarling has been writing ever since he could hold a pencil. His literary journey began with him scribbling down observations and life events much as an artist would sketch; here a little, there a little.

He is the quintessential searcher and this, along with an open acceptance of people and their lives and passions, has brought him into contact with a wonderful diverse group of artists, dissidents, minstrels and songwriters. A lifelong friendship with the artist Martin Sharp has resulted in a book that combines an inner view of Tiny Tim, the man and the performer, and also a remarkable range of artistic images by Martin.

Linda Brooks

Isn't life a joke?
Isn't the whole world a stage?
Why we all live in two different worlds
And we all have many kinds of tongues and many kinds of faces.
Why there's a face for around in the crowd
There's a face in front of our employers
And there's a face we know when the doors are closed.
It seems we all see the sunshine in front of everyone
But at night when the masks are off
And we're all by ourselves
We see ourselves as we are - nothing but pretenders, pretending
And I will keep on pretending as long as the world goes on

Tiny Tim, *The Great Pretender*

Chameleon LP

Joel Tarling

Artists enjoyed depicting Tiny. Joel drew this for one of Dave Rowe's CD projects. Joel met Tiny several times, and sat through quite a long interview. And Dave was Tiny's Australian tour manager, for the 1992 People Are Strange tour. He has worked with Martin on Tiny Tim CD projects ever since.